Programming

4 Manuscripts in 1:

Python Programming for Beginners
+
Python Crash Course
+
Machine Learning for Beginners
+
Python Machine Learning

By James Deep

Table of Contents

Python Programming for Beginners

A 7 Days Practical Guide to Fast Learn Python Programming and Coding Language (with Exercises)

Introduction

In this Python Beginner's guide, you're about to learn:

- The Most Vital Basics of Python programming. Rapidly get the dialect and begin applying the ideas to any code that you compose.
- The Useful features of Python for Beginners-including some ideas you can apply to in real-world situations and even other programs.
- Different mechanics of Python programming: control stream, factors, records/lexicons, and classes-and why taking in these center standards are essential to Python achievement
- Protest arranged programming, its impact on present-day scripting languages, and why it makes a difference.

This book has been composed specifically for Newbies and Beginners. You will be taken through each step of your very first program, and we will explain each portion of the script as you test and analyze the data.

In common computing programs, formulas are groups of individually programmed orders that are used by computers to determine outcomes and solve problems. Instead, machine learning formulas allow computers to focus only on data that is inputted and use proven stat analysis in order to deliver correct values that fall within a certain probability. What this means is that computers have the ability to break down simple data models which enables it to automate routine decision-making steps based on the specific data that was inputted.

There are many books about Python Programming on the market. Thank you so much for selecting this one! Be assured that every measure was put in place to see to it that this book contains much useful details as possible, please enjoy reading the book!

FIRST DAY

Part 1: Introduction

Python is an awesome decision on machine learning for a few reasons. Most importantly, it's a basic dialect at first glance. Regardless of whether you're not acquainted with Python, getting up to speed is snappy in the event that you at any point have utilized some other dialect with C-like grammar.

Second, Python has an incredible network which results in great documentation and inviting and extensive answers in Stack Overflow (central!).

Third, coming from the colossal network, there are a lot of valuable libraries for Python (both as "batteries included" an outsider), which take care of essentially any issue that you can have (counting machine learning).

History of Python

Python was invented in the later years of the 1980s. Guido van Rossum, the founder, started using the language in December 1989. He is Python's only known creator and his integral role in the growth and development of the language has earned him the nickname "Benevolent Dictator for Life". It was created to be the successor to the language known as ABC.

The next version that was released was Python 2.0, in October of the year 2000 and had significant upgrades and new highlights, including a cycle- distinguishing junk jockey and back up support for Unicode. It was most fortunate, that this particular version, made vast improvement procedures to the language turned out to be more straightforward and network sponsored.

Python 3.0, which initially started its existence as Py3K. This version was rolled out in December of 2008 after a rigorous testing period. This particular version of Python was hard to roll back to previous compatible versions which are the most unfortunate. Yet, a significant number of its real highlights have been rolled back to versions 2.6 or 2.7 (Python), and rollouts of Python 3 which utilizes the two to three utilities, that helps to automate the interpretation of the Python script.
Python 2.7's expiry date was originally supposed to be back in 2015, but for unidentifiable reasons, it was put off until the year 2020. It was known that there was a major concern about data being unable to roll back but roll FORWARD into the new version, Python 3. In 2017, Google declared that there would be work done on Python 2.7 to enhance execution under simultaneously running tasks.

Basic Features of Python

Python is an unmistakable and extremely robust programming language that is object-oriented based almost identical to Ruby, Perl, and Java, A portion of Python's remarkable highlights:

- Python uses a rich structure, influencing, and composing projects that can be analyzed simpler.
- It accompanies a huge standard library that backs tons of simple programming commands, for example, extremely

seamless web server connections, processing and handling files, and the ability to search through text with commonly used expressions and commands.

- Python's easy to use interactive interface makes it simple to test shorter pieces of coding. It also comes with IDLE which is a "development environment".

Common Programming Language Features of Python

I.   A huge array of common data types: floating point numbers, complex numbers, infinite length integers, ASCII strings, and Unicode, as well as a large variety of dictionaries and lists.

II.   Python is guided in an object-oriented framework, with multiple classes and inheritance.

III.   Python code can be bundled together into different modules and packages.
    Python is notorious for being a much cleaner language for error handling due to
        the catching and raising of exceptions allowed.

IV.   Information is firmly and progressively composed. Blending incongruent data types, for example, adding a string and a number together, raises an exception right away where errors are caught significantly sooner than later.

V.   Python has advanced coding highlights such as comprehending lists and iterators.

Summary

- Python effortlessly extended out by including new modules executed in a source code like C or C++.
- Python can also be inserted into another application to give an easily programmed interface.

- Python will run anyplace, including OS X, Windows Environment, Linux, and even UNIX, with informal models for the Android and iOS environments.
- Python can easily be recorded, modified and re-downloaded and distributed, be unreservedly adjusted and re-disseminated. While it is copyrighted, it's accessible under open source.
- Ultimately, Python is available free of charge.

Part 2: Installing Python

Python is both procedural and object-oriented coding language. It has an easy syntax. Python programming language is cross-platform implying that it can be run on different Operating Systems environments such as Linux, Windows platform, Mac OS X platform, UNIX platform and can be ported to .NET and Java virtual machines. Python programming language is free and open source. While most recent versions of Mac and Linux have Python preinstalled, it is recommended that one installs and runs the current version.

Installing Python

Most recent versions of Linux and Mac have Python already installed in them. However, you might need to install Python and the following are the steps for installing Python in Windows, Mac OS X or Linux.

Installing Python in Macintosh Operating System X

I.   Visit Download Python page which is the credible site and click "Download Python 3.7.2 (The version may differ from the one stated here).

II.   When the download completes, click open the package and follow the instructions given. The installation should complete with "The installation was successful" prompt.

III.   Now, visit Download Notepad++ and download the text editor and install it by opening the package and following the message prompts. The Notepad++ text editor is free and suited to help write source code (raw text programming words).

Installing Python in Linux

It is now time to issue instructions to run the source code on your OS (Operating System)

Installing in Windows

I.   Visit Download Python site which is the recommended site and click "Download Python 3.7.2 (The version may differ from the one stated here).

II.   When your download completes, open the package by clicking and follow the guidelines given. The Python installation should complete with "The installation was successful" prompt. When you install Python successfully, it also installs a program known as IDLE along it. IDLE is a graphical user interface when working with Python.

III.   Now, visit Download Notepad++ and download the text editor and install it by opening the package and following the message prompts. The Notepad++ text editor is free and suited to help write source code (raw text programming words).

Modes of Running Python

Now before we start running our first python program it is important that we understand the ways in which we can run python programs. Running or executing or deploying or firing a program simply means that we making the computer process instructions/lines of codes. For instance, if the lines of codes (program) require the computer to display some message then it should. The following are the ways or mode of running python programs. The interpreter is a special program that is installed when installing the Python package and helps convert text code into a language that the computer understands and can act on it (executing).

I.   Immediate Mode

It is a way of running python programs that are not written in a file. We get into the immediate mode by typing the word python in the command line and which will trigger the interpreter to switch to immediate mode. The immediate mode allows typing of expressions directly and pressing enter generates the output. The sign below is the Python prompt:

>>>

The python prompt instructs the interpreter to accept input from the user. For instance, typing 2+2 and pressing enter will display 4 as the output. In a way, this prompt can be used as a calculator. If you need to exit the immediate mode, type quit() or exit().

Now type 5 +3, and press enter, the output should be 8. The next mode is the Script Mode.

II.   Script Mode

The script mode is used to run a python program written in a file, the file is called a script.

The scripts can be saved to external storage such as a disk for later use. All python scripts have the file extension .py which implies that the filename ends with .py. An example is myFirstProg.py. We shall explain later how to write python scripts.

Integrated Development Environment (IDE)

An IDE provides a convenient way of writing and running Python programs. One can also use text editors to create a python script file instead of an IDE by writing lines of codes and saving the file with a .py extension. However, using an IDE can simplify the process of writing and running Python programs. The IDEL present in the Python package is an example of an IDE with a graphical user interface and gets installed along the Python language. The advantages of IDE include helping getting rid of repetitive tasks and simplify coding for beginners. IDE provides syntax highlighting, code hinting, and syntax checking among other features. There also commercial IDE such as the PyScripter IDE that performs most of the mentioned functions.

Note:

We have presented what is Python programming language, how to download and install Python, the immediate and script modes of Python IDE, and what is an IDE.

Summary

- Python can be obtained from the **Python Software Foundation** website at python.org. Typically, that involves downloading the appropriate **installer** for your operating system and running it on your machine.
- Some operating systems, notably Linux, provide a **package manager** that can be run to install Python.
- On macOS, the best way to install Python 3 involves installing a package manager called **Homebrew**. You'll see how to do this in the relevant section in the tutorial.

Part 3: Variables
First Program in Python

The rest of illustrations will assume you are running the python programs in a Windows environment.

I.   Start IDLE

II. Navigate to the File menu and click New Window

III. Type the following: print ("Hello World!")

IV. On the file, menu click Save. Type the name of myProgram1.py

V.   Navigate to Run and click Run Module to run the program.

The first program that we have written is known as the "Hello World!" and is used to not only provide an introduction to a new computer coding language but also test the basic configuration of the IDE. The output of the program is "Hello World!" Here is what has happened, the Print() is an inbuilt function, it is prewritten and preloaded for you, is used to display whatever is contained in the () as long as it is between the double quotes. The computer will display anything written within the double quotes.

Practice Exercise: Now write and run the following python programs:

- ✓ print("I am now a Python Language Coder!")

- ✓ print("This is my second simple program!")

- ✓ print("I love the simplicity of Python")

- ✓ print("I will display whatever is here in quotes such as owyhen2589gdbnz082")

Now we need to write a program with numbers but before writing such a program we need to learn something about Variables and Types.

Remember python is object-oriented and it is not statically typed which means we do not need to declare variables before using them or specify their type. Let us explain this statement, an object-oriented language simply means that the language supports viewing and manipulating real-life scenarios as groups with subgroups that can be linked and shared mimicking the natural order and interaction of things. Not all programming languages are object oriented, for instance, Visual C programming language is not object-oriented. In programming, declaring variables means that we explicitly state the nature of the variable. The variable can be declared as an integer, long integer, short integer, floating integer, a string, or as a character including if it is accessible locally or globally. A variable is a storage location that changes values depending on conditions.

For instance, number1 can take any number from 0 to infinity. However, if we specify explicitly that int number1 it then means that the storage location will only accept integers and not fractions for instance. Fortunately or unfortunately, python does not require us to explicitly state the nature of the storage location (declare variables) as that is left to the python language itself to figure out that.

Before tackling types of variables and rules of writing variables, let us run a simple program to understand what variables when coding a python program are.

✓ Start IDLE

✓ Navigate to the File menu and click New Window

✓ Type the following:

num1=4

num2=5

sum=num1+num2

print(sum)

✓ On the file, menu click Save. Type the name of myProgram2.py

✓ Navigate to Run and click Run Module to run the program.

The expected output of this program should be "9" without the double quotes.

Discussion

At this point, you are eager to understand what has just happened and why the print(sum) does not have double quotes like the first programs we wrote. Here is the explanation.

The first line num1=4 means that variable num1(our shortened way of writing number1, first number) has been assigned 4 before the program runs.

The second line num2=5 means that variable num2(our shortened way of writing number2, second number) has been assigned 5 before the program runs.

The computer interprets these instructions and stores the numbers given

The third line sum=num1+num2 tells the computer that takes whatever num1 has been given and add to whatever num2 has been given. In other terms, sum the values of num1 and num2.

The fourth line print(sum) means that display whatever sum has. If we put double quotes to sum, the computer will simply display the word sum and not the sum of the two numbers! Remember that cliché that computers are garbage in and garbage out. They follow what you give them!

Note: + is an operator for summing variables and has other users that will be discussed later.

Now let us try out three exercises involving numbers before we explain types of variables and rules of writing variables so that you get more freedom to play with variables. Remember variables values vary for instance num1 can take 3, 8, 1562, 1.

Follow the steps of opening Python IDE and do the following:

✓ The output should be 54

num1=43

num2=11

sum=num1+num2

print(sum)

✓ The output should be 167

num1=101

num2=66

sum=num1+num2

print(sum)

✓ The output should be 28

num1=9

num2=19

sum=num1+num2

print(sum)

Variables

We have used num1, num2, and sum and the variable names were not just random, they must follow certain rules and conventions. Rules are what we cannot violate while conventions are much like the recommended way. Let us start with the rules:

The Rules of When Naming Variables in Python

I. Variable names should always start with a letter or an underscore, i.e.

num1

_num1

II.   The remaining part of the variable name may consist of numbers, letters, and underscores, i.e.

number1

num_be_r

III.   Variable names are case sensitive meaning that capital letters and non-capital letters are treated differently.

Num1 will be treated differently with num1.

Practice Exercise

Write/suggest five variables for:

- ✓ Hospital department.

- ✓ Bank.

- ✓ Media House.

  Given scri=75, scr4=9, sscr2=13, Scr=18

- ✓ The variable names in above are supposed to represents scores of students. Rewrite the variables to satisfy Python variable rules and conventions.

Conventions When Naming Variables in Python

As earlier indicated, conventions are not rules per se are the established traditions that add value and readability to the way we name variables in Python.

❖ Uphold readability. Your variables should give a hint of what they are handling because programs are meant to be read by other people other than the person writing them.

number1 is easy to read compared to n1. Similarly, first_name is easy to read compared to firstname or firstName or fn. The implication of all these is that both are valid/acceptable variables in python but the convention is forcing us to write them in an easy to read form.

❖ Use descriptive names when writing your variables. For instance, number1 as a variable name is descriptive compared yale or mything. In other words, we can write yale to capture values for number1 but the name does not outrightly hint what we are doing. Remember when writing programs; assume another person will maintain them. The person should be able to quickly figure out what the program is all about before running it.

❖ Due to confusion, avoid using the uppercase 'O', lowercase letter 'l' and the uppercase letter 'I' because they can be confused with numbers. In other terms, using these letters will not be a violation of writing variables but their inclusion as variable names will breed confusion.

Practice Exercise 1

Re-write the following variable names to (1) be valid variable names and follow (2) conventions of writing variable names.

- ✓ 23doctor

- ✓ line1

- ✓ Option3

- ✓ Mydesk

✓ #cup3

Practice Exercise 2

Write/Suggest variable names that are (1) valid and (2) conventional.

✓ You want to sum three numbers.

✓ You want to store the names of four students.

✓ You want to store the names of five doctors in a hospital.

Keywords and Identifiers in Python Programming Language

At this point, you have been wondering why you must use print and str in that manner without the freedom or knowledge of why the stated words have to be written in that manner. The words print and str constitute a special type of words that have to be written that way always. Each programming language has its set of keywords. In most cases, some keywords are found across several programming languages. Keywords are case sensitive in python meaning that we have to type them in their lowercase form always. Keywords cannot be used to name a function (we will explain what it is later), name of a variable.

There are 33 keywords in Python and all are in lowercase save for None, False, and True. They must always be written as they appear below:

Note: The print() and str are functions, but they are inbuilt/preloaded functions in Pythons. Functions are a set of rules and methods that act when invoked. For instance, the print function will display output when activated/invoked/called. At this point, you have not encountered all of the keywords, but you will meet them gradually. Take time to skim through, read and try to recall as many as you can.

18

Practice Exercise

Identify what is wrong with the following variable names (The exercise requires recalling what we have learned so far)

- ✓ for=1
- ✓ yield=3
- ✓ 34ball
- ✓ m

Comments and Statements

Statements in Python

A statement in Python refers to instructions that a Python interpreter can work on/execute. An example is str='I am a Programmer' and number1=3. A statement having an equal sign(=) is known as an assignment statement. They are other types of statements such as the if, while, and for which will be handled later.

Practice Exercise

- ✓ Write a Python statement that assigns the first number a value of 18.

- ✓ Write a programming statement that assigns the second number value of 21.
- ✓ What type of statements are a. and b. above?

Multi-Line Python Statement

It is possible to spread a statement over multiple lines. Such a statement is known as a multi-line statement. The termination of a programming statement is denoted by new line character. To spread a statement overs several lines, in Python, we use the backslash (\) known as the line continuation character. An example of a multi-line statement is:

sum=3+6+7+\

9+1+3+\

11+4+8

The example above is also known as an explicit line continuation. In Python, the square brackets [] denotes line continuation similar to parenthesis/round brackets (), and lastly braces {}. The above example can be rewritten as

sum=(3+6+7+

9+1+3+

11+4+8)

Note: We have dropped the backslash(\) known as the line continuation character when we use the parenthesis(round brackets) because the parenthesis is doing the work that the line continuation \ was doing.

Question: Why do you think multi-line statements are necessary we can simply write a single line and the program statement will run just fine?

Answer: Multi-line statements can help improve formatting/readability of the entire program. Remember, when writing a program always assume that it is other people who will use and maintain it without your input.

Practice Exercise:

Rewrite the following program statements using multi-line operators such as the \, [],() or {} to improve readability of the program statements.

- total=2+9+3+6+8+2+5+1+14+5+21+26+4+7+13+31+24
- count=13+1+56+3+7+9+5+12+54+4+7+45+71+4+8+5

Semicolons are also used when creating multiple statements in a single line. Assume we have to assign and display the age of four employees in a python program. The program could be written as:

employee1=25; employee2=45; employee3=32; employee4=43.

Indentation in Python

Indentation is used for categorization program lines into a block in Python. The amount of indentation to use in Python depends entirely on the programmer. However, it is important to ensure consistency. By convention, four whitespaces are used for indentation instead of using tabs. For example:

Note: We will explain what kind of program of this is later.

Indentation in Python also helps make the program look neat and clean. Indentation creates consistency. However, when performing line continuation indentation can be ignored. Incorrect indentation will create an indentation error. Correct python programs without indentation will still run but they might be neat and consistent from human readability view.

Comments in Pythons

When writing python programs and indeed any programming language, comments are very important. Comments are used to describe what is happening within a program. It becomes easier for another person taking a look at a program to have an idea of what the program does by reading the comments in it. Comments are also useful to a programmer as one can forget the critical details of a program written. The hash (#) symbol is used before writing a comment in Python. The comment extends up to the newline character. The python interpreter normally ignores comments. Comments are meant for programmers to understand the program better.

Example

I.   Start IDLE
II.   Navigate to the File menu and click New Window
III.   Type the following:

   #This is my first comment

   #The program will print Hello World

      Print('Hello World')   #This is an inbuilt function to display

IV.   On the file, menu click Save. Type the name of myProgram5.py

Navigate to Run and click Run Module to run the program

Practice Exercise

This exercise integrates most of what we have covered so far.

- ✓ Write a program to sum two numbers 45, and 12 and include single line comments at each line of code.
- ✓ Write a program to show the names of two employees where the first employee is "Daisy" and the second employee is "Richard". Include single comments at each line of code.
- ✓ Write a program to display the student registration numbers where the student names and their registration are: Yvonne=235, Ian=782, James=1235, Juliet=568.

Multi-Line Comments

Just like multi-line program statements we also have multi-line comments. There are several ways of writing multi-line comments. The first approach is to type the hash (#) at each comment line starting point.

For Example

Start IDLE.

Navigate to the File menu and click New Window.

Type the following:

#I am going to write a long comment line

#the comment will spill over to this line

#and finally end here.

The second way of writing multi-line comments involves using triple single or double quotes: "'" or""". For multi-line strings and multi-line comments in Python, we use the triple quotes. Caution: When used in docstrings they will generate extra code but we do not have to worry about this at this instance.

Example:

Start IDLE.

Navigate to the File menu and click New Window.

Type the following:

""""This is also a great i

illustration of

a multi-line comment in Python""""

Summary

Variable are storage locations that a user specifies before writing and running a python program. Variable names are labels of those storage locations. A variable holds a value depending on circumstances. For instance, doctor1 can be Daniel, Brenda or Rita. Patient1 can be Luke, William or Kelly. Variable names are written by adhering to rules and conventions. Rules are a must while conventions are optional but recommended as they help write readable variable names. When writing a program, you should assume that another person will examine or run it without your input and thus should be well written. The next chapter will discuss Variables. In programming, declaring variables means that we explicitly state the nature of the variable. The variable can be declared as an integer, long integer, short integer, floating integer, a string, or as a character including if it is accessible locally or globally. A variable is a storage location that changes values depending on conditions. Use descriptive names when writing your variables.

SECOND DAY

Part 4: Data Types in Python

Numbers

As indicated, Python accommodates floating, integer and complex numbers. The presence or absence of a decimal point separates integers and floating points. For instance, 4 is integer while 4.0 is a floating point number.

On the other hand, complex numbers in Python are denoted as r+tj where j represents the real part and t is the virtual part. In this context the function type() is used to determine the variable class. The Python function instance() is invoked to make a determination of which specific class function originates from.

Example:

Start IDLE.

Navigate to the File menu and click New Window.

Type the following:

number=6

print(type(number))   #should output class int

print(type(6.0))   #should output class float

complex_num=7+5j

print(complex_num+5)

print(isinstance(complex_num, complex)) #should output True

Important: Integers in Python can be of infinite length. Floating numbers in Python are assumed precise up to fifteen decimal places.

Number Conversion

This segment assumes you have prior basic knowledge of how to manually or using a calculate to convert decimal into binary, octal and hexadecimal. Check out the Windows Calculator in Windows 10, Calculator version Version 10.1804.911.1000 and choose programmer mode to automatically convert.

Programmers often need to convert decimal numbers into octal, hexadecimal and binary forms. A prefix in Python allows denotation of these numbers to their corresponding type.

Number System Prefix

Octal   '0O' or '0o'

Binary   '0B' or '0b'

Hexadecimal   'oX or 'ox'

Example

print(ob1010101) #Output:85

print(ox7B+obo101) #Output: 128 (123+5)

print(oo710)   #Output:710

Practice Exercise

Write a Python program to display the following:

- 0011 11112
- 747
- 9316

Type Conversion

Sometimes referred to as coercion, type conversion allows us to change one type of number into another. The preloaded functions such as float(), int() and complex() enable implicit and explicit type conversions. The same functions can be used to change from strings.

Example:

Start IDLE.

Navigate to the File menu and click New Window.

Type the following:

int(5.3) #Gives 5

int(5.9) #Gives 5

The int() will produce a truncation effect when applied to floating numbers. It will simply drop the decimal point part without rounding off. For the float() let us take a look:

Start IDLE.

Navigate to the File menu and click New Window.

Type the following:

float(6) #Gives 6.0

ccomplex('4+2j') #Gives (4+2j)

Practice Exercise

Apply the int() conversion to the following:

- ✓ 4.1
- ✓ 4.7
- ✓ 13.3
- ✓ 13.9

Apply the float() conversion to the following:

- ✓ 7
- ✓ 16
- ✓ 19

Decimal in Python

Example

Start IDLE.

Navigate to the File menu and click New Window.

Type the following:

(1.2+2.1)==3.3 #Will return False, why?

Discussion

The computer works with finite numbers and fractions cannot be stored in their raw form as they will create infinite long binary sequence.

Fractions in Python

The fractions module in Python allows operations on fractional numbers.

Example

Start IDLE.

Navigate to the File menu and click New Window.

Type the following:

import fractions

print(fractions.my_fraction(2.5)) #Output 5/2

print(fractions.my_fraction(4)) #Output 5

print(fractions.my_fraction(2,5)) #output 2/5

NOTE

Creating my_fraction from float can lead to unusual results due to the misleading representation of binary floating point.

Mathematics in Python

To carry out mathematical functions, Python offers modules like random and math.

Start IDLE.

Navigate to the File menu and click New Window.

Type the following:

import math

print(math.pi)   #output:3.14159....

print(math.cos(math.pi)) #the output will be -1.0

print(math.exp(10)) #the output will be 22026.4....

print(math.log10(100)) #the output will be 2

print(math.factorial(5)) #the output will be 120

Practice Exercise

Write a python program that uses math functions from the math module to perform the following:

- ✓ Square of 34
- ✓ Log1010000
- ✓ Cos 45 x sin 90
- ✓ Exponent of 20

Before tackling flow control, it is important we explore logical operators.

Comparison operators are special operators in Python programming language that evaluate to either True or False state of the condition.

Program flow control refers to a way in which a programmer explicitly species the order of execution of program code lines. Normally, flow control involves placing some condition (s) on the program code lines. In this chapter, we will explore and test various flow controls in Python.

Summary

In this tutorial, you learned about the built-in **data types** and **functions** Python provides.

The examples given so far have all manipulated and displayed only constant values. In most programs, you are usually going to want to create objects that change in value as the program executes.

Part 5: Loops and Functions

LOOPS
if...else Flow Control

The if..else statement in Python is a decision making when executing the program. The if...else statement will ONLY execute code if the specified condition exists.

The syntax of if...else in Python

if test expression:

Statement(s)

Discussion
The python program will only execute the statements(s) if the test expression is True. The program first evaluates the test expression before executing the statement(s). The program will not execute the statement(s) if the test expression is False. By convention, the body of it is marked by indentation while the first is not indented line signals the end.

Challenge: Think of scenarios, real-life, where the if...else condition is required.

• If you have not enrolled for a course, then you cannot sit for the exam else sit for the exam.

• If you have paid for house rent then you will be issued with acknowledgment receipt else request for more time.

• If you are a licensed driver then you can drive to school else you hire a taxi.

• If you are tired then you can watch movies else can complete the essay.

• If you are an ethical person then you will acknowledge your mistake else you will overlook the damage caused.

• If you are committed to programming then you will practice daily else you will lose interest.

• If you have signed for email alerts you will be updated frequently else you will have to check the website daily.

• If you plead guilty to all accounts you are likely to be convicted else the merit of your case will depend on cross-examination of witnesses and evidence presented.

Note: When we use the if statement alone without the else part, it will only print/display if the condition is true, it will not cater for the alternative, the case where the first condition is not present.

Example 1

Start IDLE.

Navigate to the File menu and click New Window.

Type the following:

number=5

if number>0   #The comparison operator

  print(number, "The number is a positive number")

Discussion

The program contains the if the condition that tests if the given number satisfies the if condition, "is it greater than 0" since 5 is greater than zero, the condition is satisfied the interpreter is allowed to execute the next statement which is to extract and display the numerical value including the string message. The test condition in this program is "number>0. But think of when the condition is not met, what happens? Let us look at Example 2.

Example 2

Start IDLE.

Navigate to the File menu and click New Window.

Type the following:

number=-9

if number>0:

  print(number, "This is a positive number")

Discussion

The program contains only the if statement which tests the expression by testing of -9 is greater than zero since it is not the interpreter will not execute the subsequent program code lines. In real life, you will want to provide for an alternate in case the first condition is not met. This program will not display anything when executed because the if the condition has not been met. The test condition in this program is "number>0.

Practice Exercise

Write programs in Python using if statement only to perform the following:

- Given number=7, write a program to test and display only even numbers.
- Given number1=8, number2=13, write a program to only display if the sum is less than 10.
- Given count_int=57, write a program that tests if the count is more than 45 and displays, the count is above the recommended number.
- Given marks=34, write a program that tests if the marks are less than 50 and display the message, the score is below average.
- Given marks=78, write a program that tests if the marks are more than 50 and display the message, great performance.
- Given number=88, write a program that tests if the number is an odd number and displays the message, Yes it is an odd number.
- Given number=24, write a program that tests and displays if the number is even.
- Given number =21, write a program that tests if the number is odd and displays the string, Yes it is an odd number.

Note

The execution of statements after the if expression will only happen where the if the expression evaluates to True, otherwise the statements are ignored.

if...else Statement in Python

The if...else syntax

if test condition:

   Statements

else:

   Statements

The explanation the if statement, the if...else statement will execute the body of if in the case that the tests condition is True. Should the if...else tests expression evaluate to false, the body of the else will be executed. Program blocks are denoted by indentation. The if...else provides more maneuverability when placing conditions on the code.

Example

A program that checks whether a number is positive or negative

Start IDLE.

Navigate to the File menu and click New Window.

Type the following:

number_mine=-56

if(number<0):

   print(number_mine, "The number is negative")

else:

   print(number_mine, "The number is a positive number")

Practice Exercise

Write a Python program that uses if..else flow control to perform the following

- ✓ Given number=9, write a program that tests and displays whether the number is even or odd.
- ✓ Given marks=76, write a program that tests and displays whether the marks are above pass mark or not bearing in mind that pass mark is 50.
- ✓ Given number=78, write a program that tests and displays whether the number is even or odd.
- ✓ Given marks=27, write a program that tests and displays whether the marks are above pass mark or not bearing in mind that pass mark is 50.

Challenge:

Write a program that accepts age input from the user, explicitly coverts the age into integer data types, then uses if...else flow control to tests whether the person is underage or not, the legal age is 21. Include comments and indentation to improve the readability of the program.

if...elif...else Flow Control Statement in Python

Now think of scenarios where we need to evaluate multiple conditions, not just one, not just two but three and more. Think of where you have to choose team member, if not Richard, then Mercy, if not Richard and Mercy then Brian, if not Richard, Mercy, and Brian then Yvonne. Real-life scenarios may involve several choices/conditions that have to be captured when writing a program.

if...elif..else Syntax

if test expression:

  Body of if

elif test expression:

  Body of elif

else:

  Body of else

Remember that the elif simply refers to else if and is intended to allow for checking of multiple expressions. The if the block is evaluated first, then elif block(s), before the else block. In this case, the else block is more of a fallback option when all other conditions return false. Important to remember, despite several blocks available in if..elif..else only one block will be executed.

Example:

Three conditions covered but the only one can execute at a given instance.

Start IDLE.

Navigate to the File menu and click New Window.

Type the following:

number_mine=87

if(number>0):

  print(number_mine, "This is a positive number")

elif(number_mie==0):

print(number_mine, "The number is zero")

else:

print(number_mine, "The number is a negative number")

Discussion:

There are three possibilities but at any given instance the only condition will exist and this qualifies the use of if family flow control statement. For three or more conditions to evaluate, the if...elif..else flow statement merits.

Nested if Statements in Python

Sometimes it happens that a condition exists but there are more sub-conditions that need to be covered and this leads to a concept known as nesting. The amount of statements to nests is not limited but you should exercise caution as you will realize nesting can lead to user errors when writing code. Nesting can also complicate maintaining of code. The only indentation can help determine the level of nesting.

Example

Start IDLE.

Navigate to the File menu and click New Window.

Type the following:

my_charact=str(input("Type a character here either 'a', 'b' or 'c':"))

if (my_charact='a'):

if(my_charact='a'):

```
    print("a")

  else if:

    (my_charact='b')

    print("b")

else:

  print("c")
```

Practice Exercise

Write a program that uses the if..else flow control statement to check non-leap year and display either scenario. Include comments and indentation to enhance the readability of the program.

For Loop in Python

Indentation is used to separate the body of for loop in Python.

Note: Simple linear list takes the following syntax:

Variable_name=[values separated by a comma]

Example

Start IDLE.

Navigate to the File menu and click New Window.

Type the following:

numbers=[12, 3,18,10,7,2,3,6,1]   #Variable name storing the list sum=0   *#Initialize sum before usage, very important*

for cumulative in numbers: *#Iterate over the list*

sum=sum+cumulative

print("The sum is" ,sum)

Practice Exercise

Start IDLE.

Navigate to the File menu and click New Window.

Type the following:

Write a Python program that uses the for loop to sum the following lists.

- ✓ marks=[3, 8,19, 6,18,29,15]
- ✓ ages=[12,17,14,18,11,10,16]
- ✓ mileage=[15,67,89,123,76,83]
- ✓ cups=[7,10,3,5,8,16,13]

range() function in Python

The range function (range()) in Python can help generate numbers. Remember in programming the first item is indexed 0. Therefore, range(11) will generate numbers from 0 to 10.

Example

Start IDLE.

Navigate to the File menu and click New Window.

Type the following:

print(range(7))

The output will be 0,1,2,3,4,5,6

Practice Exercise:

Without writing and running a Python program what will be the output for:

- ✓ range(16)
- ✓ range(8)
- ✓ range(4)

Using range() and len() and indexing

Practice Exercise

Write a Python program to iterate through the following list and include the message I listen to (each of the music genre). Use the for loop, len() and range(). Refer to the previous example on syntax.

folders=['Rumba', 'House', 'Rock']

Using for Loop with Else

It is possible to include a for loop with else but as an option. The else block will be executed if the items contained in the sequence are exhausted.

Example

Start IDLE.

Navigate to the File menu and click New Window.

Type the following:

```
marks=[12, 15,17]

for i in marks:

  print(i)

else:

  print("No items left")
```

Challenge:

Write a Python program that prints all prime numbers between 1 and 50.

While Loop in Python

In Python, the while loop is used to iterate over a block of program code as long as the test condition stays True. The while loop is used in contexts where the user does not know the loop cycles required. As earlier indicated, the while loop body is determined through indentation.

Example

Start IDLE.

Navigate to the File menu and click New Window.

Type the following:

Caution: Failing to include the value of the counter will lead to an infinite loop.

Practice Exercise

- Write a Python program that utilizes the while flow control statement to display the sum of all odd numbers from 1 to 10.
- Write a Python program that employs the while flow control statement to display the sum of all numbers from 11 to 21.
- Write a Python program that incorporates while flow control statement to display the sum of all even numbers from 1 to 10.

Using While Loop with Else

If the condition is false and no break occurs, a while loop's else part runs.

Example

Start IDLE.

Navigate to the File menu and click New Window.

Type the following:

```
track = 0

while track< 4:

  print("Within the loop")

track = track + 1

else:
```

```python
print("Now within the else segment")
```

Python's Break and Continue

Let us use real-life analogy where we have to force a stop on iteration before it evaluates completely. Think of when cracking/breaking passwords using a simple dictionary attack that loops through all possible character combinations, you will want the program immediately it strikes the password searched without having to complete. Again, think of when recovering photos you accidentally deleted using a recovery software, you will want the recovery to stop iterating through files immediately it finds items within the specified range. The break and continue statement in Python works in a similar fashion.

Example

Start IDLE.

Navigate to the File menu and click New Window.

Type the following:

```python
for tracker in "bring":

  if tracker == "i":

    break

  print(tracker)

print("The End")
```

Continue Statement in Python

When the continue statement is used, the interpreter skips the rest of the code inside a loop for the current iteration only and the loop does not terminate. The loop continues with next iteration.

The syntax of Python continue

continue

Example

Start IDLE.

Navigate to the File menu and click New Window.

Type the following:

```
for tracker in "bring":
    if tracker == "i":
        continue
    print(tracker)
print("Finished")
```

The output of this program will be:

b

r

n

g

Finished

Analogy: Assume that you are running data recovery software and have specified skip word files (.doc, dox extension). The program will have to continue iterating even after skipping word files.

Practice Exercise

- Write a Python program using for loop that will break after striking "v" in the string "Oliver".
- Write a Python program that will continue after skipping "m" in the string "Lemon".

Pass Statement in Python

Like a comment, a pass statement does not impact the program as it leads to no operation.

The syntax of pass

pass

Think of a program code that you plan to use in future but is not currently needed. Instead of having to insert that code in future, the code can be written as pass statements.

Example

Start IDLE.

Navigate to the File menu and click New Window.

Type the following:

my_list={'k','i','n'}

```
for tracker in my_list:

    pass
```

Functions in Python

Functions in Python help split large code into smaller units. Functions make a program more organized and easy to manage.

In Python functions will assume the syntax form below:

def name_of_function (arguments):

   """"docstring""""

statements(s)

Example

Start IDLE.

Navigate to the File menu and click New Window.

Type the following:


```
def welcome(salute):

    """The Python function welcomes you to

    the individual passed in as

    parameter"""
```

```
print("Welcome " + salute + ". Lovely Day!")
```

Calling a Function in Python

We can call a function once we have defined it from another function or program.
Calling a function simply involves typing the function name with suitable parameters.

Start IDLE.

Navigate to the File menu and click New Window.

Type the following:

welcome('Brenda')

The output will be "Welcome Brenda. Lovely Day!'

Practice Exercise

Write a function that when called outputs"Hello (student name), kindly submit your work by Sunday".

Docstring

It is placed after the function header as the first statement and explains in summary what the function does. Docstring should always be placed between triple quotes to accommodate multiple line strings.

Calling/Invoking the docstring we typed earlier

Example

Start IDLE.

Navigate to the File menu and click New Window.

Type the following:

print(welcome._doc_)

The output will be "This function welcomes you to

the individual passed in as

parameter".

The syntax for calling/invoking the docstring is:

print(function_name. _doc_)

Python Function Return Statement

Return syntax

return [list of expressions]

Discussion

The return statement can return a value or a None object.

Example

Print(welcome("Richard"))   #Passing arguments and calling the function

Welcome Richard. Lovely Day!

None   #the returned value

Random Function in Python

Start IDLE.

Navigate to the File menu and click New Window.

Type the following:

import math

print(random.shuffle_num(11, 21))

y=['f','g','h','m']

print(random.pick(y))

random.anypic(y)

print(y)

print(your_pick.random())

Iterators

In Python, iterator refers to objects that can be iterated upon.

The for loop is used to implement iterators in Python anywhere. Iterators in Python can also be implemented using generators and comprehensions. In Python, an iterator concerns an construct that can be called several times performing same action.

Iterators in Python implement the _iter_() special method and _next_() special method which is collectively referred to as the iterator protocol.

In Python, an object becomes iterable if we can get an iterator from it for example string, tuple, and list is iterable. In operation, the iter() function calls the _iter_() method and returns an iterator from the set or list or string.

Manually Iterating Through Items in Python

The next() function is used in Python to manually loop through all the items of an iterator

Example

list_mine = [14, 17, 10, 13]

iter_list = iter(list_mine)

print(next(iter_list))

print(next(iter_list))

print(my_iter.__next__())

print(my_iter.__next__())

next(iter_list)

NOTE

The for loop provides an efficienty ay of automatically iterating through a list. The for loop can be applied on a file, list or string among others in Python.

Example

for element in list_mine:

   print(element)

Explaining the Loop

The for loop gets to iterate automatically through the Python list.

Example

for element in list_mine:

object_iter = iter(iterable)

while True:

  try:

    element = next(object_iter)

  except StopIteration:

    break

Creating Custom Iterator in Python

On the other hand, the _next_() will scan and give the next element in the sequence and will trigger the StopIteration exception once it reaches the end.

Example

class Power:

  """Will implement powers of 2

  """

  def __init__(self, max = 0):

```
    self.max = max

  def __iter__(self):

    self.m = 0

    return self

  def __next__(self):

    if self.m <= self.max:

      result = 2 ** self.m

      self.m += 1

      return result

    else:

      raise StopIteration
```

Discussion

Example

```
for j in Power(5):

  print(j)
```


Infinite Iterators

There may be situations that require continuous iteration. The situations we have tackled so far were infinite iterators and had to terminate after exhausting the items in the iterable. The iter() is an inbuilt function. The method is fired by providing two arguments. The first argument in iter() is the one being called while the other argument acts as a sentinel. Until the function returns a value equal to the Sentinel, the iterator will continue calling the function.

Example

int()

infer = iterate(int,2)

next(infer)

next(infer)

Discussion
The int() function in this program will always return value 0. Therefore, passing the function as iterate(int, 2) will return an iterator that invokes int(). The calling of int() will stop when the returned value equals 2. Since this will never happen, we will end up with an infinite iterator.

Example

Assume we want to display all odd numbers that exist.

Practice Exercise

Write a Python program that uses a custom infinite iterator to display all even numbers.

Closure Function in Python

Example

def printing(msg):

```
def printers():

    print(msg)

    return printer

custom = printing("Welcome")

custom()
```

Discussion

The printing() function was invoked with the string "Welcome" that gives us objects associated with the name. Calling custom() implied the message was remembered even though it had already completed executing the printing() function. In Python, the technique via which part of the data gets tied to the code is termed as closure. In this case, even when the variable gets out of scope, the value in the enclosing scope is remembered.

Example

```
del printing

another()

printing("Welcome")
```

NOTE

In Python, closures help provide a limited form of encapsulation. The use of enclosures can help avoid wide usage of global scope variables. Remember global scope implies that the names are accessible and modifiable at any part of the program which can create inconsistency. Closures can also be used to give an object-oriented solution to a problem.

Example

```
def product(n):

    def times(y):

        return y* number

    return times

multiply1 = times(13)

multiply1 = times(15)

print(multiply2(19))

print(multiply2(13))

print(multiply2(multiply(12)))
```

Projects

1. Implementing Simple Calculator in Python

```
def sum(m, n):

    return m + n

def minus(m, n):

    return m - n

def product(m, n):

    return m * n
```

```python
def division(m, n):

    return m / n

print("Choose an Operation.")

print("1.Sum")

print("2.Minus")

print("3.Product")

print("4.Division")

option = input("Type your choice (1/2/3/4):")

number1 = int(input("Enter number 1: "))

number2 = int(input("Enter number 2: "))

if option == '1':

    print(number1,"+",number2,"=", sum(number1,number2))

elif option == '2':

    print(number1,"-",number2,"=", minus(num1,num2))

elif choice == '3':

    print(number1,"*",number2,"=", product(number1,number2))

elif choice == '4':

    print(number1,"/",number2,"=", division(number1,number2))

else:
```

```python
        print("Check Your Selection, Out of Range")
```

2. Program to return factors of any integer

```python
def factors(m):

    print("We found factors of",m,"as:")

    for j in range(1, m + 1):

        if m % j == 0:

            print(j)

number = 400

factors(number)
```

Summary

For loops can iterate over a sequence of numbers using the "range" and "xrange" functions. The difference between range and xrange is that the range function returns a new list with numbers of that specified range, whereas xrange returns an iterator, which is more efficient. (Python 3 uses the range function, which acts like xrange). Note that the range function is zero based.

THIRD DAY

Part 6: Variable Scope and Lifetime in Python Functions

Variables and parameters defined within a Python function have local scope implying they are not visible from outside. In Python the variable lifetime is valid as long the function executes and is the period throughout that a variable exists in memory. Returning the function destroys the function variables.

Example

Start IDLE.

Navigate to the File menu and click New Window.

Type the following:

def function_my()

marks=15

print("The value inside the function is:", marks)

marks=37

function_my()

print"The value outside the function is:",marks)

Function Types

They are broadly grouped into user-defined and built-in functions. The built-in functions are part of the Python interpreter while the user-defined functions are specified by the user.

Practice Exercise

Give three examples of built-in functions in Pythons

Function Argument

Calling a function requires passing the correct number of parameters otherwise the interpreter will generate an error.

Ilustration

Start IDLE.

Navigate to the File menu and click New Window.

Type the following:

def salute(name,mesage):

    """This function welcomes to

the student with the provided message"""

print("Welcome",salute + ', ' + message)

welcome("Brenda","Lovely Day!")

Note: The function welcome() has two parameters. We will not get any error as has been fed with two arguments. Let us try calling the function with one argument and see what happens:

welcome("Brenda")   #only one argument passed

Running this program will generate an error saying "TypeError: welcome() missing 1 required positional argument. The same will happen when we pass no arguments to the function.

Example 2

Start IDLE.

Navigate to the File menu and click New Window.

Type the following:

welcome()

The interpreter will generate an error "TypeError: welcome() missing 2 required positional arguments".

Keywords Arguments in Python

Python provides a way of calling functions using keyword arguments. When calling functions using keyword arguments, the order of arguments can be changed. The values of a function are matched to the argument position-wise.

Note:

In the previous example function welcome when invoked as welcome("Brenda", "Lovely Day!"). The value "Brenda" is assigned to the argument name and "Lovely Day!" to msg.

Calling the function using keywords

Start IDLE.

Navigate to the File menu and click New Window.

Type the following:

welcome(name="Brenda", msg="Lovely Day!")

Keywords not following the order

welcome(msg="Lovely Day!", name="Brenda")

Arbitrary Arguments

It may happen that we do not have knowledge of all arguments needed to be passed into a function. Analogy: Assume that you are writing a program to welcome all new students this semester. In this case, you do not how many will report.

Example

Start IDLE.

Navigate to the File menu and click New Window.

Type the following:

*def welcome(*names):*

"""This welcome function salutes all students in the names tuple."""

for name in names:

print("Welcome".name)

welcome("Lucy","Richard","Fridah","James")

The output of the program will be:

Welcome Lucy

Welcome Richard

Welcome Fridah

Welcome James

Recursion in Python

The definition of something in terms of itself is called recursion. A recursive function calls other functions.

Example

Python program to compute integer factorials

Practice Exercise

Write a Python program to find the factorial of 7.

Python Anonymous Function

Some functions may be specified devoid of a name and this are called anonymous function. The lambda keyword is used to denote an anonymous function. Anonymous functions are also referred to as lambda functions in Python.

Syntax

lambda arguments: expression.

Lambda functions must always have one expression but can have several arguments.

Example

Start IDLE.

Navigate to the File menu and click New Window.

Type the following:

*double = lambda y: y * 2*

 # Output: 10

print(double(5))

Example 2

We can use inbuilt functions such as filter () and lambda to show only even numbers in a list/tuple.

Start IDLE.

Navigate to the File menu and click New Window.

Type the following:

first_marks = [3, 7, 14, 16, 18, 21, 13, 32]

fresh_marks = list(filter(lambda n: (n%2 == 0) , first_marks))

 # Output: [14, 16, 18, 32]

print(fresh_marks)

Lambda function and map() can be used to double individual list items.

Example 3

Start IDLE.

Navigate to the File menu and click New Window.

Type the following:

first_score = [3, 7, 14, 16, 18, 21, 13, 32]

*fresh_score = list(map(lambda m: m * 2 , first_score))*

 # Output: [6, 14, 28, 32, 36, 42, 26, 64]

print(fresh_score)

Python's Global, Local, and Nonlocal

Python's Global Variables

Variables declared outside of a function in Python are known as global variables. They are declared in global scope. A global variable can be accessed outside or inside of the function.

Example

Start IDLE.

Navigate to the File menu and click New Window.

Type the following:

```
y= "global"
def foo():
    print("y inside the function :", y)
foo()
print("y outside the function:", y)
```

Discussion

In the illustration above, y is a global variable and is defined a foo() to print the global variable y. When we call the foo() it will print the value of y.

Local Variables

A local variable is declared within the body of the function or in the local scope.

Example

Start IDLE.

Navigate to the File menu and click New Window.

Type the following:

def foo():

  x = "local"

foo()

print(x)

Discussion

Running this program will generate an error indicating 'x' is undefined. The error is occurring because we are trying to access local variable x in a global scope whereas foo() functions only in the local scope.

Creating a Local Variable in Python

Example

A local variable is created by declaring a variable within the function.

def foo():

Start IDLE.

Navigate to the File menu and click New Window.

Type the following:

  x = "local"

  print(x)

foo()

Discussion

When we execute the code, the output will be:

Local

Python's Global and Local Variable

Using both local and global variables in the same code.

Example

Start IDLE.

Navigate to the File menu and click New Window.

Type the following:

y = "global"

def foo():

  global y

  x = "local"

  *y = y * 2*

  print(y)

  print(x)

foo()

Discussion

The output of the program will be:

global global

local

We declared y as a global variable and x as a local variable in the foo().
The * operator issued to modify the global variable y and finally, we
printed both y and x.

 Local and Global Variables with the same name

Start IDLE.

Navigate to the File menu and click New Window.

Type the following:

y=6

def foo():

y=11

   print("Local variable y-", y)

foo()

print("Global variable y-", y)

Python's Nonlocal Variables

A Python's nonlocal variable is used in a nested function whose local
scope is unspecified. It is neither global nor local scope.

Example

Creating a nonlocal variable.

Start IDLE.

Navigate to the File menu and click New Window.

Type the following:

```
def outer():
    y = "local variable"
    def inner():
        nonlocal y
        y = "nonlocal variable"
        print("inner:", y)
    inner()
    print("outer scope:", y)
outer()
```

Global Keyword in Python

The global keyword I Python allows modification of the variable outside the current scope. The global keyword makes changes to the variable in a local context. There are rules when creating a global keyword:

A global keyword is local by default when we create a variable within a function.

It is global by default when we define a variable outside of a function and you do not need to use the global keyword.

The global keyword is used to read and write a global variable within a function.

The use of global keyword outside a function will have no effect.

Example

Start IDLE.

Navigate to the File menu and click New Window.

Type the following:

```
number = 3       #A global variable

def add():

    print(number)

add()
```

The output of this program will be 3.

Modifying global variable from inside the function.

```
number=3                #a global variable

def add():

    number= number + 4    # add 4 to 3
```

print(number)

add()

Discussion

When the program is executed it will generate an error indicating that the local variable number is referenced before assignment. The reason for encountering the error is because we can only access the global variable but are unable to modify it from inside the function. Using a global keyword would solve this.

Example

Start IDLE.

Navigate to the File menu and click New Window.

Type the following:

Modifying global variable within a function using the global keyword

number = 3   # a global variable

def add():

  global number

  number= number + 1 # increment by 1

  print("Inside the function add():", number)

add()

print("In main area:", number)

Discussion

When the program is run, the output will be:

Inside the function add(): 4

In the main area: 4

We defined a number as a global keyword within the function add(). The variable was then incremented by 1, variable number. Then we called the add () function to print global variable c.

Creating Global Variables across Python Modules

We can create a single module config.py that will contain all global variables and share the information across several modules within the same program.

Example

Start IDLE.

Navigate to the File menu and click New Window.

Type the following:

Create config.py

x=0

y="empty"

Then create an update.py file to modify global variables

Import config

config.x=11

config.y="Today"

Then create a main.py file to evaluate the changes in value

import config

import update

print(config.x)

print(config.y)

Discussion

Running the main.py file will generate:

11

Today

Python Modules

Modules consist of definitions as well as program statements.

An illustration is a file name config.py which is considered as a module. The module name would be config. Modules are sued to help break large programs into smaller manageable and organized files as well as promoting reusability of code.

Example:

Creating the First module

Start IDLE.

Navigate to the File menu and click New Window.

Type the following:

Def add(x, y):

"""This is a program to add two

 numbers and return the outcome"""

outcome=x+y

return outcome

Module Import

The keyword import is used to import.

Example

Import first

The dot operator can help us access a function as long as we know the name of the module.

Example

Start IDLE.

Navigate to the File menu and click New Window.

Type the following:

first.add(6,8)

Import Statement in Python

The import statement can be used to access the definitions within a module via the dot operator.

Start IDLE.

Navigate to the File menu and click New Window.

Type the following:

import math

print("The PI value is", math.pi)

Import with renaming

Example

Start IDLE.

Navigate to the File menu and click New Window.

Type the following:

import math as h

   print("The PI value is-",h.pi)

Discussion

In this case, h is our renamed math module with a view helping save typing time in some instances. When we rename the new name becomes valid and recognized one and not the original one.

From...import statement Python.

It is possible to import particular names from a module rather than importing the entire module.

Example

Start IDLE.

Navigate to the File menu and click New Window.

Type the following:

from math import pi

print("The PI value is-", pi)

Importing all names

Example

Start IDLE.

Navigate to the File menu and click New Window.

Type the following:

from math import*

print("The PI value is-", pi)

Discussion

In this context, we are importing all definitions from a particular module but it is encouraged norm as it can lead to unseen duplicates.

Module Search Path in Python

Example

Start IDLE.

Navigate to the File menu and click New Window.

Type the following:

import sys

sys.path

Python searches everywhere including the sys file.

Reloading a Module

Python will only import a module once increasing efficiency in execution.

print("This program was executed")

import mine

Reloading Code

Example

Start IDLE.

Navigate to the File menu and click New Window.

Type the following:

import mine

import mine

import mine

mine.reload(mine)

Dir() built-in Python function

For discovering names contained in a module, we use the dir() inbuilt function.

Syntax

dir(module_name)

Python Package

Files in python hold modules and directories are stored in packages. A single package in Python holds similar modules. Therefore, different modules should be placed in different Python packages.

Summary

Parameters and **variables** defined inside a function is not visible from outside. Hence, they have a local **scope**. **Lifetime** of a **variable** is the period throughout which the **variable** exits in the memory. The **lifetime** of **variables** inside a function is as long as the function executes.

Part 7: Lists in Python

We create a list in Python by placing items called elements inside square brackets separated by commas. The items in a list can be of mixed data type.

Start IDLE.

Navigate to the File menu and click New Window.

Type the following:

list_mine=[]   #empty list

list_mine=[2,5,8] #list of integers

list_mine=[5,"Happy", 5.2] #list having mixed data types

Practice Exercise

Write a program that captures the following in a list: "Best", 26,89,3.9

Nested Lists

A nested list is a list as an item in another list.

Example

Start IDLE.

Navigate to the File menu and click New Window.

Type the following:

list_mine=["carrot", [9, 3, 6], ['g']]

Practice Exercise

Write a nested for the following elements: [36,2,1],"Writer",'t',[3.0, 2.5]

Accessing Elements from a List

In programming and in Python specifically, the first time is always indexed zero. For a list of five items we will access them from index0 to index4. Failure to access the items in a list in this manner will create index error. The index is always an integer as using other number types will create a type error. For nested lists, they are accessed via nested indexing.

Example

Start IDLE.

Navigate to the File menu and click New Window.

Type the following:

list_mine=['b','e','s','t']

print(list_mine[0]) #the output will be b

print(list_mine[2]) #the output will be s

print(list_mine[3]) #the output will be t

Practice Exercise

Given the following list:

your_collection=['t','k','v','w','z','n','f']

- ✓ Write a Python program to display the second item in the list
- ✓ Write a Python program to display the sixth item in the last
- ✓ Write a Python program to display the last item in the list.

Nested List Indexing

Start IDLE.

Navigate to the File menu and click New Window.

Type the following:

nested_list=["Best",[4,7,2,9]]

print(nested_list[0][1]

Python Negative Indexing

For its sequences, Python allows negative indexing. The last item on the list is index-1, index -2 is the second last item and so on.

Start IDLE.

Navigate to the File menu and click New Window.

Type the following:

list_mine=['c','h','a','n','g','e','s']

print(list_mine[-1])   #Output is s

print(list_mine [-4]) ##Output is n

Slicing Lists in Python

Slicing operator(full colon) is used to access a range of elements in a list.

Example

Start IDLE.

Navigate to the File menu and click New Window.

Type the following:

list_mine=['c','h','a','n','g','e','s']

print(list_mine[3:5])   #Picking elements from the 4 to the sixth

Example

Picking elements from start to the fifth

Start IDLE.

Navigate to the File menu and click New Window.

Type the following:

print(list_mine[:-6])

Example

Picking the third element to the last.

print(list_mine[2:])

Practice Exercise

Given class_names=['John', 'Kelly', 'Yvonne', 'Una','Lovy','Pius', 'Tracy']

- ✓ Write a python program using slice operator to display from the second students and the rest.
- ✓ Write a python program using slice operator to display first student to the third using negative indexing feature.
- ✓ Write a python program using slice operator to display the fourth and fifth students only.

Manipulating Elements in a List using the assignment operator

Items in a list can be changed meaning lists are mutable.

Start IDLE.

Navigate to the File menu and click New Window.

Type the following:

list_yours=[4,8,5,2,1]

list_yours[1]=6

print(list_yours)   #The output will be [4,6,5,2,1]

Changing a range of items in a list

Start IDLE.

Navigate to the File menu and click New Window.

Type the following:

list_yours[0:3]=[12,11,10] #Will change first item to fourth item in the list

print(list_yours)   #Output will be: [12,11,10,1]

Appending/Extending items in the List

The append() method allows extending the items in the list. The extend() can also be used.

Example

Start IDLE.

Navigate to the File menu and click New Window.

Type the following:

list_yours=[4, 6, 5]

list_yours.append(3)

print(list_yours)   #The output will be [4,6,5, 3]

Example

Start IDLE.

Navigate to the File menu and click New Window.

Type the following:

list_yours=[4,6,5]

list_yours.extend([13,7,9])

print(list_yours)   #The output will be [4,6,5,13,7,9]

The plus operator(+) can also be used to combine two lists. The *
operator can be used to iterate a list a given number of times.

Example

Start IDLE.

Navigate to the File menu and click New Window.

Type the following:

 list_yours=[4,6,5]

print(list_yours+[13,7,9]) # Output:[4, 6, 5,13,7,9]

*print(['happy']*4)   #Output:["happy","happy", "happy","happy"]*

Removing or Deleting Items from a List

The keyword del is used to delete elements or the entire list in Python.

Example

Start IDLE.

Navigate to the File menu and click New Window.

Type the following:

list_mine=['t','r','o','g','r','a','m']

del list_mine[1]

print(list_mine) #t, o, g, r, a, m

Deleting Multiple Elements

Example

Start IDLE.

Navigate to the File menu and click New Window.

Type the following:

del list_mine[0:3]

Example

print(list_mine) #a, m

Delete Entire List

Start IDLE.

Navigate to the File menu and click New Window.

Type the following:

delete list_mine

print(list_mine) #will generate an error of lost not found

The remove() method or pop() method can be used to remove specified item. The pop() method will remove and return the last item if index is not given and helps implement lists as stacks. The clear() method is used to empty a list.

Start IDLE.

Navigate to the File menu and click New Window.

Type the following:

list_mine=['t','k','b','d','w','q','v']

list_mine.remove('t')

print(list_mine)   #output will be ['t','k','b','d','w','q','v']

print(list_mine.pop(1))   #output will be 'k'

print(list_mine.pop())   #output will be 'v'

Practice Exercise

Given list_yours=['K','N','O','C','K','E','D']

- ✓ Pop the third item in the list, save the program as list1.
- ✓ Remove the fourth item using remove() method and save the program as list2
- ✓ Delete the second item in the list and save the program as list3.
- ✓ Pop the list without specifying an index and save the program as list4.

Using Empty List to Delete an Entire or Specific Elements

Start IDLE.

Navigate to the File menu and click New Window.

Type the following:

list_mine=['t','k','b','d','w','q','v']

list_mine=[1:2]=[]

print(list_mine)   #Output will be ['t','w','q','v']

Practice Exercise

- ➤ Use list access methods to display the following items in reversed order list_yours=[4,9,2,1,6,7]

- ➤ Use list access method to count the elements in a.

- ➤ Use list access method to sort the items in a. in an ascending order/default.

Summary

Lists store an ordered collection of items which can be of different types. The list defined above has items that are all of the same type (int), but all the items of a list do not need to be of the same type as you can see below.

```
# Define a list
heterogenousElements = [3, True, 'Michael', 2.0]
```

FOURTH DAY
Part 8: Tuples in Python

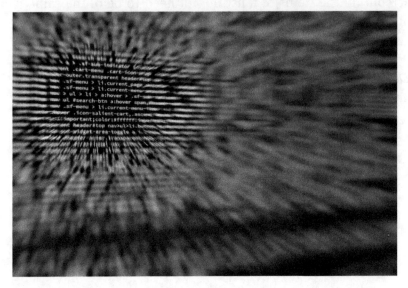

A tuple is like a list but we cannot change elements in a tuple.

Example

Start IDLE.

Navigate to the File menu and click New Window.

Type the following:

tuple_mine = (21, 12, 31)

print(tuple_mine)

tuple_mine = (31, "Green", 4.7)

print(tuple_mine)

Accessing Python Tuple Elements

Example

Start IDLE.

Navigate to the File menu and click New Window.

Type the following:

tuple_mine=['t','r','o','g','r','a','m']

    print(tuple_mine[1]) #output:'r'

    print(tuple_mine[3]) #output:'g'

Negative Indexing

Just like lists, tuples can also be indexed negatively.

Like lists, -1 refers to the last element on the list and -2 refer to the second last element.

Example

Start IDLE.

Navigate to the File menu and click New Window.

Type the following:

tuple_mine=['t','r','o','g','r','a','m']

print(tuple_mine [-2]) #the output will be 'a'

Slicing

The slicing operator, the full colon is used to access a range of items in a tuple.

Example

Start IDLE.

Navigate to the File menu and click New Window.

Type the following:

tuple_mine=['t','r','o','g','r','a','m']

print(tuple_mine [2:5]) #Output: 'o','g','r','a'

print(tuple_mine[:-4]) #'g','r','a','m'

NOTE

Tuple elements are immutable meaning they cannot be changed. However, we can combine elements in a tuple using +(concatenation operator). We can also repeat elements in a tuple using the * operator, just like lists.

Example

Start IDLE.

Navigate to the File menu and click New Window.

Type the following:

print((7, 45, 13) + (17, 25, 76))

print(("Several",) * 4)

NOTE

Since we cannot change elements in tuple, we cannot delete the elements too. However removing the full tuple can be attained using the kwyword del.

Example

Start IDLE.

Navigate to the File menu and click New Window.

Type the following:

t_mine=['t','k','q','v','y','c','d']

del t_mine

Available Tuple Methods in Python

They are only two methods available for working Python tuples.

count(y)

When called will give the item numbers that are equal to y.

index(y)

When called will give index first item index that is equal to y.

Example

Start IDLE.

Navigate to the File menu and click New Window.

Type the following:

t_mine=['t','k','q','v','y','c','d']

print(t_mine.count('t'))

print(t_mine.index('l'))

Testing Membership in Tuple

The keyword in us used to check the specified element exists in a tuple.

Start IDLE.

Navigate to the File menu and click New Window.

Type the following:

t_mine=['t','k','q','v','y','c','d']

print('a' t_mine) #Output: True

print('k' in t_mine) #Output: False

Inbuilt Python Functions with Tuple

String in Python.

Example

Start IDLE.

Navigate to the File menu and click New Window.

Type the following:

string_mine = 'Colorful'

print(string_mine)

string_mine = "Hello"

print(string_mine)

string_mine = '''Hello'''

print(string_mine)

string_mine = """I feel like I have

been born a programmer"""

print(string_mine)

Accessing items in a string

Example

Start IDLE.

Navigate to the File menu and click New Window.

Type the following:

str = 'Colorful'

print('str = ', str)

print('str[1] = ', str[1]) #Output the second item

print('str[-2] = ', str[-2]) #Output the second last item

print('str[2:4] = ', str[2:4]) #Output the third through the fifth item

Deleting or Changing in Python

In Python, strings are immutable therefore cannot be changed once assigned. However, deleting the entire string is possible.

Example

Start IDLE.

Navigate to the File menu and click New Window.

Type the following:

del string_mine

The escape sequences enable us to format our output to enhance clarity to the human user. A program will still run successful without using escape sequences but the output will be highly confusing to the human user. Writing and displaying output in expected output is part of good programming practices. The following are commonly used escape sequences.

Examples

Start IDLE.

Navigate to the File menu and click New Window.

Type the following:

print("D:\\Lessons\\Programming")

print("Prints\n in two lines")

Summary

As earlier indicated earlier, integers, floating point, and complex numbers are supported in Python. There are integers, floating and complex classes that help convert different number data types. The presence or absence of a decimal point separates integers and floating points. For instance, 4 is integer while 4.0 is a floating point number. Programmers often need to convert decimal numbers into octal, hexadecimal and binary forms. We can represent binary, hexadecimal and octal systems in Python by simply placing a prefix to the particular number. Sometimes referred to as coercion, type conversion allows us to change one type of number into another.

Inbuilt functions such as int() allows us to convert data types directly. The same functions can be used to convert from strings. We create a list in Python by placing items called elements inside square brackets separated by commas. In programming and in Python specifically, the first time is always indexed zero. For a list of five items we will access them from index0 to index4. Failure to access the items in a list in this manner will create index error.

Part 9: Strings in Python

A single or double quote in Python is used to indicate strings. The subsets of strings can be taken by using the slice operator ([:]) and []) with indexes beginning at () in the start of the string and operating their way from -1 at the end. Strings can be joined using the + (plus) sign known as the concatenation operator. The asterisk (*) is used as a repetition operator. Remember counting in programming starts from index zero (the first value)!

Example:

- ✓ Start IDLE
- ✓ Navigate to the File menu and click New Window
- ✓ Type the following:

```
str = 'Going Deep!'
print str            # Prints a complete string
print str[0]         # Prints first character of the string
print str[3:6]       # Prints characters starting from fourth to seventh
print str[3:]        # Prints string starting from the fourth character
print str * 3        # Prints string three times
print str + "I love Python" # Prints concatenated string
```

✓ On the file, menu click Save. Type the name of myProgram4.py
✓ Navigate to Run and click Run Module to run the program

The output of the program above should be:

Going Deep!

G

ng De

ng Deep!

Going Deep! Going Deep! Going Deep!

Going Deep! I love Python

Note: the # (hash sign) is used to indicate a single line comment. A comment is descriptive information about a particular line(s) of code. The comment is normally ignored by when running the program. The comment should be written after the # sign in python. Comments increase the readability of the program written.

Practice Exercise:

You will key in/type the following program statement:

str = 'I think I am now a Programmer'

a. Write a program statement that will display the entire string/statement above.

b. Write a program statement to display characters of the string from the second character to the sixth.

c. Write a single program statement that will display the entire string two times. (use *).

d. Write a program statement that will add the following at the end of the statement above, " of Python Programming Language"

String Operations

Several operations can be performed on a string making it a widely used datatype in Python.

Concatenation using the + operator, repetition using the * operator

Example

Start IDLE.

Navigate to the File menu and click New Window.

Type the following:

string1='Welcome'

string2='Again'

    print('string1+string2=',string1+string2)

*print(' string1 * 3 =', string1 * 3)*

Practice Exercise

Given string_a="I am awake" and string_b="coding in Python in a pajama"

String Iteration

The for control statement is used to continually scan through an entire scan until the specified number of times are reached before terminating the scan.

Membership Test in String

The keyword in is used to test if a sub string exists.

Example

't' in "triumph'   #Will return True

Inbuilt Python Functions for working with Strings

They include enumerate() and len().The len() function returns the length of the string.

String Formatting in Python

Single and Double Quotes

Example

Start IDLE.

Navigate to the File menu and click New Window.

Type the following:

print('They said, "We need a new team?"') # escape with single quotes

 # escaping double quotes

print("They said, \" We need a new team\"")

Python's Docstring

In Python, docstring refers to words offering a description and are written as the initial program statement in a function, module, method, or class definition. (We will handle this later on). Docstrings in Python are written using triple quotes.

Practice Exercise

This exercise will utilize several concepts that we covered earlier.

a.   Given   the   following   program   statement: Color1='red'; color1='blue'; CoLor1='yellow' explain why all the three will be treated as different variables in Python.

b.   Consider the following Python program and identify what is wrong with it.

student1_age=23   #This is the age of the first student

student2_age=19   #This is the age of the student

sotal_age=student1_age +student2_age   #Getting the sum of the ages of the

print(age)   #Displaying their ages

Part 10: Operators in Python

So far we have been using the summation (+) operator and it also doubles up as a concatenation operator (appending statements). However, we want to expand our list of operators and this leads us to basic operators in Python.

Arithmetic Operators

The multiplication (*), division (/), subtraction (-), and addition (+) are the arithmetic operators used to manipulate numbers.

Practice Exercise

Write the following programs and run it

- **Difference**

number1=35   *#declaring first number*

number2= 12   *#declaring second number*

difference=number2-number1   #declaring what the difference does

print(difference)   #Calling the print function to display what difference has

- **Multiplication**

number1=2   #declaring first number

number2= 15   #declaring second number

product=number1*number2   #declaring what the product does

print(product)   #Calling the print function to display what product has

- **Division**

number1=10   #declaring first number

number2= 50   #declaring second number

division=number2/number1   #declaring what the division does

print(division)   #Calling the print function to display what product has

Modulus

The modulus operator is used to return the integer remainder after division. The modulus=dividend%divisor.

Example

Start IDLE.

Navigate to the File menu and click New Window.

Type the following:

number1=2   *#declaring first number*

number2= 15   *#declaring second number*

remainder=number2%number1   *#declaring what the remainder does*

print(remainder)   *#Calling the print function to display remainder has*

Squaring and Cubing in Python

Squaring a number-number**2

Cubing a number-number**3

Example:

Start IDLE.

Navigate to the File menu and click New Window.

Type the following:

*Square of 3 in Python will be 3**2*

*Cube of 5 in Python will be 5**3*

- Square of 3

Start IDLE.

Navigate to the File menu and click New Window.

Type the following:

```
number=3              #declaring variable number and assigning value
3

square=number**2

print(square)         #Calling the print function to display what
square has
```

- Cube of 5

Start IDLE.

Navigate to the File menu and click New Window.

Type the following:

```
number=5              #declaring variable number and assigning value
5

cube=number**3

print(cube)           #Calling the print function to display what cube
has
```

Practice Exercise

Use python operators to write and run a python program that find the following:

- ➤ Cube of 7
- ➤ Square of 15
- ➤ Cube of 6
- ➤ Square of 11
- ➤ Cube of 8
- ➤ Square of 13

Note: We can still multiply 2 two times to get the square of 2. The reason for using the square and cube operators is to help us write compact and efficient code. Remember that the interpreter goes through each line including comments only that it ignores comments. Using the cube and square operators helps compact code and increase the efficiency of interpretation including troubleshooting as well as human readability of the code.

Operators with String in Python

In Python programming language certain operators are used to help concatenate strings. The addition sign is used to concatenate strings in Python.

Example

Start IDLE.

Navigate to the File menu and click New Window.

Type the following:

status="I am happy I know" + "how to write programs in Python"

print(status)

Python Multiplication of a string to create a sequence

*many_words="Great Programmer" * 5*

print(many_words)

Practice Exercise

✓ Use a concatenation operator to join the following strings in Python

I have realized

that programming is passion,

dedication and frequent practice.

✓ Use an operator to generate ten times the following string

Happy

Summary

We have covered what constitutes variables in Python. Variables are named storage locations and for this reason, we have variable names. There are numerical and string variables. These are known as variable types. In handling variables and indeed any other aspect of Python we will encounter and use special words known as reserved words or keywords. Keywords are fixed and must be typed the way specified. Keywords cannot be used as variable names or identifiers. Comments (preceded using #,'" or """) are for human readability aspect of a Python program. Indentation is used in Python to group lines of codes into blocks. Different types of operators such as the arithmetic operators and string operators are used to allow for manipulation of variables supported by user and inbuilt functions in Python.

FIFTH DAY

Part 11: Python Sets

The attributes of a set are that it contains unique elements, the items are not ordered, and the elements are not changeable. The set itself can be changed.

Creating a set

Example

Start IDLE.

Navigate to the File menu and click New Window.

Type the following:

set_mine={5,6,7}

  print(set_mine)

set_yours={2.1,"Great",(7,8,9)}

print(set_mine)

Creating a Set from a List

Example

Start IDLE.

Navigate to the File menu and click New Window.

Type the following:

set_mine=set([5,6,7,5])

   print(set_mine)

Practice Exercise

Start IDLE.

Navigate to the File menu and click New Window.

Type the following:

Correct and create a set in Python given the following set, trial_set={1,1,2,3,1,5,8,9}

Note

The {} will create a dictionary that is empty in Python. There is no need to index sets since they are ordered.

Adding elements to a set for multiple members we use the update() method.

For a single addition of a single element to a set we use the add()
method. Duplicates should be avoided when handling sets.

Example

Start IDLE.

Navigate to the File menu and click New Window.

Type the following:

your_set={6,7}

print(your_set)

your_set.add(4)

print(your_set)

your_set.update([9,10,13])

print(your_set)

your_set.update([23, 37],{11,16,18})

print(your_set)

Removing Elements from a Set

The methods discard(o and remove() are used to purge an item from a
set.

Example

Start IDLE.

Navigate to the File menu and click New Window.

Type the following:

set_mine={7,2,3,4,1}

print(set_mine)

set_mine.discard(2)

print(set_mine)   #Output will be {7,3,4,1}

set_mine.remove(1)

print(set_mine)   #Output will be {7,3,4}

Using the pop() Method to Remove an Item from a Set

Since sets are unordered, the order of popping items is arbitrary.

It is also possible to remove all items in a set using the clear() method in Python.

Start IDLE.

Navigate to the File menu and click New Window.

Type the following:

your_set=set("Today")

print(your_set)

print(your_set.pop())

your_set.pop()

print(your_set)

your_set.clear()

print(your_set)

Set Operations in Python

We use sets to compute difference, intersection, and union of sets.

Example

Start IDLE.

Navigate to the File menu and click New Window.

Type the following:

C={5,6,7,8,9,11}

D={6,9,11,13,15}

Set Union

A union of sets C and D will contain both sets' elements.

In Python the| operator generates a union of sets. The union() will also generate a union of sets.

Example

Start IDLE.

Navigate to the File menu and click New Window.

Type the following:

C={5,6,7,8,9,11}

D={6,9,11,13,15}

print(C|D)   #Output: {5,6,7,8,9,11,13,15}

Example 2

Using the union()

Start IDLE.

Navigate to the File menu and click New Window.

Type the following:

C={5,6,7,8,9,11}

D={6,9,11,13,15}

print(D.union(C))   #Output:{5,6,7,8,9,11,13,15}

Practice Exercise

Rewrite the following into a set and find the set union.

A={1,1,2,3,4,4,5,12,14,15}

D={2,3,3,7,8,9,12,15}

Set Intersection

A and D refers to a new items set that are shared by both sets. The & operator is used to perform intersection. The intersection() function can also be used to intersect sets.

Example

Start IDLE.

Navigate to the File menu and click New Window.

Type the following:

A = {11, 12, 13, 14, 15}

D= {14, 15,16, 17, 18}

Print(A&D)   #Will display {14,15}

Using intersection()

Example

Start IDLE.

Navigate to the File menu and click New Window.

Type the following:

A = {11, 12, 13, 14, 15}

D= {14, 15,16, 17, 18}

A.intersection(D)

Set Difference

A-D refers to a new items set are only in A but not in D. In the same way, D-A is a set of element in D but not in A. The – operator is used to compute the difference. The difference() method can also be used.

Example 1

Start IDLE.

Navigate to the File menu and click New Window.

Type the following:

A = {11, 12, 13, 14, 15}

D= {14, 15,16, 17, 18}

print(A - D)   #Output:{11,12,13}

Example 2

Start IDLE.

Navigate to the File menu and click New Window.

Type the following:

A = {11, 12, 13, 14, 15}

D= {14, 15,16, 17, 18}

print(A.difference(D))

Example 3

A = {11, 12, 13, 14, 15}

D= {14, 15,16, 17, 18}

Print(D-A)   #Output will be {18,16,17}

Set Symmetric Difference

The set of elements in both A and D except those that are common in both is known as the symmetric difference of A and D. The ^ operator is used to perform symmetric difference and the same can also be attained using the symmetric difference() operator.

Example 1

Start IDLE.

Navigate to the File menu and click New Window.

Type the following:

A = {11, 12, 13, 14, 15}

D= {14, 15,16, 17, 18}

print (A^D)   #Output:{11,12,13,16,17,18)

Example 2

A = {11, 12, 13, 14, 15}

D= {14, 15,16, 17, 18}

print(A.symmetric_difference(D)   #Output:{11,12,13,16,17,18)

Challenge: Is A^D and D^A the same?

Example: Adding elements in a Set

Paint_set = set()

paint_set.add("brown")

print(paint_set)

paint_set.update(["white", "violet"])

print(paint_set)

Superset and Subset

Start IDLE.

Navigate to the File menu and click New Window.

Type the following:

set1 = set(["A", "M"])

set2 = set(["M", "O"])

set3 = set(["M"])

issubset = set1 <= set2

print(issubset)

issuperset = set1 >= set1

print(issuperset)

issubset = set3 <= set2

```
print(issubset)
```

```
issuperset = set2 >= set3
```

```
print(issuperset)
```

Membership Tests in Sets

Example

Start IDLE.

Navigate to the File menu and click New Window.

Type the following:

```
set_mine = set("pawpaw")
```

```
print('p' in set_mine)
```

Iteration

Python commonly employs the for control statement to continually scan a set.

Example

Start IDLE.

Navigate to the File menu and click New Window.

Type the following:

```
for letter in set("pawpaw")
```

print(letter)

Inbuilt Functions with Set

Frozenset Python

Just like tuples are immutable. frozensets are immutable. To create frozensets we use the function frozenset().

Example

Start IDLE.

Navigate to the File menu and click New Window.

Type the following:

A = frozenset([11, 12, 13, 14])

D = frozenset([13, 14, 15, 16])

Summary

Set in Python is a data structure equivalent to sets in mathematics. It may consist of various elements; the order of elements in a set is undefined. You can add and delete elements of a set, you can iterate the elements of the set, you can perform standard operations on sets (union, intersection, difference).

Part 12: Python Dictionaries

While many things in Python are iterables, not all of them are sequences and a Python dictionary falls in this category. In this article, we will talk about what a Python dictionary is, how it works, and what are its most common applications.

What is a Python Dictionary?

Getting clean and actionable data is one of the key challenges in data analysis. You can't build and fit models to data that isn't usable. A Python dictionary makes it easier to read and change data, thereby rendering it more actionable for predictive modeling.

A Python dictionary holds a key: value pair. The Python dictionary is optimized in a manner that allows it to access values when the key is known.

While each key is separated by a comma in a Python Dictionary, each key-value pair is separated by a colon. Moreover, while the keys of the dictionary have to be unique and immutable (tuples, strings, integers, etcetera), the key-values can be of any type and can also be repeated any number of times. An example of a Python dictionary is shown below:

How do Python Dictionaries Work?

While there are several Python dictionary methods, there are some basic operations that need to be mastered. We will walk through the most important ones in this section.

Creating a Python dictionary

To create a Python dictionary you need to put items (each having a key and a corresponding value expressed as key: value) inside curly brackets. Each item needs to be separated from the next by a comma. As discussed above, values can repeat and be of any type. Keys, on the other hand, are unique and immutable. There is also a built-in function dict() that you can use to create a dictionary. For easier understanding note that this built in function is written as diction() in the rest of this book. Here are some examples:

Accessing Items within the Python dictionary

Accessing items in the dictionary in Python is simple enough. All you need to do is put the key name of the item within square brackets. This is important because the keys are unique and non-repeatable.

Example

To get the value of the model key:

k = thisdiction["model"]

You can also use another of the Python dictionary methods get() to access the item. Here's what it looks like.

k = thisdiction.get("model")

How to Change Values in a Python Dictionary

To change the value of an item, you once again need to refer to the key name. Here is an example.

If you have to change the value for the key "year" from 1890 to 2025:

thisdiction = {

"brand": "Mitsubishi",

"model": "Toyota",

"year": 1890

}

thisdiction["year"] = 2025

How Do You Loop Through a Python Dictionary

You can use a for loop function to loop through a dictionary in Python. By default, the return value while looping through the dictionary will be the keys of the dictionary. However, there are other methods that can be used to return the values.

To print the key names:

for k in thisdiction:

print(k)

To print the values in the dictionary, one by one:

for k in thisdiction:

print(thisdiction[k])

Another way of returning the values by using the values() function :

for k in thisdiction.values():

print(k)

If you want to Loop through both the keys and the values, you can use the items() function:

for k, m in thisdiction.items():

print(k, m)

How Do You Check if a Key Exists in the Dictionary

Here's how you can determine whether a particular key is actually present in the Python dictionary:

Say you have to check whether the key "model" is present in the dictionary:

thisdiction = {

"brand": "Mitsubishi",

  "model": "Toyota",

"year": 1890

}

if "model" in thisdiction:

print("Yes, 'model' is one of the keys in the thisdiction dictionary")

How Do You Determine the Number of Items in the Dictionary

To determine the number of key: value pairs in the dictionary we use one of the most commonly used Python Dictionary methods, len(). Here's how it works:

print(len(thisdiction))

How to add an item to the Python Dictionary

To add a new key: value pair to the dictionary, you have to use a new index key and then assign a value to it.

For instance,

thisdiction = {

"brand": "Mitsubishi",

"model": "Toyota",

"year": 1890

}

thisdiction["color"] = "pink"

print(thisdiction)

Removing Items from the Python Dictionary

Here are some of the methods to remove an item from the Python dictionary. Each approaches the same goal from a different perspective.

Method 1

This method, pop(), removes the item which has the key name that is being specified. This works well since key names are unique and immutable.

thisdiction = {

"brand": "Mitsubishi",

"model": "Toyota",

"year": 1890

}

thisdiction.pop("model")

print(thisdiction)

Method 2

The popitem() method removes the item that has been added most recently. In earlier versions, this method used to remove any random item. Here's how it works:

thisdiction = {

"brand": "Mitsubishi",

"model": "Toyota",

"year": 1890

}

thisdiction.popitem()

print(thisdiction)

Method 3

Much like the pop() method, the del keyword removes the item whose key name has been mentioned.

thisdiction = {

"brand": "Mitsubishi",

"model": "Toyota",

"year": 1890

}

del thisdiction["model"]

print(thisdiction)

Method 4

Unlike the pop() method, the del keyword can also be used to delete the dictionary altogether. Here's how it can be used to do so:

thisdiction = {

"brand": "Mitsubishi",

"model": "Toyota",

"year": 1890

}

del thisdiction

print(thisdiction) #this will cause an error because "thisdiction" no longer exists.

Method 5

The clear() keyword empties the dictionary of all items without deleting the dictionary itself:

thisdiction = {

"brand": "Mitsubishi",

"model": "Toyota",

"year": 1890

}

thisdiction.clear()

print(thisdiction)

A list of Common Python Dictionary Methods

There are a number of Python Dictionary methods that can be used to perform basic operations. Here is a list of the most commonly used ones.

Method	Description
clear()	This removes all the items from the dictionary
copy()	This method returns a copy of the Python dictionary
fromkeys()	This returns a different directory with only the key : pairs that have been specified
get()	This returns the value of the key mentioned
items()	This method returns the thuple for every key: pair in the dictionary
keys()	This returns a list of all the Python dictionary the dictionary
popitem()	In the latest version, this method deletes the recently added item
pop()	This removes only the key that is mentioned
update()	This method updates the dictionary with certain key-value pairs that are mentioned

values()	This method simply returns the values of all the items in the list

Merits of a Dictionary in Python

Here are some of the major pros of a Python library:

- It improves the readability of your code. Writing out Python dictionary keys along with values adds a layer of documentation to the code. If the code is more streamlined, it is a lot easier to debug. Ultimately, analyses get done a lot quicker and models can be fitted more efficiently.

- Apart from readability, there's also the question of sheer speed. You can look up a key in a Python dictionary very fast. The speed of a task like looking up keys is measured by looking at how many operations it takes to finish. Looking up a key is done in constant time compared with looking up an item in a large list which is done in linear time.

To look up an item in a huge list, the computer will look through every item in the list. If every item is assigned a key-value pair then you only need to look for the key which makes the entire process much faster. A Python dictionary is basically an implementation of a hash table. Therefore, it has all the benefits of the hash table which include membership checks and speedy tasks like looking up keys.

Demerits of a Python dictionary

While a Python dictionary is easily one of the most useful tools, especially for data cleaning and data analysis, it does have a downside. Here are some demerits of using a Python dictionary.

- ✓ Dictionaries are unordered. In cases where the order of the data is important, the Python dictionary is not appropriate.

- ✓ Python dictionaries take up a lot more space than other data structures. The amount of space occupied increases drastically when there are many Python Dictionary keys. Of course, this isn't too much of a disadvantage because memory isn't very expensive.

Data Structures in Python

Among the basic data types and structures in Python are the following:

- Logical: bool

- Numeric: int, float, complex

- Sequence: list, tuple, range

- Text Sequence: str

- Binary Sequence: bytes, bytearray, memoryview

- Map: dict

- Set: set, frozenset

All of the above are classes from which object instances can be created. In addition to the above, more data types/structures are available in modules that come as part of any default Python installation: collections, heapq, array, enum, etc. Extra numeric types are available from modules numbers, decimals and fractions. The built-in function type() allows us to obtain the type of any object.

Discussion

- With respect to data types, what are the differences between Python2 and Python3?

  The following are important differences:

- A division such as 5 / 2 returns integer value 2 in Python2 due to truncation. In Python3, this will evaluate to float value 2.5 even when the input values are only integers.

- In Python2, strings were ASCII. To use Unicode, one had to use the unicode type by creating them with a prefix: name = u'Saṃsāra'. In Python3, str type is Unicode by default.

- Python2 has int and long types but both these are integrated in Python3 as int. Integers can be as large as system memory allows.

- **What data structures in Python are immutable and mutable?**

  Mutable objects are those that can be changed after they are created, such as updating/adding/removing an element in a list. It can be said that mutable objects are changed in place.

  Immutable objects can't be changed in place after they are created. Among the immutable basic data types/structures are bool, int, float, complex, str, tuple, range, frozenset, and bytes.
  The   mutable   counterparts of frozenset and bytes are set and bytearray respectively.
  Among the other mutable data structures are list and dict.

With immutable objects it may seem like we can modify their values by assignment. What actually happens is that a new immutable object is created and then assigned to the existing variable. This can be verified by checking the ID (using id() function) of the variable before and after assignment.

- **What data structures in Python are suited to handle binary data?**

The fundamental built-in types for manipulating binary data are bytearray and bytes. They support memoryview that makes use of the buffer protocol to access the storage location of other binary objects without making a copy.

The module array supports storage of simple data types such as thirty-two-bit integers and double floating point values. Characters, integers and floats can be stored array types, which gives low-level access to the bytes that store the data.

- **What containers and sequences are available in Python?**

The diagram below shows List data type and its relationship to other data types.

Containers are data structures that contain one or more objects. In Python, a container object can contain objects of different types. For that matter, a container can contain other containers at any depth. Containers may also be called **collections.**

Sequences are containers that have inherent ordering among their items. For example, a string such as str = "hello world" is a sequence of Unicode characters h, e, l, etc. Note that there is no character data type in Python, and the expression "h" is actually a 1-character string.

Sequences support two main operations (for example, sequence variable seq):

- Indexing: Access a particular element: seq[0] (first element), seq[-1] (last element).

- Slicing: Access a subset of elements with syntax seq[start:stop:step]: seq[0::2] (alternate elements), seq[0:3] (first three elements), seq[-3:] (last three elements). Note that the stop point is not included in the result.

Among the basic sequence types are list, tuple, range, str, bytes bytearray and memoryview. Conversely, dict, set and frozenset are simply containers in which elements don't have any particular order. More containers are part of collections module.

- **How can I construct some common containers?**

The following examples are self-explanatory:

- str: a = '' (empty), a = "" (empty), a = 'Hello'
- bytes: a = b'' (empty), a = b"" (empty), a = b'Hello'
- list: a = list() (empty), a = [] (empty), a = [1, 2, 3]
- tuple: a = tuple() (empty), a = (1,) (single item), a = (1, 2, 3), a = 1, 2, 3
- set: a = set() (empty), a = {1, 2, 3}
- dict: a = dict() (empty), a = {} (empty), a = {1:2, 2:4, 3:9}

We can
construct bytearray from bytes and frozenset from set using their respective built-in functions.

- **What are iterables and iterators?**

  An iterable is a container that can be processed element by element. For sequences, elements are processed in the order they are stored. For non-sequences, elements are processed in some arbitrary order.

  Formally, any object that implements the **iterator protocol** is an iterable. The iterator protocol is defined by two special methods, __iter__() and __next__(). Calling iter() on an iterable returns what is called an iterator. Calling next() on an iterator gives us the next element of the iterable. Thus, iterators help us process the iterable element by element.

  When we use loops or comprehensions in Python, iterators are used under the hood. Programmers don't need to call iter() or next() explicitly.

- **Can I convert from one data type to another?**

  Yes, provided they are compatible. Here are some examples:

- int('3') will convert from string to integer

- int(3.4) will truncate float to integer

- bool(0) and bool([]) will both return False

- ord('A') will return the equivalent Unicode code point as an integer value

- chr(65) will return the equivalent Unicode string of one character

- bin(100), oct(100) and hex(100) will return string representations in their respective bases

- int('45', 16) and int('0x45', 16) will convert from hexadecimal to decimal

- tuple([1, 2, 3]) will convert from list to tuple

- list('hello') will split the string into a list of 1-character strings

- set([1, 1, 2, 3]) will remove duplicates in the list to give a set

- dict([(1,2), (2,4), (3,9)]) will construct a dictionary from the given list of tuples

- list({1:2, 2:4, 3:9}) will return a list based on the dictionary keys.

- **Should I use a list or a tuple?**

If ordering is important, sets and dictionaries should not be used: prefer lists and tuples. Tuples are used to pass arguments and return results from functions. This is because they can contain multiple elements and are immutable. Tuples are also good for storing closely related data. For example, (a, b, c) coordinates or (red, green, blue) color components can be stored as tuples. Use lists instead if values can change during the lifetime of the object.

If a sequence is to be sorted, use a list for in-place sorting. A tuple can be used but it should return a new sorted object. A tuple cannot be sorted in-place.

For better code readability, elements of a tuple can be named. For this purpose, use collections.namedtuple class. This allows us to access the elements via their names rather than tuple indices.

It's possible to convert between lists and tuples using functions list() and tuple().

- **When to use a set and when to use a dict?**

Sets and dictionaries have no order. However, from Python 3.7, the order in which items are inserted into a dict are preserved.

Sets store unique items. Duplicates are discarded. Dictionaries can contain duplicate values but keys must be unique. Since dict keys are unique, often dict is used for counting. For example, to count the number of times a word appears in a document, words can be keys and counts can be values.

Sets are suited for finding the intersection/union of two groups, such as finding those who live in a neighborhood (set 1) and/or also own a car (set 2). Other set operations are also possible.

Strings, lists and tuples can take only integers as indices due to their ordered nature but dictionaries can be indexed by strings as well. In general, dictionaries can be indexed by any of the built-in immutable types, which are considered **hashable.** Thus, dictionaries are suited for key-value pairs such as mapping country names (keys) to their capitals (values). But if capitals are the more common input to your algorithm, use them as keys instead.

- **How can I implement a linked list in Python?**

Linked list is a group of nodes connected by pointers or links. **A node** is one point of statistics or details in the linked list. Not only does it hold data but also it shows direction to the following node in a linked list that is single. Thus, the definition of a node is recursive. For a double-linked list, the node has two pointers, one that connects to the previous node and another one that connects to the next node. Linked lists can be designed to be ordered or unordered.

The head of the linked list must be accessible. This allows us to traverse the entire list and perform all possible operations. A double-linked list might also expose the tail for traversal from the end. While a Node class may be enough to implement a linked list, it's common to encapsulate the head pointer and all operations within LinkedList class. Operations on the linked lists are methods of the class. One possible implementation is given by Downey. A DoubleLinkedList can be a derived class from LinkedList with the addition of a tail pointer and associated methods.

Dictionary

When the key is known dictionaries will retrieve values.

Creating a Dictionary

A dictionary is generated by having items in curly braces demarcated by a comma. A dictionary element has a key and a matching value. The key and value in Python are captured as a pair. Normally, key: value. Keys have to be immutable and unique.

Example

Start IDLE.

Navigate to the File menu and click New Window.

Type the following:

dict_mine= {}   *#Empty dictionary*

 # dictionary with integer keys

dict_mine= {2: 'pawpaw', 4: 'rectangle'}   #dictionary with integer keys

dict_mine = {'student': 'Brenda',2:[12, 14, 13]}#dictionary with integer keys

dict_mine = dict({2:'student': 'Brenda' })

dict_mine = dict([(2, 'pawpaw'), (4, 'rectangle')])

Accessing Elements from a Dictionary

Dictionary uses keys instead of indexing to access values. The keys can be within the square brackets or with the get() method.

Example

Start IDLE.

Navigate to the File menu and click New Window.

Type the following:

dict_mine = {'name':'James', 'age': 62}

print(dict_mine['name'])

print(dict_mine.get('age'))

Add or Modify Dictionary Elements

For dictionaries, they are mutable implying that we can modify the value of current items using the assignment operator. The value will get updated if the key is already existing else we will have to add new key: the dictionary value couple.

Start IDLE.

Navigate to the File menu and click New Window.

Type the following:

dict_mine={'student':'James','age':62}

dict_mine['age'] = 37

print(dict_mine)

dict_mine['address'] = 'New York'

print(dict_mine)

Removing/Deleting Elements from a Dictionary

Example

Start IDLE.

Navigate to the File menu and click New Window.

Type the following:

my_squares={10:100,8:64,12:224}

print(my_squares.pop(2))

print(my_squares)

```
print(my_squares.popitem())

print(my_squares)

del my_squares[4]

print(my_squares)

my_squares.clear()

print(squares)

del my_squares
```

Dictionary Methods in Python

Example

Start IDLE.

Navigate to the File menu and click New Window.

Type the following:

```
scores ={}.fromkeys(['Chemistry','Spanish','Pyschology'], 0)

 print(scores)

 for item in marks.items():

 print(item)
```

Start IDLE.

Navigate to the File menu and click New Window.

Type the following:

list(sorted(scores.keys()))

Dictionary Comprehension in Python

my_squares = {y: y*y for y in range(5)}

print(my_squares)

Alternatively, the program can be written as:

my_power = {}

for y in range(5):

  power[y] = y*y

Odd Items Only Dictionary

Example

Start IDLE.

Navigate to the File menu and click New Window.

Type the following:

squares_odd={y:y*y for y in range(10) if y%2==1}

print(squares_odd)

Membership Test in a Dictionary

Using the keyword in, we can evaluate if a key is in a particular dictionary. The membership tests should be used for dictionary keys and not for dictionary values.

Example

Start IDLE.

Navigate to the File menu and click New Window.

Type the following:

my_squares = {10: 100, 6: 36, 8: 64, 11: 121}

print(11 in my_squares)

print(36 in squares)

Practice Exercise

Given:

square_dict={2:4,6:36,8:64}

- Use membership to test if 6 exist in the dictionary.
- Use membership, test if 36 exist in the dictionary.

Iteration in a Dictionary

We use the for loop to iterate through each key in a particular dictionary.

Inbuilt Functions

Example

Start IDLE.

Navigate to the File menu and click New Window.

Type the following:

your_squares = {2: 4, 4: 16, 6: 36, 8: 64, 10: 100}

print(len(your_squares))

print(sorted(your_squares))

for i in squares:

  print(your_squares[i])

Practice Exercise

Give the following set, setm=set(["Blue","Yellow"])

- ✓ Write a working program to copy the set elements.
- ✓ Display the new set.
- ✓ Clear the set.
- ✓ Print the latest status of the set.

Given the setr=set(["Knock","Up"])

- ✓ Write a simple program to copy the set elements.
- ✓ Write a working program to display the latest status of the set.
- ✓ Write a simple program clear the elements of the set.
- ✓ Display the latest status of the set.
- ✓ Delete the entire set using del.

Given m=frozenset([11,12,13,14,15]) and n=([13,14,15,16,17])

* Use the isdisjoint() to test of the sets have no shared elements.
* Write a program to return a new set with items in the set that are not in the others.
* Write a union of sets m and n.
* Write an intersection of sets n and m.
* Write a program to pop an item in set n.
* Write a program that appends element 21 to the set m.
* Check to see if set m has element 14 using a built-in keyword.
* Use discard() to drop all items in the set m.

Given this set second_set = {"berry", "pineaple", "melon"}

* Write a Python program to update the set with these elements at a go "mango","guava", "plum"
* Find the length of this set using the len().
* Use remove() to clear the set.

Given {(, 17, 19, 21)

* Use set constructor set() to construct a set named third_set in Python.
* Use the add() method to add "Kim" to the set.
* Pop an element from the set using pop().
* Update the set using update() to include {43,41,40}

Given setq=([13,2,17,8,19])

* Find the minimum value in the set using inbuilt features of Python.
* Find the maximum value in the set using inbuilt features of Python.

Given setb=([5,"K", 8, 1])

147

❖ Use the for a statement to write a Python program that iterates through the set elements.

Given

diction1={11:12,12:27}

diction2={13:52,13:57}

❖ Create a python program to concatenate the dictionaries in one.

Summary

At the end of the day, a Python dictionary represents a data structure that can prove valuable in cleaning data and making it actionable. It becomes even more valuable because it is inherently simple to use and much faster and more efficient as well. Of course, if you are looking for a career in data science, a comprehensive course with live sessions, assessments, and placement assistance might be just what you need.

In python, the attributes of a set include having items that are not ordered, items that are unique and each element in a set is unchangeable. Adding elements to a set for multiple members we use the update() method. For a single addition of a single element to a set, we use the add() method. Duplicates should be avoided when handling sets. Using the keyword in, we can evaluate if a key is in a particular dictionary. The membership tests should be used for keys and not for values.

SIXTH DAY

Part 13: Object-Oriented Programming in Python

Object and Class in Python

Python supports different programming approaches as it is a multi-paradigm. An object in Python has an attribute and behavior.

Example

Car as an object:

Attributes: color, mileage, model, age.

Behavior: reverse, speed, turn, roll, stop, start.

Class

It is a template for creating an object.

Example

class Car:

NOTE:

By convention, we write the class name with the first letter as uppercase. A class name is in singular form by convention.

Syntax

class Name_of_Class:

From a class, we can construct objects by simply making an instance of the class. The class_name() operator creates an object by assigning the object to the empty method.

Object/Class Instantiation

From our class Car, we can have several objects such as a first car, second care or SUVs.

Example

Start IDLE.

Navigate to the File menu and click New Window.

Type the following:

my_car=Car()

   pass

Practice Exercise

✓ Create a class and an object for students.
✓ Create a class and an object for the hospital.
✓ Create a class and an object for a bank.
✓ Create a class and an object for a police department.

Example

Start IDLE.

Navigate to the File menu and click New Window.

Type the following:

class Car:

category="Personal Automobile"

  def __init__(self, model, insurance):

   self.model = model

   self.insurance =insurance

subaru=Car("Subaru","Insured")

toyota=Car("Toyota","Uninsured")

print("Subaru is a {}".format(subaru._class_.car))

print("Toyota is a {}".format(toyota._class_.car))

print("{} is {}".format(subaru.model, subaru.insurance))

print("{} is {}".format(toyota.model, toyota.insurance))

Methods

Functions defined within a body of the class are known as methods and are basic functions. Methods define the behaviors of an object.

Example

Start IDLE.

Navigate to the File menu and click New Window.

Type the following:

```
def __init__(self, model, insurance):

    self.model = model

    self.insurance =insurance

  def ignite(self, ignite):

    return "{} ignites {}".format(self.model, ignition)

  def stop(self):

    return "{} is now stopping".format(self.model)

subaru=Car("Subaru","Insured")

print(subaru.ignite("'Fast'"))

print(subaru.stop())
```

NOTE

The methods ignite() and stop() are referred to as instance methods because they are an instance of the object created.

Practice Exercise

- ✓ Create a class Dog and instantiate it.
- ✓ Create a Python program to show names of two dogs and their two attributes from a.

Inheritance

A way of creating a new class by using details of existing class devoid of modifying it is called inheritance. The derived class or child class is the newly formed class while the existing class is called parent or base class.

Example

Start IDLE.

Navigate to the File menu and click New Window.

Type the following:

class Dog:

  def __init__(self):

    print("Dog is available")

  def whoisThis(self):

    print("Dog")

```python
    def walk(self):

        print("Walks gently")

class Spitz(Dog):      #Child class

    def __init__(self):

        super().__init__()

        print("Spitz is now available")

    def whoisThis(self):

        print("Pitbull")

    def wag(self):

        print("Strong")

pitbull = Pitbull()

pitbull.whoisThis()

pitbull.walk()

pitbull.wag()
```

Discussion

We created two Python classes in the program above. The classes were Dog as the base class and Pitbull as the derived class. The derived class inherits the functions of the base class. The method _init_() and the function super() are used to pull the content of _init_() method from the base class into the derived class.

Encapsulation in Python

Encapsulation in Python Object Oriented Programming approach is meant to help prevent data from direct modification. Private attributes in Python are denoted using a single or double underscore as a prefix.

Example

Start IDLE.

Navigate to the File menu and click New Window.

Type the following:

"__" or "_".

```
class Tv:

    def __init__(self):

        self.__Finalprice = 800

    def offer(self):

        print("Offering Price: {}".format(self.__finalprice))

    def set_final_price(self, offer):

        self.__finalprice = offer

t = Tv()

t.offer()

t.__finalprice = 950

t.offer()
```

 # using setter function

t.setFinalPrice(990)

t.sell()

Discussion

The program defined a class Tv and used _init_(o methods to hold the final offering price of the TV. Along the way, we attempted to change the price but could not manage. The reason for the inability to change is because Python treated the _finalprice as private attributes. The only way to modify this value was through using a setter function, setMaxPrice() that takes price as a parameter.

Polymorphism

In Python, polymorphism refers to the ability to use a shared interface for several data types.

Start IDLE.

Navigate to the File menu and click New Window.

Type the following:

class Tilapia:

   def swim(self):

     print("Tilapia can swim")

   def fly(self):

     print("Tilapia cannot fly")

```
class Shark:

    def jump(self):

        print("Shark can't fly")

    def swim(self):

        print("Shark can swim")

def jumping_test(fish):

    fish.jump()

bonny = Tilapia()

biggy = Shark()

jumping_test(bonny)

jumping_test(biggy)
```

Discussion

The program above has defined two classes Tilapia and Shark all of which share the method jump() even though they have different functions. By creating common interface jumping_test() we allowed polymorphism in the program above. We then passed objects bonny and biggy in the jumping_test() function.

Practice Exercise

- ✓ In a doctor consultation room suggest the class and objects in a programming context.
- ✓ In a football team, suggest programming class and objects.
- ✓ In a grocery store, suggest programming class and objects.

Class Definition in Python

The keyword def is used to define a class in Python. The first string in a Python class is used to describe the class even though it is not always needed.

Example

Start IDLE.

Navigate to the File menu and click New Window.

Type the following:

class Dog

'"Briefly taking about class Dog using this docstring'"

   Pass

Example 2

Start IDLE.

Navigate to the File menu and click New Window.

Type the following:

Class Bright:

"My other class"

b=10

def salute(self):

print('Welcome')

print(Bright.b)

print(Bright.salute)

print(Bright.__doc__)

Object Creation in Python

Example from the previous class

Open the previous program file with class Bright

student1=Bright()

Discussion

The last program will create object student1, a new instance. The attributes of objects can be accessed via the specific object name prefix. The attributes can be a method or data including the matching class functions. In other terms, Bright.salute is a function object and student1.salute will be a method object.

Example

Start IDLE.

Navigate to the File menu and click New Window.

Type the following:

class Bright:

   "Another class again!"

   c = 20

```
def salute(self):

    print('Hello')

student2 = Bright()

print(Bright.salute)

print(student2.salute)

student2.salute()
```

Discussion

We invoked the student2.salute() despite the parameter 'self' and it still worked without placing arguments. The reason for this phenomenon is because each time an object calls its method, the object itself is passed as the first argument. The implication is that student2.salute() translates into student2.salute(student2). It is the reason for the 'self; name.

Constructors

Start IDLE.

Navigate to the File menu and click New Window.

Type the following:

```
class NumberComplex

class ComplexNumber:

    def __init__(self,realnum = 0,i = 0):
```

```
    self.real = realnum

    self.imaginarynum = i

  def getData(self):

    print("{0}+{1}j".format(self.realnumber,self.imaginarynum))

complex1 = NumberComplex(2,3)

complex1.getData()

complex2 = NumberComplex(5)

complex2.attribute = 10

print((complex2.realnumber,        complex2.imaginarynumber,
complex2.attribute))

complex1.attribute
```

Deleting Objects and Attributes

The del statement is used to delete attributes of an object at any instance.

Example

Start IDLE.

Navigate to the File menu and click New Window.

Type the following:

```
complex1 = NumberComplex(2,3)
```

del complex1.imaginarynumber

complex1.getData()

del NumberComplex.getData

complex1.getData()

Deleting the Entire Object

Example

Start IDLE.

Navigate to the File menu and click New Window.

Type the following:

complex1=NumberComplex(1,3)

del complex1

Discussion

When complex1=NumberComplex(1,3) is done, a new instance of the object gets generated in memory and the name complex1 ties with it. The object does not immediately get destroyed as it temporarily stays in memory before the garbage collector purges it from memory. The purging of the object helps free resources bound to the object and enhances system efficiency. Garbage destruction Python refers to automatic destruction of unreferenced objects.

Inheritance in Python

In Python inheritance allows us to specify a class that takes all the functionality from the base class and adds more. It is a powerful feature of OOP.

Syntax

class ParentClass:

  Body of parent class

class ChildClass(ParentClass):

  Body of derived class

Example

Start IDLE.

Navigate to the File menu and click New Window.

Type the following:

class Rect_mine(Rect_mine):

  def __init__(self):

   Shape.__init__(self,4)

  def getArea(self):

   s1, s2, s3,s4 = self.count_sides

   perimeter = (s1+s2+s3+s4)

area = (s1*s2)

print('The rectangle area is:' %area)

Example 2

r = rect_mine()

r.inputSides()

Type b1 : 4

Type l1 : 8

Type b2 : 4

Type l1:   8

r.dispSides()

Type b1 is 4.0

Type l1 is 8.0

Type b2 is 4.0

Type l1 is 8.0

r.getArea()

Method Overriding in Python

When a method is defined in both the base class and the derived class, the method in the child class/derived class will override the parent/base class. In the above example, _init_() method in Rectangle class will override the _init_() in Shape class.

Inheritance in Multiple Form in Python

Example

Start IDLE.

Navigate to the File menu and click New Window.

Type the following:

In this case, MultiInherit is derived from class Parent1 and Parent2.

Multilevel Inheritance

Inheriting from a derived class is called multilevel inheritance.

Example

Start IDLE.

Navigate to the File menu and click New Window.

Type the following:

class Parent:

    pass

class Multilevel1(Parent):

    pass

class Multilevel2(Multilevel1):

  pass

Discussion

Multilevel1 derives from Parent, and Multilevel2 derives from Multilevel1.

Method Resolution Order

Example

Start IDLE.

Navigate to the File menu and click New Window.

Type the following:

print(issubclass(list,object))

print(isinstance(6.7,object))

print(isinstance("Welcome",object))

Discussion

The particular attribute in a class will be scanned first. The search will continue into parent classes. This search does not repeat searching the same class twice. The approach or order of searching is sometimes called linearization of multiderived class in Python. The Method Resolution Order refers to the rules needed to determine this order.

Operator Overloading

Inbuilt classes can use operators and the same operators will behave differently with different types. An example is the + that depending on context will perform concatenation of two strings, arithmetic addition on numbers, or merge lists. Operating overloading is an OOP feature that allows assigning varying meaning to an operator subject to context.

Making Class Compatible with Inbuilt Special Functions

Example

Start IDLE.

Navigate to the File menu and click New Window.

Type the following:

class Planar:

    def __init__(self, x_axis= 0, y_axis = 0):

      self.x_axis = x_axis

      self.y_axis = y_axis

    def __str__(self):

      return "({0},{1})".format(self.x_axis,self.y_axis)

Discussion

planar1=Planar(3,5)

print(planar1)   *#The output will be (3,5)*

Using More Inbuilt Methods

Example

Start IDLE.

Navigate to the File menu and click New Window.

Type the following:

class Planar:

   def __init__(self, x_axis= 0, y_axis = 0):

     self.x_axis = x_axis

     self.y_axis = y_axis

str(planar1)

format(planar1)

Discussion

It then follows that each time we invoke format(planar1) or str(planar1), Python is in effect executing planar1._str_() thus the name, special functions.

Operator + Overloading

The _add_() function addition in a class will overload the +.

Example

Start IDLE.

168

Navigate to the File menu and click New Window.

Type the following:

class Planar:

   def __init__(self, x_axis= 0, y_axis = 0):

     self.x_axis = x_axis

     self.y_axis = y_axis

   def __str__(self):

     return "({0},{1})".format(self.x_axis,self.y_axis)

   def __add__(self,z):

     x_axis = self.x_axis + z.x_axis

     y_axis = self.y_axis + z.y_axis

     return Planar(x_axis,y_axis)

Practice Exercise

- Print planar1 + planar2 from the example above.

Discussion

When you perform planar1+planar2 in Python, it will call planar._add_(planar2) and in turn Planar._add_(planar1, planar2).

Revisit Logical and Comparison Operators

Practice Exercise

- ❖ Given x=8, y=9, write a Python program that uses logical equals to test if x is equal to y.
- ❖ Write a program that evaluates x!=y in Python programming language.
- ❖ Write and run the following program

> *m = True*
>
> *n = False*
>
> *print('m and n is',m and n)*
>
> *print('m or n is',m or n)*
>
> *print('not m is',not n)*

- ❖ From the program in c., which program statement(s) evaluates to True, or False.
- ❖ Write and run the following program in Python

> *m1 = 15*
>
> *n1 = 15*
>
> *m2 = 'Welcome'*
>
> *n2 = 'Welcome'*
>
> *m3 = [11,12,13]*
>
> *n3 = [11,12,13]*
>
> *print(m1 is not n1)*

print(m2 is n2)

print(m3 is n3)

❖ Which program statement(s) generate True or False states in e.
❖ Write and run the following program

m = 'Welcome'

n = {11:'b',12:'c'}

print('W' in m)

print('Welcome' not in m)

print(10 in n)

print('b' in n)

❖ Which program statement(s) in g. return True or False states.

The special functions needed for overloading other operators are listed below.

Comparison Operators Overloading

In Python, comparison operators can be overloaded.

Example

class Planar:

  def __init__(self, x_axis= 0, y_axis = 0):

    self.x_axis = x_axis

self.y_axis = y_axis

def __str__(self):

    return "({0},{1})".format(x_axis,y_axis)

def __lt__(self,z):

    *self_magnitude = (x_axis ** 3) + (y _axis ** 3)*

    *z_magnitude = (z.x_axis ** 3) + (z.y_axis ** 3)*

    return self_magnitude < z_magnitude

Practice Exercise

a. Perform the following to the example above Planar(1,1)

b. Again perform Planar(1,1) in the above example.

c. Finally, perform Planar(1,1) from the above example.

Summary

Python supports different programming approaches as it is a multi-paradigm. An object in Python has an attribute and behavior. From a class, we can construct objects by simply making an instance of the class. The class_name() operator creates an object by assigning the object to the empty method. The keyword def is used to define a class in Python. The first string in a Python class is used to describe the class even though it is not always needed. When a method is defined in both the base class and the derived class, the method in the child class/derived class will override the parent/base class. In the above example, _init_() method in Rectangle class will override the _init_() in Shape class.

Inbuilt classes can use operators and the same operators will behave differently with different types. An example is the + that depending on context will perform concatenation of two strings, arithmetic addition on numbers, or merge lists. Operating overloading is an OOP feature that allows assigning varying meaning to an operator subject to context.From a class, we can construct objects by simply making an instance of the class. The class_name() operator creates an object by assigning the object to the empty method.

The _init_() function is a special function and gets called whenever a new object of the corresponding class is instantiated. Functions defined within a body of the class are known as methods and are basic functions. Methods define the behaviors of an object. In Python, polymorphism refers to the ability to use a shared interface for several data types. An illustration is a program that has defined two classes Tilapia and Shark all of which share the method jump() even though they have different functions. By creating common interface jumping_test() we allowed polymorphism in the program above. We then passed objects bonny and biggy in the jumping_test() function.

Part 14: File Management and Exception Handling in Python

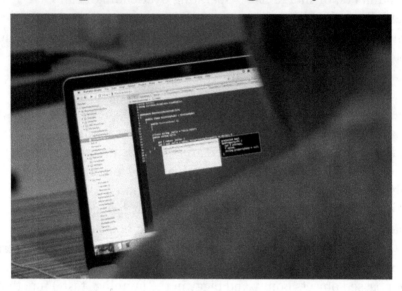

File Methods in Python

These methods enable the user to manipulate files in an easy and efficient manner. The methods are preloaded and the user only needs to understand where they can apply.

Directory in Python

Python allows us to arrange several files into different directories for easier handling. The collection of files and subdirectories in Python is known as a directory. The os module in Python contains methods for working with directories.

Getting Current Directory in Python

The keyword getcwd() method is used to get the current working directory. The method will return the current working directory in a string form. The getwcwdb()is also used to get a directory.

Changing Directory

The chdir() method helps modify the existing directory. However, the new path we intend to create should be given a string as a method. The path elements can be separated using the backward slash\ or the forward slash/.

Example

Start IDLE.

Navigate to the File menu and click New Window.

Type the following:

os.chdir('C:\\Tutorial')

print(os.getcwd())

Practice Exercise

Use the chdir() to change a directory in the Python root folder on your computer.

Files and List Directories

The listdir() method in Python is used to determine all files and subdirectories within a directory.

The listdir() method accepts a path and gives a file lists and subdirectories in that particular path. The listdir() will return from the current working directory if no path is specified.

Example

Start IDLE.

Navigate to the File menu and click New Window.

Type the following:

print(os.getcwd())

C:\Tutorial

os.listdir()

os.listdir('D:\\')

Creating a New Directory

The mkdir() method can be used to create a new directory. The method accepts the path of the new directory and will create a new directory in the current working directory in case the particular path is not defined.

os.mkdir('week2')

os.listdir()

File or a Directory Renaming in Python

In Python, the rename()method is used to rename a file or a directory. The old name is given as the argument 1 and the new name is given as argument 2.

Practice Exercise

Create a directory using the Python method and name it Lesson. Rename it using a Python method to Python Lessons.

Removing File or Directory in Python

The remove() method is used to delete a file in Python. Likewise, rmdir() is used to remove an empty directory.

Example

Start IDLE.

Navigate to the File menu and click New Window.

Type the following:

os.listdir()

['mine_direct']

os.rmdir('mine_direct')

Errors and Exceptions

When the Python interpreter encounters errors it will raise exceptions. For instance, dividing a number by zero will lead to an exception.

Example of an Error

Start IDLE.

Navigate to the File menu and click New Window.

Type the following:

if y < 3

   if y < 3

at runtime errors can still occur like when we open a file that does not exist. A file may not exist because it has been renamed and we are accessing using the old name or the file has been deleted. The file could have the same name but has changed the file extension. Python will create an exception object whenever these runtime error types occur.

Inbuilt Exceptions in Python

Python has several inbuilt exceptions that are flagged when associated errors arise. The local() method can help list all inbuilt exceptions in Python.

Exception Handling in Python

If exceptions occur, the execution of a program stops and the exception is passed to the calling process for handling. If the exception is not handled, a program will crash. Thought: Have you tried opening a smartphone app that says "the app has stopped". Can you imagine a program that crashes if it cannot file the image you trying to attach? Exception handling is critical in creating effective programs and also for security. Can you imagine if a hacker realizes that your program will crash and require restarting each time it fails to load an image, the hacker will have a leeway disrupting your software. Fortunately, exception handling allows us to anticipate and give way forward to a program should it encounter an exception.

Handling an Exception by Catching the Exception in Python

Start IDLE.

Navigate to the File menu and click New Window.

Type the following:

import sys

my_list= ['b', 1 ,3]

```
for entry in my_list:

    try:

        print("Our entry is", my_entry)

        r = 1/int(my_entry)

        break

    except:

        print("Unfortunate",sys.exc_info()[0],"has occured.")

        print("Try again.")

        print()

print("The reciprocal of the number",my_entry,"is",r)

import sys
```

User Defined Exception

Sometimes a user may need to create own exceptions that best align with your programming needs and these are known as user-defined exceptions.

A user has to create a new class and derive from the class, Exception class.

Summary

Files are used for future storage. To read from a file we need to open it and once through with it, we have to close it to free the resources tied with the file in Python. The inbuilt function open() in Python is used to launch a file. When this function is invoked, a file object is accessed and loaded sometimes referred to as a handle and it is used to modify or read the file accordingly. For the readlines() method, it will scan the entire file lines. After reading the entire file, the reading method will report empty status. The reason for empty status is because there are no more arguments for the method to process. The read() will go through each line in the file till there is no more lines to scan.

The 'r' is used to launch the file for reading and is the default. The 'w' is preferred when launching a file for writing. For exclusive file creation, we use the 'x' mode. The operation will be unsuccessful if the file already we want already exists. The other mode, 'a' is used to launch a file for adding data at the file end while retaining earlier content. The 'a' model will create a new file in case it does not exist. For the 't' mode, it will launch the file in default text mode. The 'b' mode is sued to launch the file in binary mode. Lastly, the '+' mode is used for launching the file to allow reading and writing.

SEVENTH DAY

Part 15: Memoization, Modules, and Packages

This is the method of caching a functional call's results. When you go through and memorize a function, you are only able to evaluate it by looking up the results that you obtained the first time that you had put those parameters to your function.

The log for this is often known as the Memoization cache. In some situations, you are going to find that the lookup failed. This simply means that the function wasn't able to call using those parameters. Only at that time would running your function really be necessary.

Memoization doesn't make much sense unless the function is deterministic, or you can simply accept the result as out of date. But, if your function is expensive, a big speedup would happen when you use this process. Let's back up a bit and see what this all means.

As a programmer, you know that when you do a recursion, it is going to make it easy for you to break up a big problem into pieces that are smaller and more manageable. Try considering iterative sets against the recursive solutions for a Fibonacci sum. Recursive solutions are often simpler when you are reading and then writing a branching problem. You will notice that graph traversals, mathematical series, and tree traversals are often done with recursion. Even though it does offer you a ton of convenience, the computational time that comes with recursion can be very big.

Doing Manual Memoization

The first approach that we are going to use is going to require you to take advantage of a feature out of Python, one that most people are not that excited about, to add state to a function. We can do that with the following code:

```
def fib_default_memoizedn, cache = {}):
if n in cache: ans=cache[n]
elif n<= 2:ans =1
cache[n]=ans else:
ans=fib_default_memoized(n-2)+fib_default_memoized(n-1)
cache[n]=ans

ı
```

RETURN ANS

The basic logic that comes with this is pretty obvious. The cache is going to be the results dictionary of your previous calls to the fib_default_memoized(). The 'n' parameter is the key. It is going to be the nth Fibonacci number. If this is true, then you are done. But if it is not true, then you have to take the time to evaluate this as the version of the native recursive and keep it in the cache before the return of the results.

The thing here is 'cache' is the function's keyword parameter. Python is usually going to evaluate the keyword parameters only one time, which is when you import the function. This means that if there are any issues with mutability in your parameter, it is only going to be initialized one time. This is usually the basis of small bugs that happen in the program, but in this case, you are going to mutate your parameter in order to take advantage of it.

Manual Memoization: Objects

Some programmers who use Python argue that going through and mutating your formal parameters is a bad idea. For others, especially those who like to work with Java, the argument for this is that all functions that have state need to be turned into objects. An example of how this would look like in your compiler includes the following: class Fib():

```
CACHE = {}
```

```
DEF__CALL__(SELF, n):
if n in self.cache: ans = self.cache[n] if n <= 2:
ans = 1 self.cache[n] = ans else:
ans = self(n-2) + self(n -1) self.cache[n] = ans
```

RETURN ANS

If you are doing this one, the call dunder method is going to be used to make the Fib instances behave like a function. The Cache is shared by all the Fib instances because that is its class attribute. When you are looking at Fibonacci numbers, this is a desirable thing to do. However, if your object made calls to a server well defined in the constructor, and the result was going to depend on the server, this may not be a good thing. Instead, you would need to move it over to an object attribute by taking it right to the ' init ' part. Either way, you will get the speed up process from this.

Manual Memoization: Using 'Global"

Another thing that we can work on with this process is manual memoization with the help of the 'Global' function. You can go through and evade your default parameters and some of the hacky mutations simply by adding in 'global'. This is one thing that sometimes gets a bad reputation with programmers, but it is a good one to learn how to use. Many times you would use the global here declaration because it works better, but you would use the same kind of coding that we had above.

Decorators

The last thing we are going to talk about here is a decorator. This is simply a higher order function. What this means is that the function is going to be the argument and then it will return to you another function. When it comes to these decorators, the returned function is going to usually be the original function, which has been augmented to be more functional. An example of this would be to make decorate that is going to allow you to print text each time a function is called. The way that you can write this out is:

def output_decorator(f): def f_(f)
f()
*print('Ran f...') return f_*

You can take the decorated version to replace the f. You just need to do 'F=output_decorator(f)'. Just by calling the f(), you are going to get your decorated version. Python is going to make this even easier if you just use the following syntax to help.

@output_decorator def f()
#...define f...

Now, if you go through and try to do this, you will find that the result from the output_decortor is not that motivating. But you can go beyond this and augment the operation of the function itself. For example, you could include a type of cache with the decorator and then intercept the calls to the function if needed.

But if you try to write out your own decorator, there are times when you get confused in the particulars of the argument passing, and then getting really stuck with the introspection of Python when you figure this out. Introspection is the capacity to determine when you run the program, the type of an object. This is one of the strengths of the Python language, but if you are using a decorator, things can become messy.

If you are going to use one of the decorators, be careful with what you are doing here. You want to make sure that you understand how to make them work and that you actually need to use it in your code. Otherwise, you may run into some issues with the code, and it may not interpret in the compiler the right way.

Python Modules

Modules consist of definitions as well as program statements. An illustration is a file name config.py which is considered as a module. The module name would be config. Modules are sued to help break large programs into smaller manageable and organized files as well as promoting reusability of code.

Example

Creating the First module

Start IDLE.

Navigate to the File menu and click New Window.

Type the following:

Def add(x, y):

""""This is a program to add two

numbers and return the outcome""""

outcome=x+y

return outcome

Module Import

The keyword import is used to import.

Example

Import first

The dot operator can help us access a function as long as we know the name of the module.

Example

Start IDLE.

Navigate to the File menu and click New Window.

Type the following:

first.add(6,8)

Import Statement in Python

The import statement can be used to access the definitions within a module via the dot operator.

Start IDLE.

Navigate to the File menu and click New Window.

Type the following:

import math

print("The PI value is", math.pi)

Import with renaming

Example

Start IDLE.

Navigate to the File menu and click New Window.

Type the following:

import math as h

  print("The PI value is-",h.pi)

Discussion

In this case, h is our renamed math module with a view helping save typing time in some instances. When we rename the new name becomes valid and recognized one and not the original one.

From...import statement Python.

It is possible to import particular names from a module rather than importing the entire module.

Example

Start IDLE.

Navigate to the File menu and click New Window.

Type the following:

from math import pi

print("The PI value is-", pi)

Importing All Names

Example

Start IDLE.

Navigate to the File menu and click New Window.

Type the following:

from math import*

print("The PI value is-", pi)

Discussion

In this context, we are importing all definitions from a particular module but it is encouraged norm as it can lead to unseen duplicates.

Module Search Path in Python

Example

Start IDLE.

Navigate to the File menu and click New Window.

Type the following:

import sys

sys.path

Python searches everywhere including the sys file.

Reloading a Module

Python will only import a module once increasing efficiency in execution.

print("This program was executed")

import mine

Reloading Code

Example

Start IDLE.

Navigate to the File menu and click New Window.

Type the following:

import mine

import mine

import mine

mine.reload(mine)

Dir() Built-In Python function

For discovering names contained in a module, we use the dir() inbuilt function.

Syntax

dir(module_name)

Python Package

Files in python hold modules and directories are stored in packages. A single package in Python holds similar modules. Therefore, different modules should be placed in different Python packages.

Summary

A module is a Python object with arbitrarily named attributes that you can bind and reference. Simply, a module is a file consisting of Python code. A module can define functions, classes and variables. A module can also include runnable code.
A package is a collection of Python modules: while a module is a single Python file, a package is a directory of Python modules containing an additional __init__.py file, to distinguish a package from a directory that just happens to contain a bunch of Python scripts.

Part 16: Time and Date

The module datetime in Python enables us to work with times and dates.

Getting Current Time and Date

```
import datetime
datetime_today=datetime.datetime.now()
print(datetime_today)              #Will return the current time and date
```

Discussion

We imported the datetime module using the import datetime statement. The datetime class is defined in the datetime module. The now() method is invoked to create a datetime object containing the local date and time now.

Example

```
import datetime
date_today=datetime.date.today()
print(date_today)
```

Discussion

In this program we used the today() method specified in the date class to extract date object.

Understanding the Datetime Module

Python allows us to use the dir() function to extract a list containing all attributes of a module.

Example

```
import datetime
print(dir(datetime))
```

The commonly used classes in the datetime module include date Class, time Class, datetime Class, and timedelta Class among others.

Date Object

import datetime

t = datetime.date(2018, 5, 6)

print(t)

Discussion

The date() in the example is a constructor of the date class and the constructor accepts three arguments: year, month and day.

Example 2

from datetime import date

b=date(2018,5,6)

print(b)

Practice Exercise

- ✓ In example 2 explain what is b
- ✓ Explain the statement 'from datetime import date'.

Example 3

Using the today() class method we can create a date object containing the current date.

```
from datetime import date

day = date.today()

print("Date today =", today)
```

Timestamp

It is also possible to create date objects from a time stamp. The fromtimestamp() method we can create a current date object.

Example

```
from datetime import date
timetoday = date.fromtimestamp(1235153363)
print("Date =", timetiday)
```

Printing Current Date

Example

```
from datetime import date

timetoday = date.timetoday()

print("Current year:", timetoday.year)
print("Current month:",timetoday.month)
print("Current day:", timetoday.day)
```

Time Object

The local time is a time object instantiated from the time class.

Example

```
from datetime import time

m = time()
print("m =", m)

n = time(11, 34, 56)
print("n =", n)

p = time(hour = 11, minute = 34, second = 56)
print("p =", p)

f = time(11, 34, 56, 234566)
print("f =", f)
```

Print Hour to Microsecond

Example

```
from datetime import time

m = time(11, 34, 56)

print("hour =", m.hour)
print("minute =", m.minute)
print("second =", m.second)
print("microsecond =", m.microsecond)
```

Datetime Object

Example

```
from datetime import datetime

m = datetime(2019, 1, 15)
print(m)

n = datetime(2018, 10, 27, 22, 56, 58, 351270)
print(n)
```

Discussion

The datetime() constructor takes three arguments year, month and day.

Print Year to the Minute

Example

```
from datetime import datetime

m = datetime(2018, 10, 27, 25, 54, 53, 351270)
print("year =", m.year)
print("month =", m.month)
print("hour =", m.hour)
print("minute =", m.minute)
print("timestamp =", m.timestamp())
```

Using Timedelta

In Python, a timedelta object represents the difference between two times or dates.

```
from datetime import datetime, date

time1 = date(year = 2019, month = 1, day = 12)
time2 = date(year = 2018, month = 11, day = 22)
time3 = time1 - time2
print("time3 =", time3)

time4 = datetime(year = 2018, month = 7, day = 12, hour = 7, minute = 9, second = 33)
time5 = datetime(year = 2019, month = 6, day = 10, hour = 5, minute = 55, second = 13)
time6 = time4 - time5
print("time6 =", time6)

print("type of time3 =", type(time3))
print("type of time6 =", type(time6))
```

Getting Difference Between Two Timedelta Objects

```
from datetime import timedelta

time1 = timedelta(weeks = 4, days = 10, hours = 2, seconds = 56)
time2 = timedelta(days = 6, hours = 11, minutes = 8, seconds = 34)
time3 = time1 - time2

print("time3 =", time3)
```

Discussion

In this program, we created timedelta objects time1 and time2 and their difference displayed on the screen.

From Datetime Import Timedelta

```
time1 = timedelta(seconds = 33)
time2 = timedelta(seconds = 54)
time3 = time1 - time2

print("time3 =", time3)
print("time3 =", abs(time3))
```

Duration in Seconds

```
from datetime import timedelta

time = timedelta(days = 4, hours = 2, seconds = 56, microseconds = 31423)
print("total seconds =", time.total_seconds())
```

NOTE

In Python one can find the sum of two times and date using the + operator. It is also to divide and multiply a timedelta object by floats and integers.

Format Datetime in Python

Formatting datetime attributes are achieved through strftime() and strptime() methods. In Python the strftime() method is specified under classes datetime, date and time.

Using the method will format a string from a given datetime, date or time object.

Example

```
from datetime import datetime

now = datetime.now()

time = now.strftime("%H:%M:%S")
print("time:", time)

string1 = now.strftime("%m/%d/%Y, %H:%M:%S")
print("string1:", string1)

string2 = now.strftime("%d/%m/%Y, %H:%M:%S")
# dd/mm/YY H:M:S format
print("string2:", string2)
```

Discussion

In this program, the following are format codes %m, %Y,%H, and %d and the strftime() method accepts one or more format codes and a gives a formatted string. In the program, time, string1, and string2 are strings.

From strptime() to datetime

In Python, the strptime () will create a datetime object from a specified string that represents date and time.

Example

```
from datetime import datetime

date_mine = "15 March, 2017"
print("date_mine =", date_mine)

object_date = datetime.strptime(object_date, "%d %B, %Y")
print("object_date =", object_date)

Discussion
In Python, the strptime() accepts two arguments namely a string capturing date and time, and format code
Timezone in Python
A third party module pytZ is recommended for handling timezone needs in Python.
from datetime import datetime
import pytz
local = datetime.now()
print("Local:", local.strftime("%m/%d/%Y, %H:%M:%S"))
Mumbai_tz = pytz.timezone('Asia/India')
datetime_Mumbai = datetime.now(Mumbai_tz)
print("NY:", datetime_Mumbai.strftime("%m/%d/%Y, %H:%M:%S"))
Lagos_tz = pytz.timezone('Africa/Lagos')
datetime_Lagos = datetime.now(Lagos_tz)
print("Lagos:", datetime_Lagos.strftime("%m/%d/%Y, %H:%M:%S"))
```

Discussion

In this program, the Mumbai_tz and Lagos_tz are datetime objects holding current time and date of their corresponding timezone

199

Summary

Example: Python get today's date.
Here, we imported date class from the datetime module. Then, we used date.today() method to get the current local date. By the way, today variable will be a date object. You can use strftime() method to create string representing date in different formats from this object.

Conclusion

Thank you for making it through to the end of this book. I hope it was informative and able to provide you with all of the tools you need to achieve your goals whatever they may be.

The next step is to take a look at some of the topics and the things that we discuss in this book, and put them to use. There are many different things that you will be able to do with the Python language, and this book aimed to help you get started with a few of the more complex parts that you may want to add into your code.

When you are done, you will be able to combine this information with your basics and make some really powerful codes.

When you have spent some time working on the Python language and you are ready to take your skills to the next level and develop some strong codes that can do so much in just a few lines, make sure to read through this book to help you get started!

Python Crash Course

The Ultimate Step-By-Step Guide to Learn, Understand, and Master Python Programming and Computer Coding Language (From Beginners to Advanced)

Introduction

The following chapters will discuss all of the different parts of learning how to do some of your coding in the Python language. There are a lot of different reasons why you will want to learn how to work with the Python language, and we want to make sure that we can take some of the steps of the different part by step and learn how to make them work for our needs. There are a lot of options out there for learning how to code and get things done with programming, but you will find that the Python language is going to be one of the best ones to work with. And this guidebook will show you why that is.

This guidebook is going to spend some time taking a look at some of the basics of the Python language. We will look at what Python is all about, where it comes from, and even the steps that are needed to install this language and all of the necessary files on your computer, no matter what operating system you are working with at the time.

Once we have some of the basics of coding in the Python language down, it is time for us to move on to the next step. In this one, we are going to explore a few other important parts that come with Python including how to handle things like the variables and the strings, how to work with lists, tuples, and operators, and some of the Python functions to get things done. All of these are important to writing out some of the various codes that you want to handle in the Python language, and should not be missed out on.

Once we have some of the basic parts of the Python language down and ready to go, it is time for us to work on some of the actual codes that we need to write to gain some expertise in this kind of language. We will look a bit at how to write out own classes while gaining a deeper understanding of the OOP aspect of Python, how to write out conditional statements loops, and even some exceptions of your own.

To finish off some of the topics that we need to know to get started with programming in Python, there are a few more things that a beginner should understand to get the best results. We will spend our time in these chapters with a look at Python encapsulation and what this means for keeping certain parts of your code private and secrete, what the databases and dictionaries mean in this language, and how to work with CGI and GUI in this language as well.

There are so many great things that we are going to take a look at when it is time to work with the Python language. This guidebook is going to spend some time taking a look at some of the most important parts that come with this kind of language, and how even a beginner can get started and make this language their own. When you are ready to learn a bit more about this language and what it can do for you, make sure to check out this guidebook to help out!

Chapter 1: What is the Python Language?

History and Evolution

Since computers were first invented, many people have had the job to make them more useful. To make this happen, there are a ton of programming tools that have been developed over the years to turn the instructions the computer is given into code that the computer can execute. When this first started, assembly language was the main type. While it did allow you to create programming that was tailored and then optimized for the low memory systems of that time, it was hard to learn, read, and maintain and only a few people could use it.

As computer technology grew and many systems became more complex, the programming languages needed to change as well. Some higher-level languages including Lisp, Cobol, and Fortran were produced to produce punch cards which the computers were able to read and then execute the instructions that were found on the card. Programming with this kind of tool was a lot easier than the languages in the past, allowing more people to write the complex programs they needed.

As time started to go on, there were a lot of improvements that were made to some of the technology that we are working with now, and it has resulted in a lot of better storage methods when it comes to our programs and more. For example, some of those punch cards have been replaced with a type of magnetic tape and then it was all moved over to work with a disc drive. As these new inventions came out, the tools to work on these programs improved as well.

Basic was one of the first coding languages that was designed to be easy to read through and this one was developed in the 1960s. then in the 1970s, we saw the introduction of Pascal and C, and these became tools that helped us to get a really simple and structured kind of programming language that would help a programmer to get the efficient code that they want. You will find that the structured languages like these would not have to rely on the go-to statement found in some of the other languages. Instead, these programs would rely on a flow that has features including conditional statements, functions, and loops like we will talk about later in this guidebook. These features were nice because they would allow a new programmer to make their own applications with the help of standalone reusable routines, which would then be able to lower the amount of time that it would take to develop the program, and even debug it so that the program would work the way that you would like.

It was in the 1980's when the next big advancement in programming happened This was where C++, and a few other languages, turned into OOP languages, or object-oriented programming languages. There are a number of these that are now available and usable, but they were useful because they helped us to hold onto our information better. While these tools of OOP languages were powerful and had some new capabilities when it came to coding, many times they would be seen as special because they could cut out some of the challenges that came with coding.

As the use and the popularity of computers started to grow, and it becomes common for more people to use them, it was also an important factor to have a language for programming that was easy to use, one that we can use on a lot of different platforms. Because of this need, the language that we know as Python today was developed.

Python is going to be a general-purpose programming language. Whether you are a beginner or someone who has been in the coding world for some time, you will find that this language is easy to learn while still making sure that there is a lot of power behind it to get those codes done. You are able to use this for a lot of different purposes, from some general housekeeping tasks for your system to just having fun and making your programs and games. Of course, when you compare this language to some of the others out there, you will also notice that Python is going to have a lot of rules and structures that you must follow to get this to work. No matter what codes you would like to write in Python, you will need to follow the rules and ensure that the compiler is ready to handle it all. The good news is that the rules are pretty simple with this language and you will find that this language is simple, powerful, and compact all in one. As a beginner, it is easier to catch onto this kind of coding language than you think, and before long, and with the help of this guidebook, you will be able to get everything to work the way you would like and will be writing your codes in no time.

In the past, a lot of people were worried about learning a coding language. They worried that these languages were too tough to learn, that they would just get frustrated, and that only those who had spent their whole lives around computers could even attempt to write their codes. And maybe with some of the older codes, this was true. Thanks to a lot of the newer codes that have been introduced recently, the idea that only those gifted in computer programming could code has faded away. With many of the codes that are coming out now, including Python, anyone can learn a few of the syntaxes for what they want to do, or even find some premade codes online and make some changes. And since many of these codes are open-sourced, it is easier than ever to learn how to use them and develop the codes to meet your needs.

You will find that many of the modern languages that are used for coding are going to be a lot better and easier to use than what we were able to find in the past with most coding languages. Gone are the days that even professionals would run into troubles regularly when it was time to find the bugs in the system. Now it is possible for anyone and everyone to learn how to use this coding language for these needs. And this is mainly because we have a lot of great OOP languages to work within Python.

The Benefits of Python

There are a lot of benefits that come with using the Python coding language for all of your programming needs. It is often seen as one of the best general-purpose coding languages that you can work with, and with the ease of use and learning, and all of the great features that come with it, it is no wonder that this language is a favorite for a lot of people along the way.

It is Easy to Work with

The first benefit that most people are going to enjoy when it comes to using the Python language is that it is very easy to use. This language was designed for use with a beginner, and the whole purpose is to make sure that anyone, even those who may not be well-versed in doing any kind of programming at all, will be able to learn and write some of the codes of their own that they would like. This language is meant to help a beginner, someone who has never had a chance to work with coding in the past, learn how to do some of this coding, and get the results that they would like. There are also a lot of different things that you are able to do when you work with the Python coding language. It is designed to help with almost any kind of coding that you are interested in handling, from some of the basics of writing your own projects all the way to helping out with data analysis and machine learning if you so choose. There is just so much that you are able to do with this kind of language and many people are jumping on board to learn how to work all of these different angles with ease thanks to the Python coding language.

It Has Lots of Power

Even though this is a coding language that is meant to help us out with some of the basics of coding, you will find that there is quite a bit of strength and power behind what we can do with it. Even more advanced problems can be easily handled when we are looking at this kind of language, and you will find that with the added extensions and libraries that are available with Python, it is easy to figure out how to write codes that work with some complex coding and programming problems

Some people hear about how easy it is to work with Python and they worry that there is not going to be enough strength and power behind it in order to get started. They think they need to go with another option because this one will not have the strength of the features that are needed to get things done. But, once you mess around with some of the codes that we will do with this language, you will find that it is going to have plenty of the power and a ton of the features, that you need to get anything done.

Many Libraries to Work With

While we are at it, you will find that a lot of the libraries and extensions that come with the Python language are going to be really great as well. You can already do a lot of work with the standard Python language, but you will also find that there are additional libraries that work well with Python and can help us to expand out what we are able to do with programming in this language. From libraries that can help us out with math, science, machine learning, data science, and more, you will find that the Python coding language is one of the best options for you to work with. From here, we will also find that the Python language is going to be one that is able to work well with others. For some of the basics that we will discuss in this guidebook, this is not going to seem like that big of a deal. But when we get into some things like machine learning and data science with this language, the fact that we can combine Python with other languages is going to help us get more done.

Easy to Read

We will also see that the Python coding language is going to be a great option to work with when you want to make sure that things stay organized and easy to read through. There are a lot of other coding languages out there that you can choose from, but that does not mean that they are the right ones for you. In most cases, beginners are going to find that working with an OOP language, just like Python is, is one of the best ways to keep the information organized and easy to use.

It is an OOP Language

The fact that Python is an OOP language is going to be good news for you. We will explore this a bit more in the next few chapters, but this basically means that the code is split up into classes, and then the objects that show up in the code will fit into one of these classes. This is the best way to make the code as efficient as possible, and will ensure that you are able to bring up the right parts, at the right times so that your code will work the way that you want.

As we can see here, there are a lot of different benefits that come with working in the Python language, and how well you will be able to use it. Sure, there are a lot of other coding languages out there that you are able to choose to work with. But none are going to provide us with as many benefits and features as we are going to be able to see with the Python language.

The Basics of the Python Language

Now that we know a bit more about the Python language and some of the things that we are able to do in order to see results with this kind of language, it is time to learn a few of the different basic parts that are needed in this kind of coding language before you even write out a single code with it at all. There are a lot of different parts that come into play, so let's dive right in and get started.

Python Keywords

The first thing that we need to take a look at in this section is the Python keywords. Just like with other languages that we may work with, we will find that these are reserved words that we are able to use to provide a command to our compiler. You should make sure that they are only used in the proper place in your code and that you are not bringing them up randomly, or you will end up with an error in the code that you are writing. These are reserved because they are meant to provide your compiler with the instructions that it needs in order to handle your coding at that time. these keywords are already programmed into the compiler to make sure that it behaves well. Because of this, you will find that they are going to be important to any kind of code that you are trying to write. Make sure that you learn what these works are all about, and how they are going to work with the compiler, so that you can be on the lookout.

Naming Our Identifiers

Your identifiers can be important to your code as well, and in Python, there are quite a few identifiers to work with too. You will find that they come in at a lot of different names and you may seem them as functions, entities, variables, and classes. When you are naming an identifier, you can use the same information and the same rules will apply for each of them, which makes it easier for you to remember the rules.

The first rule to remember is when you name these identifiers. You have many options when you are naming your identifiers. For example, you can rely on both uppercase and lowercase letters with naming, as well as any number and the underscore symbol. You can also combine any of these together. One thing to remember here is that you can't start the name with a number and there shouldn't be any spaces between the words that you write out. So, you can't write out 3words as a name, but you can write out words3 or threewords. Make sure that you don't use one of the keywords that we discussed above or you will end up with an error.

When you pick out the identifier name, you can follow the rules above, and try to pick out a name that you can remember. Later on, when writing the code, you will need to pull it back up, and if you give it a name that is difficult to remember, you could run into problems or raise errors because things aren't showing up the way that you want. Outside of these rules, you will be fine naming the identifiers anything that you want.

Control Flow Basics

In many languages, the control flow that comes with it is going to be an important thing as well. The control flow that comes with Python is going to be pretty important as well because it helps us to know whether or not we are correctly writing the code. There are going to be a few strings that we need to pay careful attention to because they need to be read by the compiler properly.

If you are not using the control flow in the right manner, then you will end up with the compiler being confused and then you will get some error messages. The good news here is that we are going to spend some time looking at a lot of examples of codes in this guidebook, and you will be able to figure out what is right and what is wrong with the control flow that you are working with.

Python Comments

The next thing that we need to spend some time on is the comments. As you are working with some of the codes that you would like to write, you may find that there are some situations where you would like to add in a little note, or some other explanation on what is being written inside of that particular code. And you want to be able to do this without causing the compiler to get confused or making it impossible to finish up the code without an error.

These are little notes that can be important to others who are using or reading through the code, but we do not want them to show up in the code when it is executed. And this is going to be known as a comment in the Python language, as well as with some of the other coding languages that you want to work with. Any comment that you write out with Python will be ignored and passed over by the compiler, as long as you use the # symbol ahead of what you are writing. This symbol is going to tell the compiler that you are writing out a comment, and that it should avoid reading that comment and instead move on to another part of the code to handle.

With the Python language, you technically are able to add in as many of these comments as you would like to help explain to yourself or others what you have written at that part of the code. If you would like to have one on every other line of the code, then this is technically allowed. Keep in mind though that this is going to make your code look a bit messy and unprofessional, so it is generally something that is avoided. Just add in the number of comments that are needed and don't go overboard, and your code will work great.

We will talk about the next two topics a bit more in some of the following chapters because they are so important to what we are going to be doing throughout our coding experience, but they still deserve a bit of mention here. We are going to take some time to look at two more important topics that are the basis of your Python code, whether these codes are simple or more complex, including the operators and variables.

Variables

Variables are another part of the code that you will need to know about because they are so common in your code. The variables are there to help store some of the values that you place in the code, helping them to stay organized and nice. You can easily add in some of the values to the right variable simply by using the equal sign. It is even possible for you to take two values and add it to the same variables if you want and you will see this occur in a few of the codes that we discuss through this guidebook. Variables are very common and you will easily see them throughout the examples that we show.

Operators

Then we are able to move on to some of the operators that you will be able to use. While you are coding you will quickly notice that these operators are all over the place. And there are quite a few of them that you are able to handle along the way as well. Learning how to work with these operators can make code writing a little bit easier, and will help us to make sure that our codes will work the way that we want.

Operators are pretty simple parts of your code, but you should still know how they work. You will find that there are a few different types of them that work well. For example, the arithmetic functions are great for helping you to add, divide, subtract, and multiply different parts of the code together. There are assignment operators that will assign a specific value to your variable so that the compiler knows how to treat this. There are also comparison operators that will allow you to look at a few different pieces of code and then determine if they are similar or not and how the computer should react based on that information.

These are just a few of the different parts of working with the Python code that we are able to focus on. These parts are going to be critical to ensuring that we are not going to lose out on some of the work that we need to handle, and can make it easier for us to understand some of the more complex codes that we will focus on at a later time. Make sure to review these parts and gain a good understanding of how they work to help make it a bit easier when it is time to work with the codes that are coming up.

Chapter 2: Everything You Need to Know to Install Python

Before you are able to work with any of the coding that we want to do with Python or anything else that comes in this guidebook, we need to take a moment to learn more about how to install and download this language on your own computer. The good news is that the Python language can work on any operating system that you would like. You are not limited based on the system that you want to work with, which is another great benefit that you will be able to enjoy when it is time to work with this kind of language.

With this in mind, we want to make sure that we know all of the rules that need to be in place to install Python appropriately, no matter what kind of operating system you are working with. We are going to take a look at the three biggest systems out there that you can work with including Mac OS X, Windows, and the Linux operating system to help us get started.

Installing On the Mac Operating System

First on the list is the Mac OS X system. If you are working with a computer that has this on it, you may find that there is already a version of Python 2 on that system. Many of the Mac computers are going to come pre-installed with the Python library on them, which makes it easier to use them and get the results that you would like overall. The version you have though is going to depend on which type of computer you have and how long you have owned it. To check out which version of Python 2 is on your system, you can type in the following prompt in your command terminal:

Python – V

This is going to show you the version you get so a number will come up. You can also choose to install Python 3 on this system if you would like, and it isn't required to uninstall the 2.X version on the computer. To check for the 3.X installation, you just need to open up the terminal app and then type in the following prompt:

Python3 – V

The default on OS X is that Python 3 is not going to be installed at all. If you want to use Python 3, you can install it using some of the installers that are on Python.org.

This is a good place to go because it will install everything that you need to write and execute your codes with Python. It will have the Python shell, the IDLE development tools, and the interpreter. Unlike what happens with Python 2.X, these tools are installed as a standard application in the Applications folder.

Being able to run the IDLE and the Python shell is going to be dependent on which version you choose and some of your own personal preferences. You can use the following commands to help you start the shell and IDLE applications:

- For Python 2.X just type in "Idle"
- For Python 3.X, just type in "idle3"

As we brought up a bit before, when you take the time to download and install Python 3, you will be able to install the IDLE in your Applications folder. Doing all of this from the Python website, www.python.org, is the best option because it will ensure that you have the right files and more that are needed to complete this process.

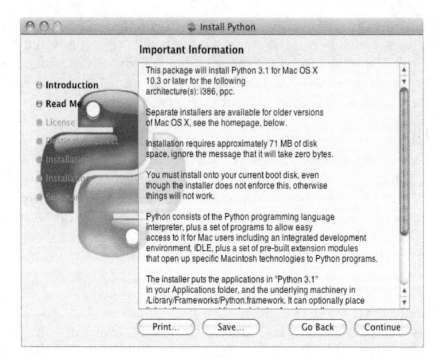

The image above is a good one for us to work with because it shows us an example of the pup-ups that we are going to see when it comes to working with installing this on Mack. You can easily click on Continue after reading through the information, and do this a few times, and it will be set up and ready to go for our needs.

The Windows Operating System
The next operating system that we need to take a look at is how to add this to the Windows system. The Windows system is a popular option to work with because it will allow you the opportunity to do a lot of neat features, and many programmers and individual users alike are going to rely on this to get their work done. One thing that we have to notice here though is if we do use the Windows system, we will have to go through the full process of downloading and installing the Python language.

The reason for this is that Windows has its own version of a coding language already installed. Because of this, it is not going to already have Python installed as well. This doesn't mean that the Python language will not work with Windows. It works fine and you won't run

218

into any issues at all. But you do need to go through the process and actually install it on your system.

The steps that we will need to take in order to download and install Python on a Windows system will include:

1. The first step is going to include going to the official Python Page in order to download the page and then look for the installer for a Windows system. You are able to choose the version of Python you would like to work with, but most programmers are going to go with the latest version of Python 3 that is out.

    a. The default here is that the installer is going to choose a version of Python that is 32-bit. There is an option for the 64-bit as well so you can change this if you would like.

2. After you are done with this part, you are able to right-click on your installer to get things going, and then select that you would like to Run as Administrator at this part. There are going to just be two options for you to choose from. Our choice here is to go with Customize Installation.

3. When you click on that to start the installation, you are going to end up on the following screen with a lot of options. You want to make sure that all of the boxes under "Optional Features" are clicked, and then you can move on.

4. While you are still under the category for the Advanced Options, you will be able to pick out the best location for you to have the Python language installed on your computer. Click on Install from here. This is going to take a few moments for the installation to happen so give it some time and then close the installer.

5. Next, we need to go through the process that is needed to set the PATH variable for the system so that it is going to include

all of the directories that we need. This is going to include any packages and other components that we will need later.

There are a number of steps that we are able to use for this one including:

a. The first step to work on here is to open up our Control Panel in Windows. The way that we can do this is to click on our taskbar, type in the words "Control Panel" and then click on the icon that shows up.

b. Inside of this Control panel when it opens up, we want to do a search for the Environment. Then click on the Edit the System Environment Variables. From here, we are going to be able to click on the button for Environment Variables.

c. Go to the section that is marked for the User Variables. You get two options to work with here. You are able to create one of your own variables, or you can make some edits to the PATH variable that is there.

d. If there isn't already a variable that is present for PATH on your system, then you will need to go through this and create one. We can start this by clicking on New. Make the name for the PATH variable anything that you would like and what you can remember and add in the necessary directories that you want. Click on close so that you are out of the dialogs of this and go to the last step.

Now that you are at this part, we are able to open up the command prompt. We can do this by clicking on our Start Menu, then Windows System, and then the Command Prompt. From here we want to type in the word "python". This is going to help us to load up the interpreter for Python and then we are able to get started with our coding.

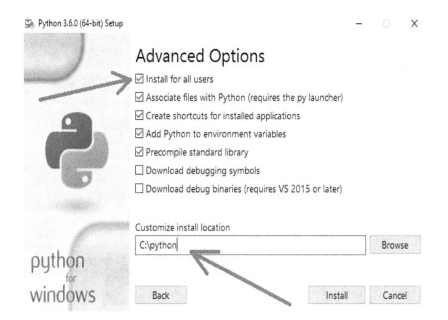

During this process, you are going to end up with a screen that asks you some of the Advanced options that you would like to use. Often you will want to leave the checks on the parts that are already there, but you do not need to do this though. You can change up the options to fit what you need. You can also consider coming up with a customized location in order to keep this organized, and to ensure that you are going to be able to get this set up the right way. Pick a location that you will be able to remember and pull out later on.

The Linux System

And the final operating system that we need to spend some time on here is how to install Python on a Linux system. Just like with the Mac OS X we need to stop and check whether there is one of the Python 3 versions already on the computer or now. You are able to open up the command prompt that comes with this operating system, and work with the code below to check:

$ python3 - - version

If you are on Ubuntu 16.10 or newer, then it is a simple process to install Python 3.6. you just need to use the following commands:

```
$ sudo apt-get update
$ sudo apt-get install Python3.6
```

If you are relying on an older version or Ubuntu or another version, then you may want to work with the deadsnakes PPA, or another tool, to help you download the Python 3.6 version. The code that you need to do this includes:

```
$ sudo apt-get install software-properties-common
$ sudo add-apt repository ppa:deadsnakes/ppa
# suoda apt-get update
$ sudo apt-get install python3.6
```

The good news here is that if you are working with other distributions of Linux, it is likely that you already have Python 3 installed on the system. If not, you can use the distribution's package manager. And if the package of Python 3 is not recent enough, or not the right one for you, you can go through and use these same steps to help install a more recent version of Python on your computer as needed.

As we can see here, working with the Python coding language is going to be a simple process that anyone can do, and when we get it down and learn ow to make it work for our needs, we will be able to write any of the codes that we want. Most of the installation steps for any of the operating systems above are going to be simple, and then you are ready to go writing some of your own codes in the Python language.

Chapter 3: The Python Variables and Strings

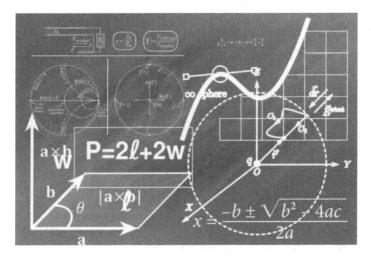

The next topic that we need to take a look at for this guidebook is the idea of the Python strings and variables. You will find that these are going to help us to keep the code going well, and will ensure that we are getting the most out of the codes that we try to write. The variables are going to help us to assign the values that we want to different parts of the code, and the strings are going to provide us with some of the text characters that we need in the code. Both of these are going to come together to help us to get some of the results that we are looking for in Python. Let's take a look at how each of these will be able to work and how we are able to make sure that this will work the way that we want.

The Python Variables

The Python variables are an important thing to work with as well. A variable, in simple terms, is often just going to be a box that we can use to hold onto the values and other things that show up in our code. They will reserve a little bit of the memory of our code so that we are able to utilize it later one. These are important because they allow us to pull out the values that we would like to use at a later time without issues along the way.

These variables are going to be a good topic to discuss because they are going to be stored inside of the memory of our code. And you will then be able to assign a value over to them, and pull them out in the code that you would like to use. These values are going to be stored in some part of the memory of your code, and will be ready to use when you need. Depending on the type of data that you will work with, the variable is going to be the part that can tell your compiler the right place to save that information to pull it out easier.

With this in mind, the first thing that we need to take a look at is how to assign a value over to the variable. To get the variable to behave in the manner that you would like, you need to make sure that a minimum of one value is assigned to it. Otherwise, you are just save an empty spot in the memory. If the variable is assigned properly to some value, and sometimes more than one value based on the code you are using, then it is going to behave in the proper manner and when you call up that variable, the right value will show up.

As you go through and work with some of the variables you have, you may find that there are three main options that are able to use. Each of these can be useful and it is often going to depend on what kind of code you would like to create on the value that you want to put with a particular variable. The three main types of variable that you are able to choose from here will include:

- Float: this would include numbers like 3.14 and so on.
- String: this is going to be like a statement where you could write out something like "Thank you for visiting my page!" or another similar phrase.
- Whole number: this would be any of the other numbers that you would use that do not have a decimal point.

When you are working with variables in your code, you need to remember that you don't need to take the time to make a declaration to save up this spot in the memory. This is automatically going to happen once you assign a value over to the variable using the equal sign. If you want to check that this is going to happen, just look to see that you added that equal sign in, and everything is going to work. Assigning a value over to your variable is pretty easy. Some examples of how you can do this in your code would include the following:

x = 12   *#this is an example of an integer assignment*
pi = 3.14   *#this is an example of a floating point assignment*
customer name = John Doe #this is an example of a string assignment

There is another option that we are able to work with on this one, and one that we have brought up a few times within this section already. This is where we will assign more than one value to one for our variables. There are a few cases where we are going to write out our code and then we need to make sure that there are two or more values that go with the exact same variable.

To make this happen, you just need to use the same kind of procedure that we were talking about before. Of course, we need to make sure that each part is attached to the variable with an equal sign. This helps the compiler know ahead of time that these values are all going to be associated to the same variable. So, you would write out something like a = b= c= 1 to show the compiler that all of the variables are going to equal one. Or you could do something like 1 = b = 2 in order to show that there are, in this case, two values that go with one variable.

The thing that you will want to remember when you are working with these variables is that you have to assign a value in order to make the work happen in the code. These variables are also just going to be spots in your code that are going to reserve some memory for the values of your choice.

The Python Strings

The next topic that we need to take a look at in this chapter is going to be all about the strings. These strings are going to help us to learn more about how we can control some of the different parts of our codes, and will make it easier to understand what the string is. as a review, a string is just going to include a series of text characters that are found in our code for us to use.

Now, when you are working with these strings, you will find that there are some different types of operators that you are able to use when you bring them up. An operator is simply a symbol that is able to perform a specific operation that is inside of your code. When we are in this kind of situation, the operation is going to be performed on the strings. Some of the operators that you are going to be able to find here will include some of the following:

1. The concatenation operator: This is going to be the type of operator that you will use when it is time to take those strings and concatenate them.

2. Repetition operator: This is going to be the type of operator that you are able to use when you would like to get more than one copy of your string, and often many of these copies. You are able to use this one and then choose the number of times you would like to see the string repeat.

3. Slice operator: This is going to be an operator that will take a look through the chosen string, and then will figure out the specific character that you would like to work with from there. Any time that we bring this one up, you will need to remember that the first character of your string is going to be zero.

4. Range slice operator: This is another operator that we are able to use because it can retrieve a range of characters out of the index, rather than just one character to you. If you would just like to have it showcase out one part, or one word, of that string, then you would need to work with this operator.

5. In operator: This operator is going to spend some time searching for a specified character in your target string. If you do have that specific character found in the string, then you will get the True answer returned to you. But if the operator is not able to find that answer in the string, then the False answer is going to be returned to you.

6. No in operator: This is the operator that will work in the opposite manner as the in operator. It is going to search for a specified character in your string. But if the operator is not able to find that character in the string, then you will get the

True answer returned. If that character is found in the string, then it is going to return False.

As we are working on some of the strings that we want to handle, you will find that there are a lot of options that are going to be available for you to use at any time. these strings come with a lot of functions and will help you to add more options and features to some of the codes that you are trying to write. Some of the different functions that are going to work well when you design strings in Python will include:

- Capitalize(): This one is going to take the first letter of the string and capitalize it for you.
- Center(width, char): This is going to return to you a string that is at least the specified width and then it will be created by padding the string with the character.
- Count(str): This is going to return the number of times that a particular string is contained in another string.
- Find(str): This is going to return the index number of the substring in the string.
- Isalpha(): This is going to check if all the characters of a string are alphabetic characters.
- Isdigit(): This part is going to check whether the string contains just numbers or digits or if there is a mixture.
- Islower): This function is going to take a look to see if the string you are checking has all lower case characters.
- Len(): This is going to let you know the length of the string
- Isupper(): This one is going to check to see if all the characters in the string are upper case.
- Lower(): This will give you a return that has all the string in lower case letters.
- Replace(): This is going to take the string that you have and replace it with a new string
- Upper(): This is going to return the string in upper case.
- Split(): This is going to split up the string based on the split character.

Chapter 4: Handling Python Operators, Tuples, and Lists

This chapter is going to take some time to delve into a few of the other parts that we need to know when it is time to work with the Python language. In this chapter, we are going to spend our time looking at how to work with the operators, as well as what the similarities and the differences between tuples and lists are. Let's dive in and learn more about these topics and how you can make them work for your needs.

The Python Operators

The Python operators are going to be pretty diverse and can do a lot of different things in your code based on how you use them. When we are talking about the operators, there are going to be quite a few different types that you are able to work with in the code. Let's explore a bit more about these operators and how we are able to use these for our needs as well.

Arithmetic Operators

The first type of operator that we are going to take a look at is the arithmetic operators. These are going to be similar to the signals and signs that we would use when we do mathematical equations. You can work with the addition, subtraction, multiplication, and division symbols in order to do the same kinds of actions on the different parts of the code that you are working with. These are common when you want to do something like add two parts of the code together with one another.

You have the freedom to add in as many of these to your code as you would like, and you can even put more than one type in the same statement. Just remember that you need to work with the rules of operation and do these in the right order in order to make it work the way that you would like. Otherwise, you will be able to add in as many of these to the same code as you need to make it work.

Operator	Description	Exan
+	Adds two operands	A + B
-	Subtracts second operand from the first	A - B
*	Multiply both operands	A * B
/	Divide numerator by denumerator	B / A
%	Modulus Operator and remainder of after an integer division	B % /
++	Increment operator, increases integer value by one	A++
--	Decrement operator, decreases integer value by one	A-- w

The above is going to be some of the different operators that you are able to work with that fit into this category. Working with these will ensure that we are able to handle the work, and that we will be able to use inside of our codes.

Comparison Operators

After looking at the arithmetic operators, it is also possible for us to work with the comparison operators. These comparison operators are going to be good to work with because they will let you take over two, and sometimes more, values and statements in the code and then see how they are going to compare to one another. This is one that we will use often for a lot of codes that are going to rely on Boolean expressions because it ensures that the answer you get back with be false and true. So your statements in this situation are going to be the same as each other, or they will be different.

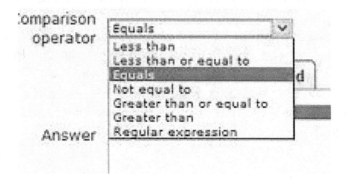

There are a lot of times when we are going to be able to work with these comparison operators to get the most out of the programming that we are doing. You need to consider these ahead of time and make sure that we are going to be able to get the results that we need in our code.

Logical Operators

Next we are going to be looking at the logical operators. These may not be used as often as the other options, but it is still some time for us to look it over. These operators are going to be used when it is time to evaluate the input that a user is able to present to us, with any of the conditions that you are able to set in your code. There are going to be three types of logical operators that we are able to work with, and some of the examples that you are going to use in order to work with this in your code includes:

- Or: with this one, the compiler is going to evalue x and if it is false, it will then go over and evaluate y. If x ends up being true, the compiler is going to return the evaluation of x.
- And: if x ends up being the one that is fase, the compiler is going to evaluate it. If x ends up being true, it will move on and evaluate y.

- Not: if ends up being false, the compiler is going to return True. But if x ends up being true, the program will return false.

A	B	A AND B	A OR B	NO
False	False	False	False	True
False	True	False	True	True
True	False	False	True	Fals
True	True	True	True	Fals

The chart above is going to show us a bit more about the logical operators that we are able to work with as well. This can give us a good idea of what is going to happen when we use each of the operators for our own needs as well.

Assignment Operators

And the final type of operator that we are going to take a look at is the assignment operator. This is going to be the kind of operator that will show up, and if you take a look at some of the different codes that we have already taken a look at in this guidebook, you will be able to see them quite a bit. This is because the assignment operator is simply going to be an equal sign, where you will assign a value over to a variable throughout the code.

So, if you are looking to assign the number 100 over to one of your variables, you would just need to put the equal sign there between them. This can be used with any kind of variable and value that you are using in your code, and you should already have some familiarity with getting this done ahead of time. It is also possible for you to go through and take several values, assigning them to the same variable if that is best for your code. As long as you have this assignment operator, or the equal sign, in between it, you will be able to add in as many values over to the variable that you would like.

Working with these operators is a simple thing to work with, but you will find that they show up in your coding on a regular basis. You are able to use them to add your variables together, to use other mathematical operators, to assign a value over to the variable, or even a few values to your same variable. And you are able to even take these operators to compare two or more parts of the code at the same time and see I they are the same or not. As we can already see, there are so many things that we will be able to do when it comes to using these operators.

Understanding Tuples and Lists

One thing that you will see on a regular basis when you are working with the Python language is that there seems to be a big difference between the lists and the tuples that you will see with this kind of coding language. These are going to seem similar, but there are some differences that we need to be aware about, and learning what these are, and how we can work with them, can make a difference in the kinds of codes that we can write.

The Lists

To keep it easy, we are going to start with a list. A list is basically going to be a collection of objects that are kind of arbitrary, somewhat akin to what we are going to see as an array in other languages of coding, but there will be more flexibility that comes with it. Lists are going to be defined when we are able to enclose them off with a comma-separated sequence of objects in some square brackets. There are a few different characteristics that we are going to see in these Python lists, and they will include:

1. The lists are going to be ordered
2. Lists are going to be dynamic
3. Lists are going to be mutable
4. Lists can be nested to be nested to an arbitrary depth
5. The elements that are part of the list can be accessed by the index.
6. Lists are going to contain some objects that are a bit arbitrary.

The Tuples

With this in mind, we then need to take a look at what the Python tuple is going to be about. Python is going to provide us with another type that is going to be an ordered collection of objects that we are able to call a tuple. Tuples are going to be pretty similar to the lists

232

that we already talked about, but there are a few properties that make them different.

These will include:

1. Tuples are going to be defined by enclosing the elements in parentheses instead of a square bracket.
2. The tuple is going to be immutable.

This is going to bring out one more question that we need to explore. When would we use a list, and when would it be better in our code to work with a list like we talked about before. There are benefits and negatives to each one, and often it is going to depend on what you want to see happen in the code. Some of the reasons why you would want to use a tuple instead of a list is going to include the following:

1. The tuple will allow for a faster execution of the program when you are using a tuple than it is for an equivalent list. This is not going to be as noticeable when your tuple or list is small, but it is something to consider when you have a longer list or tuple.
2. Sometimes you do not want to make it in your code for the data to receive any modifications. If the values in the collection are going to remain constant for the life of the program, then using a tuple instead o a list is going to guard against modifications that could happen on accident.
3. There is also another type of data that we are able to explore in here a bit, and that we will look at a bit more as we go through this guidebook, known as a dictionary. This dictionary is going to require, as one of the components, a value that is immutable. A tuple can be used for this kind of purpose, while a list can't.

Working with the Python programming language and understanding when the different parts are going to come into play, including the differences between lists and tuples and the other parts of this coding language in order to write some of the codes that you are looking for overall.

Chapter 5: The Python Functions

When you are working with a language like Python, there will be times when you will need to work with something that is known as a function. These functions are going to be blocks of reusable code that you will use in order to get your specific tasks done. But when you define one of these functions in Python, we need to have a good idea of the two main types of functions that can be used, and how each of them works. The two types of functions that are available here are known as built-in and user-defined.

The built-in functions are the ones that will come automatically with some of the packages and libraries that are available in Python, but we are going to spend our time working with the user-defined functions because these are the ones that the developer will create and use for special codes they write. In Python though, one thing to remember no matter what kind of function you are working with is that all of them will be treated like objects. This is good news because it can make it a lot easier to work with these functions compared to what we may see with some other coding languages.

Built-in Functions

abs()	divmod()	input()	open()	staticmethod()
all()	enumerate()	int()	ord()	str()
any()	eval()	isinstance()	pow()	sum()
basestring()	execfile()	issubclass()	print()	super()
bin()	file()	iter()	property()	tuple()
bool()	filter()	len()	range()	type()
bytearray()	float()	list()	raw_input()	unichr()
callable()	format()	locals()	reduce()	unicode()
chr()	frozenset()	long()	reload()	vars()
classmethod()	getattr()	map()	repr()	xrange()
cmp()	globals()	max()	reversed()	zip()
compile()	hasattr()	memoryview()	round()	__import__()
complex()	hash()	min()	set()	
delattr()	help()	next()	setattr()	
dict()	hex()	object()	slice()	
dir()	id()	oct()	sorted()	

The user-defined functions that we are going to talk about in the next section are going to be important, and can really expand out some of the work that we are doing as well. But we also need to take a look at some of the work that we are able to do with our built-in functions as well. The list above includes many of the ones that are found inside of the Python language. Take some time to study them and see what they are able to do to help us get things done.

Why are User Defined Functions So Important?

To keep it simple, a developer is going to have the option of either writing out some of their own functions, known as a user-defined function, or they are able to go through and borrow a function from another library, one that may not be directly associated with Python. These functions are sometimes going to provide us with a few advantages depending on how and when we would like to use them in the code.

Some of the things that we need to remember when working on these user-defined functions, and to gain a better understanding of how they work, will include:

235

- These functions are going to be made out of code blocks that are reusable. It is necessary to only write them out once and then you can use them as many times as you need in the code. You can even take that user-defined function and use it in some of your other applications as well.
- These functions can also be very useful. You can use them to help with anything that you want from writing out specific logic in business to working on common utilities. You can also modify them based on your own requirements to make the program work properly.
- The code is often going to be friendly for developers, easy to maintain, and well-organized all at once. This means that you are able to support the approach for modular design.
- You are able to write out these types of functions independently. And the tasks of your project can be distributed for rapid application development if needed.
- A user-defined function that is thoughtfully and well-defined can help ease the process for the development of an application.

Now that we know a little bit more about the basics of a user-defined function, it is time to look at some of the different arguments that can come with these functions before moving on to some of the codes that you can use with this kind of function.

Options for Function Arguments

Any time that you are ready to work with these kinds of functions in your code, you will find that they have the ability to work with four types of arguments. These arguments and the meanings behind them are something that will be pre-defined, and the developer is not always going to be able to change them up. Instead, the developer is going to have the option to use them, but follow the rules that are there with them. You do get the option to add a bit to the rules to make the functions work the way that you want. As we said before, there are four argument types you can work with and these include:

1. Default arguments: In Python, we are going to find that there is a bit different way to represent the default values and the syntax for the arguments of your functions. These default values are going to be the part that indicates that the argument of the function is going to take that value if you don't have a value for the argument that can pass through the call of the function. The best way to figure out where the default value is will be to look for the equal sign.

2. Required argument: The next type of argument is going to be the required arguments. These are the kinds of arguments that will be mandatory to the function that you are working on. These values need to go through and be passed in the right order and number when the function is called out, or the code won't be able to run the right way.

3. Keyword arguments: These are going to be the argument that will be able to help with the function call inside of Python. These keywords are going to be the ones that we mention through the function call, along with some of the values that will go all through this one. These keywords will be mapped with the function argument so that you are able to identify all of the values, even if you don't keep the order the same when the code is called.

4. Variable arguments: The last argument that we are going to take a look at here is the variable number of arguments. This is a good one to work with when you are not sure how many arguments are going to be necessary for the code that you are writing to pass the function. Or you can use this to design your code where any number of arguments can be passed, as long as they have been able to pass any of the requirements in the code that you set.

Writing a Function

Now that we have a little better idea of what these functions are like and some of the argument types that are available in Python, it is time for us to learn the steps that you need to accomplish all of this.

There are going to be four basic steps that we are able to use to make all of this happen, and it is really up to the programmer how difficult or simple you would like this to be.

We will start out with some of the basics, and then you can go through and make some adjustments as needed. Some of the steps that we need to take in order to write out our own user-defined functions include:

1. Declare your function. You will need to use the "def" keyword and then have the name of the function come right after it.
2. Write out the arguments. These need to be inside the two parentheses of the function. End this declaration with a colon to keep up with the proper writing protocol in this language.
3. Add in the statements that the program is supposed to execute at this time.
4. End the function. You can choose whether you would like to do it with a return statement or not.

An example of the syntax that you would use when you want to make one of your own user-defined functions includes:

def userDefFunction (arg1, arg2, arg3, ...):
    program statement1
    program statement2
    program statement3
    ....
    Return;

Working with functions can be a great way to ensure that your code is going to behave the way that you would like. Making sure that you get it set up in the proper manner, and that you are able to work through these functions, getting them set up in the manner that you would like, can be really important as well. There are many times when the functions will come out and serve some purpose, so taking the time now to learn how to use them can be very important to the success of your code.

Chapter 6: Python as an OOP Language and Working with the Python Classes

One thing that you will notice as an important part of the Python program is that it is divided up into classes. This is going to allow you a great method to work with in Python because it can help you to organize the code that you have, and keep everything in order as much as possible. The neat thing about Python is that it works with these classes, and allows you a chance to make easy to use codes that are able to work well without all of the mess and complications that come with some of the other coding languages.

The classes that come with the Python language can be very important. These are going to ensure that we are going to be able to get the most out of some of the codes that we want to create, and will make it easier to ensure that there is enough organization that is going on as well. And when we use these classes as boxes that can hold onto some of he objects of our code, this will ensure that all of the parts are going to show up when they should.

The one thing that we have to remember with this is that we are able to add in any object that we would like to a class. But it needs to make sense why that object is in the class. The objects in the same class have to have something similar to one another, and it must make sense why they are in that same class together.

In Python, we are going to learn how to work with a few of our own classes, mainly because it is the organizing structure that comes with Python and will help us to add in some organization and will ensure that nothing in your code will get lost. To make one of these classes though, we need to pick out the right keywords, like what we talked about before. You can give the class any name that you would like, just make it something that you will be able to remember easily, and then ensure that it shows up in the code after the keyword you need.

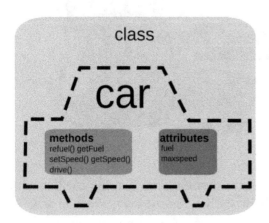

The image above is a good way to help us to learn more about how these OOP languages will work, and what we are able to do with them. We have a class of car, and then all of the methods and attributes that go with them. They all fit together inside of the class of car, even though there are a lot of different attributes that we have been able to work with, including those that are in the image and more.

After we have gone through the steps that are needed to handle our class, we also need to go through and name our own subclass. This subclass will show up in some of the parenthesis Add in the semicolon at the end to maintain some of the programming etiquette that we need.

How to Write a Class

Writing a class at this point is going to sound a bit more complicated than it needs to be. That is why we need to stop here and get a good look at an example of how this kind of coding would work with Python. Then we are able to go through a bit more later and discuss what the different parts mean, and why they are important. To start, the coding that you can use with creating your own Python class will include:

```
class Vehicle(object):
#constructor
def_init_(self, steering, wheels, clutch, breaks, gears):
self._steering = steering
self._wheels = wheels
self._clutch = clutch
self._breaks =breaks
self._gears  = gears
#destructor
def_del_(self):
    print("This is destructor....")
#member functions or methods
def Display_Vehicle(self):
    print('Steering:' , self._steering)
    print('Wheels:', self._wheels)
    print('Clutch:', self._clutch)
    print('Breaks:', self._breaks)
    print('Gears:', self._gears)
#instantiate a vehicle option
myGenericVehicle = Vehicle('Power Steering', 4, 'Super Clutch', 'Disk Breaks', 5)

myGenericVehicle.Display_Vehicle()
```

If you would like, you can try out this code. Just open up your text editor and type the code inside. As you work on writing this out, you will notice that a few of the topics we have already discussed in this guidebook show up in this code. Once you have a chance to write out and then execute this code, let's divide it up and see what happened above. While we are here, we need to explore a bit about the importance of accessing the various members that come in a class. You need to set it up so that the text editor as well as your compiler are going to be able to recognize any of the classes that you would like to create. This will make it easier for them to execute the code in the proper manner. To do this, make sure that your code is set up properly.

Working with the Access Class

The good news is that there are going to be a number of methods that we are able to use in order to ensure that we can access the class members and that everything falls into place the way that we would like. The method that we are going to use though is known as the accessor method. This one is the most common that you will see, and it is going to be an efficient method to get the work done.

To help you get a better understanding of some of the ways that you can access the various members of the class that you made, we need to take a look at the following code:

```
class Cat(object)
        itsAge = None
        itsWeight = None
        itsName = None
        #set accessor function use to assign values to the fields or
member vars
        def setItsAge(self, itsAge):
        self.itsAge = itsAge

        def setItsWeight(self, itsWeight):
        self.itsWeight = itsWeight

        def setItsName(self, itsName):
        self.itsName =itsName
        #get accessor function use to return the values from a field
        def getItsAge(self):
```

```
    return self.itsAge
    def getItsWeight(self):
    return self.itsWeight

    def getItsName(self):
    return self.itsName

objFrisky = Cat()
objFrisky.setItsAge(5)
objFrisky.setItsWeight(10)
objFrisky.setItsName("Frisky")
print("Cats Name is:", objFrisky.getItsname())
print("Its age is:", objFrisky.getItsAge())
print("Its weight is:", objFrisky.getItsName())
```

Before we move on, type this into your compiler. If you have your compiler run this, you are going to get some results that show up on the screen right away. This will include that the cat's name is Frisky (or you can change the name to something else if you want), that the age is 5 and that the weight is 10. This is the information that was put into the code, so the compiler is going to pull them up to give you the results that you want. You can take some time to add different options into the code and see how it changes over time.

While there are a number of steps that we need to take with this kind of coding, classes are not going to be difficult to work with. These are also going to be the perfect part of the code to help you take care of the information, and keep it in order so that it is able to make more sense. You get the option o creating any kind of class that you want to work with, and fill it up with the objects that work the best for your needs.

Chapter 7: The Conditional Statements in Python

Another fun thing to work with when you are in the Python language is the conditional statements. These are going to be known by a lot of different names, such as the if statements and the decision control statements. But they are going to be a great option when you would like the program to learn how to do a few things on its own, without you having to think about all of the possible inputs before you even start.

There are going to be times when you would like to make sure that your code behaves in the right manner and can make some decisions on its own when you are not able to be there to monitor it all and hope that it all fits into the right place. Any time that you have a part of your code that will allow the user to put in any kind of answer that they want all on their own, rather than just selecting from a few options, then you are going to find that the conditional statements are the best ones to work with.

In this chapter, we are going to take a look at the three most common options of the conditional statements that you are likely to use with some of your codings. The three that we are going to focus on the most are the if statement, the if else statement, and the elif statement. These will all work in a slightly different manner from one another, but they can all add some great things to your code, so we are going to spend our time taking a look at them and how they are going to work for our needs.

The If Conditional Statements

The first thing we are going to look at is regular if statement. This keeps things simple and will ensure that we are set and ready to handle some of the basics of these conditional statements. This one is based on the idea that the answer the user gives is either true or it is false depending on what conditions you have set. If the user adds in input that the program is going to see as true, then your program will see this and will continue on to the next step. But if the user does put in an answer that is seen as false for that part of the code, then the program will just end because nothing is set up to handle this issue along the way. As we can see here already, there is the potential for some problems when you are working with this kind of coding. But we are still going to take a quick look at this to see how it works and to get the basic idea of these conditional statements, and then move on to how we can change things on to fix this issue. A good example of how the, if the statement is able to work, will be below:

```
age = int(input("Enter your age:"))
if (age <=18):
        print("You are not eligible for voting, try next election!")
print("Program ends")
```

Let's explore what is going to happen with this code when you put it into your program. If the user comes to the program and puts that they are younger than 18, then there will be a message that shows up on the screen. In this case, the message is going to say "You are not eligible for voting, try next election!" Then the program, as it is, is going to end. But what will happen to this code if the user puts in some age that is 18 or above?

With the if statement, nothing will happen if the user says that their age is above 18. The if statement just has one option and will focus on whether the answer that the user provides is going to match up with the conditions that you set with your code. The user has to put in that they are under the age of 18 with the if statement in this situation, or you won't be able to get the program to happen again.

As we have already mentioned with this one, the if statement could end up causing us a few problems when we are coding. You want to make sure that the user is able to put in any answer that is the best for them, not the "right" answer, and you want to make sure that the program you are writing is still going to be able to respond and give some kind of answer to the user along the way. Some of the users who come to your website or program will have an age that is higher than 18, and it is going to be confusing and look bad if they put that answer in and can't get the program to work.

The If Else Conditional Statement
This is why we are going to move on to the if else statement. This one is used a lot more often than we see with the if statement, and it is able to handle some of the problems that we saw with the if statement. This kind of statement is going to work with some of the topics that we had above and make some changes to fix the issues and ensure that this all works.

Let's say that we are still working with the same kind of program that we had above. But this time we want to make sure that we have some kind of result show up on the screen, no matter what answer the user inputs into our program this time. so, with this one, we are going to work to separate out the users based on their age. There will be a group who is above 18 and one that is under 18, and a response from the system based on this. The code that we would be able to use to help us write out our own if else statement is going to be below:

age = int(input("Enter your age:"))
if (age <=18):
        print("You are not eligible for voting, try next election!")
else
        print("Congratulations! You are eligible to vote. Check out your local polling station to find out more information!)

246

print("Program ends")

As you can see, this really helps to add some more options to your code and will ensure that you get an answer no matter what results the user gives to you. You can also change up the message to say anything that you want, but the same idea will be used no matter the answer that the user gives.

You have the option to add in some more possibilities to this. You are not limited to just two options as we have above. If this works for your program, that is just fine to use. But if you need to use more than these two options, you can expand out this as well. For example, take the option above and expand it to have several different age groups. Maybe you want to have different options come for those who are under 18, those that are between the ages of 18 and 30, and those who are over the age of 30. You can separate it out in that way and when the program gets the answer from the user, it will execute the part that you want. The cool thing with this is there are a lot of different options and programs that we are able to write that work with this. Maybe we want to create our own program that allows the user to go through and pick out one of their favorite types of candy. There are a ton of different types of candy, and they go by so many different names that it is really hard to list them all out and be prepared for this ahead of time. But the if else statement would be able to help us to handle all of this.

With this one, we would just pick out a certain number of candy choices that we would like, maybe the top six, and then list out a response that goes with that. And then we would use our else statement at the end in order to catch all of the answers that did not fit in with the original six that we listed out. This ensures that no matter what input the user adds to the system, they are going to get some kind of response out of the process as well.

The else statement in all of this is going to be an important thing to make sure it is there because it is responsible for catching all of the answers that are left that the user could potentially give to you. If you don't have this statement placed in the code, or not in the right part of the code, it is not going to be able to catch all of the other possible inputs of the user as you would like.

Now that we have had a chance to talk about the if statement and the if else statement, it is time for us to move on to our elif statements. These are a unique part of programming in the Python language, and they are going to help us add in another level to some of the conditional statements that we are able to work with. This kind of conditional statement is going to allow for a user to pick out a few choices that you present to them, and then, depending on what answer or choice the user goes with, the program is going to execute the code and provide the results that go with that answer.

The Elif Conditional Statement
You will find that these elif statements are going to show up in a lot of different places. One option is going to be when they show up in the games that you play. If you have ever gone through and played a game or been on another kind of program where you are given a menu style of choices to make, then you have already had some experience with these elif statements doing their work. These statements are a good one to work with when you would like to provide the user with some more options, rather than just limiting them to a few
When you work with this kind of elif statement, you are going to find it gives you some freedoms. You are able to choose how many statements are going to show up in this kind of code. There are no minimum or maximums as long as you go through and write out the syntax in the proper manner. You may want to make sure that you do not add in too many of these though because that can clog up the system a bit and makes it hard for the user to choose what they would like to go with.
To help us see what is going on with these elif statements and to make sure that we are going to complete the work that we need with one of these, it is good to take a look at the syntax of the elif statements to see how it works. A good example of these elif statements will include the following:
if expression1:
statement(s)
elif expression2:
statement(s)
elif expression3:

statement(s)
else:
statement(s)

This is a pretty basic syntax of the elif statement and you can add in as many of these statements as you would like. Just take that syntax and then place the right information into each part and the answer that is listed next to it. Notice that there is also an else statement at the end of this. Don't forget to add this to your code so that it can catch any answer that the user puts in that isn't listed in your elif statements.

To help you better understand how these elif statements work and how the syntax above is going to work, let's take a look at a little game that you can create using these statements:

```
Print("Let's enjoy a Pizza! Ok, let's go inside Pizzahut!")
print("Waiter, Please select Pizza of your choice from the menu")
pizzachoice = int(input("Please enter your choice of Pizza:"))
if pizzachoice == 1:
        print('I want to enjoy a pizza napoletana')
elif pizzachoice == 2:
        print('I want to enjoy a pizza rustica')
elif pizzachoice == 3:
        print('I want to enjoy a pizza capricciosa')
else:
        print("Sorry, I do not want any of the listed pizza's, please bring a Coca Cola for me.")
```

With the example above, you will find that the user is able to make some choices about what they would like to "order" from your system, and then they will click on the option that goes with this. If they want to order one of the types of pizzas, for example, they just need to click on that and will happen in the program. You can mix this up based on what you would like to see happen in the code that you are writing, but it will end up following the same basic idea in the code you are writing if you use the elif statement.

As we can see from this chapter, there are a lot of options and choices that you can go with when working on a conditional statement. They are going to provide you with a lot of power with the coding that you want to do and can make it easier for you to create some of the different kinds of codes that you would like. Make sure to take some time to explore a few of these options, and learn how you can make them work for your needs.

Chapter 8: The Python Loops

The next topic that we will need to take some time to discuss in this coding language is an idea that is known as a loop. These are going to be important to the codes that you want to write, and they can work well when you combine them with a few of the conditional statements that we talked about before. Loops are a good way to clean up your program, they can ensure that you will see a lot of work done with just a few lines of code, and it is really a great way for us to make the code intense and powerful, without having to rewrite a bunch of things or learn a lot of complicated processes.

You will find that these loops are going to be helpful when you are writing out any of the codes you want that should repeat something a number of times. This repeating needs to happen at least a few times in your code, but you want to do this without making the code messy and without having to go through and write out those lines a bunch of times either. It isn't as big of a deal to write out a few lines or write the same line two or three times. But when you think about writing out the same line of code one hundred times or more, then you can see why there is some appeal in writing loops that can handle those lines in just a few lines instead.

For example, maybe you are going through and working on your own code where you want to be able to list out the numbers from one to 50.

You don't really want to spend all of your time writing that many lines of code so that the compiler can learn what it should do. When you add in a loop, you will find that it can do some of the work for you. These loops basically tell the compiler to repeat itself until you set up a condition that tells it to stop.

Multiplication Tables								
10 x 1	=	10	11 x 1	=	11	12 x 1	=	12
10 x 2	=	20	11 x 2	=	22	12 x 2	=	24
10 x 3	=	30	11 x 3	=	33	12 x 3	=	36
10 x 4	=	40	11 x 4	=	44	12 x 4	=	48
10 x 5	=	60	11 x 5	=	55	12 x 5	=	60
10 x 6	=	60	11 x 6	=	66	12 x 6	=	72
10 x 7	=	70	11 x 7	=	77	12 x 7	=	84
10 x 8	=	80	11 x 8	=	88	12 x 8	=	96
10 x 9	=	90	11 x 9	=	99	12 x 9	= 108
10 x 10	= 100		11 x 10	= 110		12 x 10	= 120	
10 x 11	= 110		11 x 11	= 121		12 x 11	= 132	
10 x 12	= 120		11 x 12	= 132		12 x 12	= 144	

To write out a table like the one above, you have two options. You can go through and type in all of the parts one at a time. Or you can go through and use a loop and get it done in just a few lines of codes. We will take a look at the nested loop in a few pages and show you exactly how we are able to work with these loops for our needs.

While this is a process that can sometimes sound a bit complex, you will find that these loops can actually be pretty easy to work with. These loops are basically there to tell your compiler that it needs to repeat the same block of code more than one time. The compiler will continue reading through the same block of code against until the inserted condition is met and ready to be used. So, if you want to allow the code to count from one to 50, you would just tell the compiler to read through the same lines of code until the output is higher than 50. We will take a look at a few of the codes that you will be able to write out that can handle this problem for us. Of course, when writing a loop condition, you need to be careful about getting the condition set up. If you don't set up your condition from the beginning, then the program will just keep reading the code over and over again, getting stuck in a continuous loop. You need to have a condition or a break in your code to help it stop and move on to the next thing the program should do.

With the traditional methods of coding that you may have used in the past, you would have to write out every line of code. Even if there were some similar parts of code that were the same, or you were basically retyping the same piece of code over and over again, that is how you had to do it as a beginner because that is the only way that you knew how to do things.

With the help of these loops, you can get rid of that way of thinking. You can combine a lot of lines of code into just a few and instead convince the compiler to read through that same line as many times as you need. If you need it to do it 100 times, then that is what the compiler will do. With one line of code, thanks to these loops, you can get a ton of things done without having to write out 100 lines, or more, of code.

With all of this said, there are a few options that you are able to choose when it is time to try out the loops. The method that you are going to pick will depend on what you would like to see happen in the program, and even how many times you are hoping that the compiler will go through the loop at a minimum. We are going to take some time now to look at the three most popular types of loops that are likely to show up in some of the programmings that you do including the nested loop, the while loop, and the for a loop.

The While Loop

On our list, we are going to start out with the while loop. This while loop is going to be the type of loop that we will use if we would like to make sure our code will go through the cycle at least a minimum number of times. You are able to set how many times you would like the loop to happen when you are writing out the code to make sure that the loop will go through the process for as long as you need it too.

With this kind of loop in Python, your goal will not be to have the code go through a cycle an indefinite number of times, but you do want to make sure that it is able to do it a specific number of times, the amount that will ensure your code works how you would like. Going back to our earlier example, if you want to have the program count from one to 50, you want to make sure that this program is going to head through the loop 50 times to finish it all off. With this option, the loop will go through the process a minimum of one time, and then will check out whether the conditions of that loop have been met or not. It will put up the number one, then check to see whether this output meets the conditions, see that it does not, put in the number two, and continue this loop until it sees that it is at a number that is higher than 50.

This is a simple kind of loop that we are able to work with and we are going to see how we can put it to practical use for some of the work that we want to do. To get a better idea of how we are able to get these loops to work, let's take a look at some of the sample codes of a while loop and see what is going to happen when it gets to work:

```
counter = 1
while(counter <= 3):
        principal = int(input("Enter the principal amount:"))
        numberofyeras = int(input("Enter the number of years:"))
        rateofinterest = float(input("Enter the rate of interest:"))
        simpleinterest    =    principal    *    numberofyears    *
rateofinterest/100
        print("Simple interest = %.2f" %simpleinterest)
        #increase the counter by 1
        counter = counter + 1
        print("You have calculated simple interest for 3 time!")
```

Before we move on, take this code and add it to your compiler and let it execute this code. You will see that when this is done, the output is going to come out in a way that the user can place any information that they want into the program. Then the program will do its computations and figure out the interest rates, as well as the final amounts, based on whatever numbers the user placed into the system. With this particular example, we set the loop up to go through three times. This allows the user to put in results three times to the system before it moves on. You can always change this around though and add in more of the loops if it works the best for your program.

Working with the For Loop

Now that we have had a chance to look at the while loop and see all of the benefits that we are able to get when working with that kind of loop, it is time for us to move on to the third type of loop that we are able to use in this kind of coding. There are times when we will need to work with a slightly different idea in some of the coding that we want to do, and this is where we will want to bring in the for loop. Many times the work that you will do with the while loop can also be done with the loop, and this loop is seen as the traditional form of working on loops so you are more likely to see this one a lot in the coding you do.

With the for loop that we are going to work with, you will find that you can set all of this up so that the user will not be the one who goes through and provides the information to the loop on when it should stop. Instead, the loop will be set up to go over the iteration in the order that things are going to show up in the statement that you write, and then this information is the kind that will show up on the screen. With this one, you will be noticed that there isn't really going to be much of a need for input from any outside force or even from the user, at least until your loop is done and reaches the end.

A good example of working with the for loop is going to include:

```
# Measure some strings:
words = ['apple', 'mango', 'banana', 'orange']
for w in words:
print(w, len(w))
```

When you work with the for loop example that is above, you are able to add it to your compiler and see what happens when it gets executed. When you do this, the four fruits that come out on your screen will show up in the exact order that you have them written out. If you would like to have them show up in a different order, you can do that, but then you need to go back to your code and rewrite them in the right order, or your chosen order. Once you have then written out in the syntax and they are ready to be executed in the code, you can't make any changes to them.

The Nested Loop

And finally, we are going to take a look at the final type of loop, the one that is known as the nested loop. This one is going to work in a slightly different manner than we may see with the for loop and the while loop, but there are times when it can come in handy and will help us to get a lot of things done in our coding. When we do decide to work with one of the nested loops, you are basically taking one loop, and then placing it so that it goes inside of another loop. Then it is set up that both of these loops will continue to run until everything is done. This may seem like a silly thing to add to some of the codings that we do, and it may seem overly complicated for what we want to accomplish. but there are a lot of times when we will need this to show up in our codes. For example, maybe we want to create a code that is able to write out a multiplication table for us. Maybe you want to have it set up so that it can multiply from one time one all the way to ten times ten.

If you went through and wrote this out by hand, which you certainly can if you would like, this would take an enormous amount of code to get it done and to ensure the program is going to behave how you want. This is a lot of time and wasted energy though since you can easily just work with the nested loop to get it all done. This can get the work done in just a few lines of code, rather than hundreds of lines of code, and can save time. The code that you are able to use in order to create a nested loop and make your own multiplication table will include:

#write a multiplication table from 1 to 10
For x in xrange(1, 11):
       For y in xrange(1, 11):
       Print '%d = %d' % (x, y, x*x)

When you got the output of this program, it is going to look similar to this:

$1*1 = 1$
$1*2 = 2$
$1*3 = 3$
$1*4 = 4$
All the way up to $1*10 = 2$
Then it would move on to do the table by twos such as this:
$2*1 = 2$
$2*2 = 4$

And so on until you end up with 10*10 = 100 as your final spot in the sequence.

Go ahead and put this into the compiler and see what happens. You will simply have four lines of code, and end up with a whole multiplication table that shows up on your program. Think of how many lines of code you would have to write out to get this table the traditional way that you did before? This table only took a few lines to accomplish, which shows how powerful and great the nested loop can be.

These loops are an important part of any code that you would like to write and taking the time to learn how to use them, and the different steps that you are able to use to make them work for your needs can be important as well. There are a lot of reasons that you would want to make a loop and make sure that it is added to your code. You will be able to use this as a method to get a ton of coding done, and rather than taking up a lot of time and lines and making your code look messy, you can clean it up with one of the three loops above.

Chapter 9: Handling Your Own Exceptions

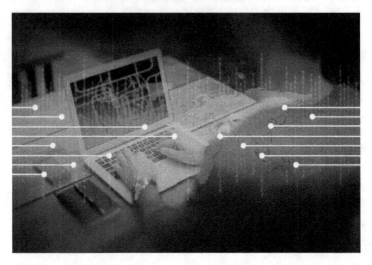

Another great thing that we are able to do when it comes to working with our Python language is known as exception handling. This is going to be a unique topic that we are going to spend a little bit of time on here because of its importance, but in the beginning, it is going to sound a little bit confusing. Don't worry though because you will catch on quickly, and it won't be long before you are able to raise an exception, make changes to the exception, and even create some of your own exceptions that will be unique to the code that you are working with.

As you are going through some of the work that you need to handle in your code, you may find that there are going to be a few exceptions that the program is already going to bring out for you. And then there are also going to be a few that you will want to write on your own to ensure that the program is going to work the way that you would like. You will be able to find some of the automatic ones already in the standard library for Python. A good example of this is when you or the user will try to divide by zero in the code. The Python language will automatically not allow this to happen, so it is going to raise one of these exceptions for it. But if there is a special kind of exception that you want to work with when you are working on your own codes, and you will be able to add this in as well.

Now, the first part of this process is to raise an exception that the compiler will be able to recognize because of the standard library of Python. If the user does one of the things that will automatically bring it up the way that we want. This could be something simple like using an improper statement in our code, or misspelling one of our classes so that the computer is not sure what you are looking for when you try to search or it at another time. These are things that the compiler is going to see as errors already, and you will need to go through and learn how to handle these.

As a programmer, it is going to be your job, and a good idea, to know some of the kinds of exceptions that are going to be found in this kind of standard library with Python. This is going to be helpful to work with because it is going to tell us what to add into our codes, and when an exception is going to turn up for you. Some of the exceptions that the standard library of Python will already know about, and the different keywords that we need to be aware of will include:

- Finally—this is the action that you will want to use to perform cleanup actions, whether the exceptions occur or not.
- Assert—this condition is going to trigger the exception inside of the code
- Raise—the raise command is going to trigger an exception manually inside of the code.
- Try/except—this is when you want to try out a block of code and then it is recovered thanks to the exceptions that either you or the Python code raised.

How to Raise An Exception

The first thing that we are going to take a look at here is how to raise up an exception inside of your code. We are going to work with some of the automatic ones that are going to show up. When you see these, you want to make sure that you are prepared and that you know what you are able to do to handle these, and ensure that they are easier to work with and understand.

If you are working on a new code and you notice that there is a potential kind of issue that is showing up, or you want to go through the steps and figure out why your program is doing something that seems a bit off, then you may be able to check with the compiler and see that at this time, it is raising up a new exception for you. This is due to the fact that your program ran a bit, had a chance to take a look through the code, and found that it was not able to proceed. You then have to go through and check it out to figure out what is wrong and how you can fix this kind of issue. The good thing to remember here is that many times the issues you are dealing with will be simple, and you will be able to fix them pretty easily. For example, if you are going through your code and trying to bring up a file, and you provided it with the wrong name, either when you first named it or when it was time to call it up, your compiler is going to go through and raise a new exception. The program took the time to look through your code and noticed that there was stuff going on that it was not able to help you out with at all, and so it raised this exception.

A good way for you to really get into some of these exceptions and see how they work is to actually take some time to write out your own examples and get some practice with them. This helps us to see what is going to happen when the compiler is able to raise up one of the exceptions. The code that you are able to use in order to see what happens with your compiler when you do it is going to be below:

```
x = 10
y = 10
result = x/y #trying to divide by zero
print(result)
```

The output that you are going to get when you try to get the interpreter to go through this code would be:

```
>>>
Traceback (most recent call last):
        File "D: \Python34\tt.py", line 3, in <module>
        result = x/y
ZeroDivisionError: division by zero
>>>
```

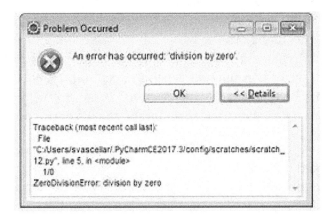

The picture above is going to be a good example of what is going to show up when we try to divide by zero. We are able to change up the message to make it work with what we should see within the code.

When you take a look at this example, your compiler is going to bring up an error, simply because you or the user is trying to divide by zero. This is not allowed with the Python code so it will raise up that error. Now, if you leave it this way and you run the program exactly how it is, you are going to get a messy error message showing up, something that your user probably won't be able to understand. It makes the code hard to understand, and no one will know what to do next. A better idea is to look at some of the different options that you can add to your code to help prevent some of the mess from before. You want to make sure that the user understands why this exception is being raised, rather than leaving them confused in the process. A different way that you can write out this code to make sure that everyone is on the same page includes:

x = 10
y = 0
result = 0
try:
    result = x/y
    print(result)
except ZeroDivisionError:

print("You are trying to divide by zero.")

As you can see, the code that we just put into the compiler is going to be pretty similar to the one that we wrote above. But we did go through and change up the message to show something their when the user raises this exception. When they do get this exception, they will see the message "You are trying to divide by zero" come up on the screen. This isn't a necessary step, but it definitely makes your code easier to use!

How to Define My Own Exceptions

The next thing that we need to take a look at is some of the steps that we are able to use in order to raise our own exceptions. With the work that we did above, we spent our time handling any of the automatic exceptions that were found by the program and that the standard library of Python was going to recognize. Then we went a bit further and found out some of the steps that we are able to use in order to personalize the message that comes with that exception, rather than just leaving it in an automatic manner that most non-programmers, or your regular users, are not going to understand.

Now that we have that out of the way, it is time for us to take our exception writing skills to the next level, and really learn how we can write some of our own exceptions to fit the kinds of codes that we are writing. This is not going to come into play all of the time, but sometimes it can really be helpful in make sure you are going to get everything done the way that you would like.

For example, maybe you are working on some new program or code, and you want to set it up so that your users are only going to be able to add in input of certain numbers, and then not allow some of the other numbers. Or you could have an exception that will show up when the user tries to guess more than three times. These are both things that could come up in a game, and having the process set up to handle these, and raising some of your own exceptions can make a big difference.

Keep in mind with some of these kinds of exceptions that they are unique to the program that you are creating. If you don't specifically add these exceptions into the mix, then the compiler won't recognize that there is anything wrong here, and will just keep going. You are able to add in as many of these exceptions, and any kind of exception that you would like, and it is going to follow a fairly similar idea to what we say before. The code that we are going to use to ensure that this happens the way that we want though will include:

```
class CustomException(Exception):
def_init_(self, value):
        self.parameter = value
def_str_(self):
        return repr(self.parameter)

try:
        raise CustomException("This is a CustomError!")
except CustomException as ex:
        print("Caught:", ex.parameter)
```

When you finish this particular code, you are done successfully adding in your own exception. When someone does raise this exception, the message "Caught: This is a CustomError!" will come up on the screen. You can always change the message to show whatever you would like, but this was there as a placeholder to show what we are doing. Take a moment here to add this to the compiler and see what happens.

There are a lot of different times when you will want to work with exception handling. This is something that we are going to focus on more and more when we bring in some of the advanced types of codes that are possible with Python. There are many times that you can work with both types of exceptions that were discussed in this chapter, and you will find that they are going to help you to get more done overall. Make sure to practice some of the codes above to make sure that you have exception handling down and ready to go.

Chapter 10: Python Encapsulation

The next topic that we need to take some time to learn about in this guidebook is the idea of data encapsulation. This is going to refer to the process of sending data. And we want to send this data where the data is augmented with successive layers of control information before it is transmitted to go across the network. The reverse that we are going to see with this kind of encapsulation is going to be known as decapsulation, which is when we refer to those successive layers from before being removed, or unwrapped, at the receiving end of the network.

When you are working on coding, the variable of your object is not always going to be something that you can access directly. To prevent there being an accidental change, the variable of an object can sometimes only be changed in certain situations, such as with the method or methods of those objects. These variables are going to be known as private variables.

The methods that are there to ensure the correct values are set are important. If you have an incorrect value that have been set then this kind of method is going to return an error to you. You will find that while working with the encapsulation idea, Python is not going to come with a private keyword. This is a little bit different than what we are going to find with some of the other object-oriented programming languages that are out there. this doesn't mean that you are lost though. You will be able to go through and use the process of encapsulation in order to get the work done. It is also important to learn a bit about the differences between encapsulation and abstraction. With abstraction, which is a similar idea, we are using a mechanism that is going to represent all of the essential features of that part of the code, without having to include any of the implementation details. With abstraction, we are hiding the implementation. With encapsulation, we are trying to hide the information.

Python is going to follow the idea that we're all adults when it comes to hiding the methods and the attributes that are in our codes. What this means is that we need to place some trust in the other programmers who go through and try to use any of your classes. You need to stick with some of the plain attributes as much as possible because these are easier to work with, and can make sure that your code has fewer problems in the long run.

The Getter and Setter

Now, as you go through with this, it is tempting to use the getter and setter methods that you want to use, rather than the attributes. But for the most part, the only time that you will want to use the getters and the setters is to make sure that you can change up the implementation a bit later on if it is needed. However, you will find that with some of the newer versions of Python, including Python2.2 and later will allow doing certain things with properties:

1. Protected members: Protected members will be those that are only going to be accessible only from within the class and all of the subclasses. This is something that we are going to see with Java and C++ quite a bit. How are we going to be able to accomplish this in Python though? This is done by a process known as the convention. When we are able to prefix the name of a member with just one underscore, we are basically telling others that we don't want it to be touched, unless it is going to be a subclass that is there.

2. Private members: In addition to working with some of the protected members, we are also going to work with the private members. There is going to be a method in Python that is used to define private that has a double underscore that is in front of the function and the variable name. this is going to be the right way to hide these when you would like to try and access them from outside of the class.

   a. Remember here that the Python language is not going to have a real private method, so one underline that shows up at the beginning of the attribute or the method means that you should not be able to access the method. But this is going to be a convention, and it is still possible for us to access the variable with the use of just one underscore. In addition, we are still able to access the private variables even when we bring in the double underscore.

Putting It All Together

Let's take a quick look at how this is going to work with our class. Remember that we talked about the private members with some of our coding above, but let's look at an example of how we are able to access this private member data with the help of a process that is known as name mangling. The process that we will use to make this happen includes:

```
class Person:
def __init__(self):
self.name = 'Manjula'
self.__lastname = 'Dube'

def PrintName(self):
return self.name +' ' + self.__lastname

#Outside class
P = Person()print(P.name)
print(P.PrintName())
```

print(P.__lastname)
#AttributeError: 'Person' object has no attribute '__lastname'

As we can see already, there are a lot of differences from what we are going to see with encapsulation and data hiding within the Python language. This is especially true when we compare this process to some of the work that we are able to do with other coding languages as well. But there are still some methods that we are able to do around this in order to get some of the results that we are looking for in the process.

With Python, instead of working with the private keyword, you are going to rely on the convention: a class variable that should not be accessed directly is going to be prefixed with the help of an underscore. If you have worked with some of the other coding languages in the past, you will find that it is going to be a bit harder to work with and can take you some time to see results. But the good news is that if this is the first coding language that you are working with, it is not going to take up much more of your effort and it can be easier for you to work with. The coding that you are able to do to make this happen includes:

lass Robot(object):
　def __init__(self):
　　self.a = 123
　　self._b = 123
　　self.__c = 123

obj = Robot()
print(obj.a)
print(obj._b)
print(obj.__c)

Take some time to add this to your compiler and run it to see what is going to happen. You may then find that there is going to be an error and an underscore that shows up. When we end up with a single underscore, this means that we are working with a private variable. This means that you do not want to access it directly. But nothing is going to stop you from doing this, except the convention.

Then we are going to work with a double underscore. This is going to be a private variable. This is going to make it a bit harder to reach that particular variable, but it is still possible in some cases. Remember that both are going to be accessible in some cases. Python is going to have some private variables by convention, but you still need to be careful about what is able to reach which part throughout this process. While we are on this process, we need to spend a few minutes talking about the getters and the setters. The private variables are intended to be changed with the methods that are known as getter and setter. You are able to use these to provide some indirect access to your private variables. An example of how you would be able to go through and write out this kind of code would include:

```
class Robot(object):
  def __init__(self):
    self.__version = 22

  def getVersion(self):
    print(self.__version)

  def setVersion(self, version):
    self.__version = version

obj = Robot()
obj.getVersion()
obj.setVersion(23)
obj.getVersion()
print(obj.__version)
```

The values with this method will be changed inside of the class methods that you are working with. This is a simple example of what we are able to work with, but we are able to go through and do some additional checks if we would like to. For example, one of the checks that you will want to do is see whether or not the value is too large or not negative based on your own conditions.

What to Keep In Mind

As you go through this process, there are a number of things that we need to keep in mind when it is time to access the private functions or the private members that we want to work within this language.

Some of the things that we need to keep track of when we work in this language by accessing the parts that we want to keep private will include:

1. When you write out one of the attributes that need to go with an object, and that attribute does not exist, the system of Python is not going to send up an error or complain about this. Instead, it is just going to go through and create a brand new attribute for you to use.
2. Private attributes are not ones that the Python system is going to protect. This was a design decision that you will work with.
3. For the most part, the private attributes that you want to work with are going to be masked. The reason for this is that there should never be a clash that happens in the inheritance chain. The masking is going to be done by some implicit renaming throughout the code. Private attributes will still need to come with a real name.

Chapter 11: Python Databases & Dictionaries and How to Work with Them

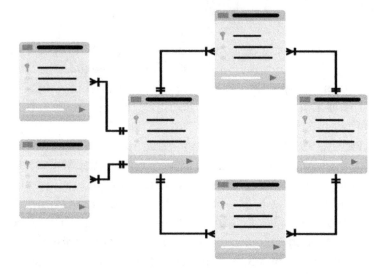

The databases and the dictionaries that are found in the Python language are going to be important parts of coding in this kind of language. When we are able to use this in the proper manner, we will be able to search and use the data that we want, and we will find that the dictionaries will be able to help us out with some of the extra features and more that we need to work with inside of this kind of language.

When we are able to combine these together we have the features and more that are needed to keep our codes as strong as possible. Let's dive into both of these and see what we are able to do with the Python databases and Python dictionaries.

The Python Database
There are a number of databases that are going to work well when we want to make sure that the Python language is going to work the way

that we want. We have to make sure that we know what these databases are capable of, and that we are able to use them in the proper manner and more.

There are many times when the Python language is going to rely on these databases. This becomes even more apparent when we are working on things like data science and machine learning. Being able to work with these databases will make a world of difference, and can help us to gather up, and analyze some of the different types of data that we need to complete these processes. The good news is that there are a lot of different options that we are able to bring out when it is time to work with the databases in Python, and some of these will include:

1. DB-API: The Python Database API is going to be useful because it is going to define a standard kind of interface for the Python database access modules. Nearly all of the modules for Python databases are going to conform to this kind of interface in some manner.

2. SQLAlchemy: This is going to be a very commonly used toolkit for a database that you are able to use. Unlike some of the other libraries, it not only provides us with an ORM layer to work with, but it can provide us with a generalized API for helping us to write out database-agnostic code without SQL being present.

3. Records: Records are another choice that you can make that is an SQL library that is minimalistic. You will find that this one is designed for sending out some raw SQL queries for various databases. Data can be used programmatically or we are able to export to a number of useful data formats overall.

4. PlugSQL: This is another simple interface for Python to help organize and using the parameterized and handwritten form of SQL. It is going to be an anti-ORM that will be lo-fi for the most part, but it is still going to present a nice, simple, and clean interface in Python.

5. Django ORM: This is going to be the interface with Python that is going to be used by Django in order to provide us with some access to the database. It is going to be based on the ideas of models, and abstraction that is going to make it a bit easier to manipulate the data you have in Python. The basics of this one will include:
    a. Each model is going to be a Python class that is going to subclass the djgano.db.models.Model
    b. Each attribute of the model is going to represent a field in the database.
    c. Django is going to give you some database access to the API to make queries that are automatically generated.

6. Peewee: This is another type of ORM that will focus on being a lightweight version that provides us with support for Python 2.6+ and 3.2+. It is also going to, by default, help us support PostgreSQL, MySQL, and SQLite. The model layer is going to be similar to find with Django ORM, and it is going to have a few methods to help us query the data.

7. PonyORM: This is going to be a different kind of ORM that focuses on a different approach in order to query the database. Instead of writing out the work in a Boolean expression or an SQL-like language, the generator syntax of Python is going to be used. There is also a graphical schema editor that is able to generate the PonyORM entities for you.

8. SQLObject: The final thing that we are going to take a look at here is working with the database known as SQLObject. This one is able to support a wide variety of databases to help you get your work done and it works with some of the newer versions of Python as well.

As we can see here, there are a lot of different databases that we are able to work with, and they can all help us to get the results that we would like in no time. When it is time to use Python to help us gather up more information about our industry and more things, then working with the database is going to be one of the best ways to do this. Make sure to focus on the database that is going to be the best for your needs.

CSV File

Name	Phone	S1	S2	S3
Joe	123-456-7890	0.36708695	0.67513519	0.56813032
Bob	098-765-4321	0.44835032	0.2889662	0.04135565
Bob	098-765-4321	0.14615163	0.96273868	0.84140746
Bob	098-765-4321	0.18719318	0.04837126	0.56654116
Steve	768-098-1234	0.28967208	0.97307346	0.7299056
Steve	768-098-1234	0.72702782	0.79337758	0.50868288
Steve	768-098-1234	0.88013836	0.08682228	0.64708199

SQLite Table 1

ID	S1	S2	S3
1	0.36708695	0.67513519	0.56813032
2	0.44835032	0.288966205	0.04135565
2	0.14615163	0.962738682	0.84140746
2	0.18719318	0.04837126	0.56654116
3	0.28967208	0.973073461	0.7299056
3	0.72702782	0.793377577	0.50868288
3	0.88013836	0.086822281	0.64708199

SQLite Table 2

ID	Name	Phone
1	Joe	123-456-7890
2	Bob	098-765-4321
3	Steve	768-098-1234

The chart above is going to give us a good look at how we are able to work with a database when we are handling some of the work that we need to do in the Python language. Taking the time to add in the entries will help us to set this all up and get it to work for things like data science and more later on.

The Python Dictionaries

Python is going to provide us another type of data that we are able to use known as a dictionary. This is going to be similar to working with a list, or a collection of objects. We are going to spend some time taking a look at some of the basic parts of a dictionary in Python, and how we are able to access and manage the data that happens in a dictionary. Once you are done, this is going to be enough to help us know when to use the dictionary, the appropriate type of data, and how to do this work as well.

There are a few things that a list and a dictionary are going to have in common, which is going to make it seem, in some cases, like you are working with the same thing. Some of the similarities that come with this include:

1. Both are going to be mutable.
2. Both the dictionary and the list will be dynamic. This means that we will be able to get them to shrink and grow as needed.
3. Both the dictionary and the list are able to be nested. A list is able to contain another list, and a dictionary will be able to contain another dictionary. A dictionary also has the ability to contain a list and vice versa as well.

However, there are going to be a few times when the dictionary is going to differ from some of the lists that you would like to use as well. Dictionaries are going to differ, for the most part, from lists primarily in how the elements are going to be accessed overall. These include:

1. The elements of a list are going to be accessed by the position that they have on the list through the process of indexing.
2. Dictionary elements are accessed via keys.

With this in mind, we are going to take a look at how to define our own dictionary. Dictionaries are going to be the implementation of Python for a structure of data that we usually call an associative array. A dictionary is going to consist of a collection of key-value pairs.

Each of these pairs is important because they are going to map the key to its associated value. You are able to go through and define a dictionary simply by enclosing a comma-separated list of key-value pairs in the curly braces. And then you can work with a colon in order to separate out each of the keys from the value that is associated with it.

It is easy to see a lot of examples of how this is going to work in your code. We are going to add in a look at a dictionary, one that is going to define a map of a location to the name of its corresponding Major League Baseball team as well:

>>> MLB_team = {
...   'Colorado' : 'Rockies',
...   'Boston' : 'Red Sox',
...   'Minnesota': 'Twins',
...   'Milwaukee': 'Brewers',
...   'Seattle' : 'Mariners'
... }

With this in mind, we are able to go through and create one of our own dictionaries as well. In Python, we are able to create our own dictionary by placing the sequence of elements that we want to use within curly {} braces, and then we will separate it out by a comma. Dictionary will hold a pair of values, one being the key, and then the other one is going to hold a corresponding pair element that is going to be the key: value.

Values in a dictionary can be any type of data that you would like, and you can duplicate it as much as possible. However, you need to make sure that the keys you are using are not repeatable and that you make them immutable.

```
In [12]:  #take the list of sellerID from Xvariable file
          from collections import defaultdict
          keys = ['31', '53', '57', '57', '57', '82', '82
          values = ['70803', '70901', '70801', '70801', '

          d = {}
          for k,v in zip(keys, values):
              d.setdefault(k, []).append(v)
          d
```

```
Out[12]:  {'1037': ['70803'],
           '1068': ['70803', '70803', '70805', '70805'],
           '1088': ['70803'],
           '1217': ['70809'],
           '1361': ['70804',
            '70804',
            '70804',
            '70804',
            '70804',
            '70804',
            '70804',
```

With the above, we are able to get a good look at what we are able to do when it comes to handling our own dictionaries in this language. The Python dictionaries are able to bring up a lot of the things that we are looking for when it is time to get organization and more in all of our work and coding as well.

Dictionaries are also going to be crated with the function that is already found in Python known as dict()> An empty dictionary is something that you are able to just work with that and the curly braces and that is it. Dictionary keys are going to be case sensitive. This means that you can have the same name, but different cases, with the key will still have it treated in a different manner.

With this in mind, let's take a look at how we would be able to write out some of this code to make it work for our needs. A good example of working with a few of the different things that you need for the dictionary will include:

```
# Creating an empty Dictionary
Dict = {}
print("Empty Dictionary: ")
print(Dict)


# Creating a Dictionary
# with Integer Keys
Dict = {1: 'Geeks', 2: 'For', 3: 'Geeks'}
print("\nDictionary with the use of Integer Keys: ")
print(Dict)


# Creating a Dictionary
# with Mixed keys
Dict = {'Name': 'Geeks', 1: [1, 2, 3, 4]}
print("\nDictionary with the use of Mixed Keys: ")
print(Dict)


# Creating a Dictionary
# with dict() method
Dict = dict({1: 'Geeks', 2: 'For', 3:'Geeks'})
print("\nDictionary with the use of dict(): ")
print(Dict)
```

```
# Creating a Dictionary
# with each item as a Pair
Dict = dict([(1, 'Geeks'), (2, 'For')])
print("\nDictionary with each item as a pair: ")
print(Dict)
```

During this time, it is also possible for us to add in some elements in our dictionary. There are a number of methods that we are able to use to make this happen. For example, we can use the defining value with the key in order to just add one of the values at a time. Updating an existing value is also possible in our dictionary because we can use the method of update() to do this. In some cases, you are even able to add in some of the nested key values to this to help create an even stronger dictionary.

One thing to remember here is that when you are adding a value, which is completely acceptable in this kind of coding if the key-value already exists, then the value is going to be updated. But if the value doesn't exist when you start, then you will get a new key along with its corresponding value, to add to your dictionary.

The next thing that we can do is access the elements that we need out of the dictionary. In order to access the different items that are in the dictionary, you need to refer to the name of its key. Key can be used inside of the square brackets as well. There is also going to be the get() method that will also help us when it is time for us to access and use the element that comes from one of your dictionaries.

Looking at the process to remove elements out of the dictionary can be important as well. In this kind of dictionary, the deletion of keys can be done when you are working with the keyword of del. Using this keyword helps because it can help you to either delete specific values form the dictionary, or even the whole dictionary if you would like. There are a number of other functions that you can use as popitem() and pop() can also be used for helping us to delete the arbitrary values and the specific values from the dictionary. All the items that are in your specific dictionary can be deleted in one fell swoop if you would like with the help of the clear() method. Items in the nested dictionary can go through the process of being deleted as well with the del keyword and providing over a specific nested key and a particular key that you would like to delete out of that kind of dictionary.

Another thing to keep in mind with this is if you use the code "del Dict" it is going to end up deleting the whole dictionary. And if you go through and try to print this after the deletion, you are going to get an error as well.

There are a few different methods that we are able to use when it comes to handling the dictionary that you would like to handle. Some of the different methods that we need to focus on to help us gain the control that we want with our dictionary includes:

1. Copy(): This method is going to return for us a shallow copy of our dictionary.
2. Clear(): This method is going to help us remove all of the different items out of our dictionary.
3. Pop(): This one is going to remove and then will return an element that is in your dictionary that has the specific key that you are looking for.
4. Popitem(): This method is going to remove the arbitrary key-value pair from the dictionary, and will make sure that it is returned to you as a tuple.
5. Get(): This is going to be a conventional method that will make it easier to access the value we need with a key.
6. Dictionary_name.values(): This method is going to return a list of all the values available in a given dictionary.
7. Str(): This one is going to help us produce a printable string that is going to be a representation of our dictionary.
8. Update(): This one will add in the dictionary dict2's key-values pairs to the dictionary.
9. Keys(): When you use this method, we are going to get a list of the dictionary keys that we want to work with.
10. Items(): This one is going to return to us a list of dict's, or the key and value, in tuple pairs.
11. Has_key(): This one is going to return to us true if the key in the dictionary dict, false if not.

12. Fromkeys(): This method is going to create a new dictionary that is going to have the keys out of the seq and the values set to value.

13. Type(): This method is going to help us to return the type of the variable that we were able to pass.

14. Cmp(): This is going to help us to compare the elements of both dict.

There are a lot of times when we will want to work with the idea of a dictionary in our code, and we have already taken some time to explore how this will work, and why it is so important to some of the codes that we would like to write. Make sure to spend some time looking this over and seeing just how we are going to be able to make the dictionary work for your project.

Chapter 12: Working with GUI and CGI in This Language

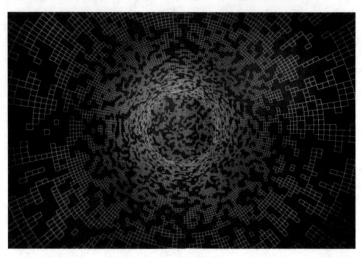

To more important parts that we need to talk about when it comes to working with the Python language is the idea of working with the GUI and the CGI of your computer. You will find that both of these are going to be things that Python is able to handle, and when we are able to put it all together, it is easier to handle some of the more complex things that we would like. So, let's dive right in and see what we are able to do with these two topics.

Getting Familiar with GUI

The first thing that we are going to take a look at here is how to work with the topic of GUI In Python. The GUI is going to stand for Graphical User Interface, and it is often going to be similar to the little different icons that we will see on our operating system that allow us to get online or into another program, without having to open up the command line and then writing that in as well. There are times when you will need to go through and write out the commands and the codes that you want to work with, but there are also going to be times when the GUI is going to be the best option that you would like to use.

Python is going to provide us with a few different options when it is time to write out some GUI based programs that work for our needs. These can include a few options like:

1. Tkinter: This is often the easiest option that we are able to work with. It is going to be the standard in Python for GUI and it is going to be used for this kind o thing the most.
2. JPython: This is going to be a Python platform for Java that is providing us with some scripts in Python that help us to get all of this done with the help of the Java language as well.
3. wxPythn: This is going to be one of the options that are bundled with Python and going to be an alternative of Tkinter as well.

Now that we know a bit more about the Tkinter program, we are going to take a look at some of the sample examples that we are able to work with here. IN this program, it is shown how Tkinter is going to be used with the help of Python in order to build up windows, and some buttons and the events that we want to have associated with these buttons as well.

The code that we are able to use for this one will include:

```
import Tkinter as tk
from Tkinter import *
from Tkinter import ttk

class karl( Frame ):
   def __init__( self ):
      tk.Frame.__init__(self)
      self.pack()
      self.master.title("Karlos")
      self.button1 = Button( self, text = "CLICK HERE", width = 25,
               command = self.new_window )
      self.button1.grid( row = 0, column = 1, columnspan = 2, sticky =
W+E+N+S )
   def new_window(self):
      self.newWindow = karl2()
```

```
class karl2(Frame):
    def __init__(self):
        new =tk.Frame.__init__(self)
        new = Toplevel(self)
        new.title("karlos More Window")
        new.button = tk.Button( text = "PRESS TO CLOSE", width = 25,
                    command = self.close_window )
        new.button.pack()
    def close_window(self):
        self.destroy()
def main():
    karl().mainloop()
if __name__ == '__main__':
    main()
```

As we go through with this, we are going to see that there are going to
be a few standards that we are able to work with the GUI's and some
of the attributes that go with it. Some of these are going to include
options like bitmaps, anchors, cursors, colors, fonts, and dimensions.

What is CGI?

Until this point, a lot of the programming that we are able to do,
whether it is with Python or another option, was not related that much
to the network or for being online. But now it is time for us to move
onto a bit of work with CGI. As the name suggests, CGI is going to
mean the Common gateway interface for everything that we need to
accomplish. CGI is going to be one of the more essential parts that we
need to learn when it is time to work with HTTP.

To make it simple, this CGI is going to be a set of standards that is able
to define the method that is considered standard when it is time to
pass information or web-user requests to an application program, and
then to get data back from it in order to pass that data on to the users
you are working with. This is going to be an exchange of the
information that happens between the web-server and a custom script.
When the user goes through this process and actually requests the web
page that they want to work with, the server, when the process is
working well, will send them that web page, rather than another one,

that was requested. This is because the web server that you are working with is usually going to pass the information to all of the different programs of application that will process this data, and then it will make sure that an acknowledged message is going to show up. This may seem like a fairly basic process, but there are going to be a number of steps that happen with it. And the techniques that are used here, the ones that make sure that the data and the information are based back and forth between the application and the server will be CGI or Common Gateway Interface. It is as simple as that.

With this in mind, the first thing that we are going to take a look at is the first step of the process. Think about what happens when a user clicks on a hyperlink in order to browse on a particular URL or a web page that we have searched. To help us get started, there are a few steps that we are able to use, and these steps are going to include the following:

1. The browser is able to contact the web server of HTTP with a demand for the URL that is needed.
2. Then the URL is going to go through some parsing.
3. The system is going to look for the filename that was requested in the first step.
4. It is going to be able to find that file unless there is something wrong with the web page that was requested and will send it back.
5. The web browser is able to take these responses to form the webserver.
6. As the server response, it is either going to show you the file that it received, which is hopefully the website you asked for if all went well, or it is going to show us an error message.

Now, keep in mind with this one that it is possible to set up this HTTP server because when a certain directory is requested, then the file will not be sent back sometimes. Instead, it is going to be executed in this situation as a program, and then the output of that program is going to be the part that is displayed back to the browser you are using.

From here, we need to take a look at how we can configure the CGI that we want to work with. There are a number of steps that we are able to use to make this happen will include some of the following:

1. First, we want to be able to find out which user is running the web server at that time.
2. Then we will move on and check for the server configuration to help us figure out if we are then able to run in the scripts that are needed for that directory we are looking out.
3. Check out the permissions that are on that particular file.
4. Make a clear assurance that scripts you are making are readable and that the webserver user is going to be able to execute it as well.
5. Make sure that the scripts of Python have the first line set up in order to refer to the web server that the interpreter is able and willing to run.

And before we end with the discussion of CGI, we need to figure take a look at the structure of writing out one of these programs. The output of the script for CGI in Python is going to consist of two different sections, and they are going to be separated out thanks to a blank line. the first part is going to be there to show us the number of headers that we are meant to work with and that will be able to help us to describe back to our client what kind of data is following next. A good example of how this code is supposed to look and how we can structure out one of our CGI programs in Python will include the following:

print ("Content-Type : text/HTML")

 # then comes the rest hyper-text documents
print ("<html>")
print ("<head>")
print ("<title>My First CGI-Program </title>")
print ("<head>")
print ("<body>")
print ("<h3>This is HTML's Body section </h3>")

```
print ("</body>")
print ("</html>")
```

Working with both the GUI and the CGI is going to be important with many of the projects that you are able to do within the Python coding language. When you are able to put all of these pieces together and see the great results, and you learn when you should pull each one up and use it, you will find that it is easier than ever to add in the amount of success that you would like to have in the process.

Conclusion

Thank you for making it through to the end of *Python Crash Course*. I hope it was informative and able to provide you with all of the tools you need to achieve your goals whatever they may be. The next step is to start using some of the different topics that we have discussed in this guidebook to your advantage and learn how to work with the Python language. There are a lot of different parts that can come with this kind of coding language, and learning how they all fit together and trying out some of the different codes that are present is one of the best ways to get hands-on and ready to go with this process.

This guide spent some time taking a look at some of the different tasks that you are able to do with the Python language, and how you are able to make this the right option for you as well. This book is meant to teach you all of the different parts that come with coding in general, but even more specifically what you are able to do with the help of this language whether you are starting as a total beginner or if you have been doing programming for a long period of time.

Working with coding is not always as easy as we would like, but you will find that when you take on the OOP language of Python, and you learn how to handle some of the basics, there is very little that you won't be able to do with your work. Trying out a few of these options and learning how to make it all fit together to write some fantastic codes.

There may be a lot of different options that you are going to work with when it is time to handle some of your biggest coding challenges. But the best one to choose is going to be Python. It has all of the strength that you are looking for, a lot of ease to learn and to read, and so much more. When you are ready to get your crash course in the Python language and you are ready to hit the ground running, make sure to check out this guidebook to get started.

Machine Learning for Beginners

An Introductory Guide to Learn and Understand Artificial Intelligence, Neural Networks and Machine Learning

Introduction

The stage has always been set for thinkers to come up with theories explaining the rise of intelligent machines. As Philip K. Dick puts it, it is all green lights to think that androids dream of electric sheep. Well, the answer is no. Scientific facts have evolved with time to a point in space where the human imagination is full of conflicting images from science fiction. Contrary to the ideas portrayed in most Hollywood blockbusters, I believe that the human species do not face a struggle for existence with the autonomous robotics. On the contrary, the human species is edging closer to the last age of artificial intelligence. As a leaner, it's vital to understand the basis of machine learning. You also need to comprehend the challenges most emerging interested candidates encounter in the learning process.

Machine learning (ML) forms one of the major components of artificial intelligence. Machine learning algorithms are tuned to learn from existing data and information. The concept of machine learning delves in the idea that computers, like human beings, can perform their task without explicit programming. The algorithms only need to learn and advance.

In the current world, machine learning algorithms have empowered computers to interact with human beings. The machines can independently operate machines (yes, devices can operate machines), write match reports, and detect abnormalities in different systems. I possess firm resolve that machine learning at its best will positively influence the actions and production processes in most industries. For this reason, it is essential to explicitly explain the concept to enable everyone to have a grasp and the know-how on the most exciting topic in the world of technology

In this book, I will give my readers a quick trip through the concept of machine learning to impart the knowledge necessary to further advance in the field. So seat back and...lights, camera, action.

Chapter 1: Introduction to Machine Learning

MACHINE LEARNING

The thought of machine learning seems ambiguous, considering that they are not intelligent. By nature, machines perform designated tasks ranging from controlling traffic to exploring space. The various devices used today have made work more manageable and effective. However, machines lack intelligence, which makes them considerably different from humans. Through the sense of vision, smell, taste, tactility, and hearing, the human brain, receives and processes data. The neural system transports the collected data to prompt action. Resultantly, the brain sends commands to the different body parts to act per the demands. The brain stores the experience in the form of memory, which can enable one to react accordingly when a situation repeats itself in the future. On the contrary, a machine cannot comprehend the gathered data. Despite exposure to specific information, it cannot classify or store it for future experiences. With the advent of advanced technology, developers are creating machines to solve problems that were initially meant for humans. The development of these machines involves enabling them to 'think' and 'understand' issues so that they can address them just like humans. Over the years, computers have gained precedence as intelligent machines. They can perform tasks and solve diverse problems after encoding a set of programming instructions. The CPU functions like the human brain, which primary aim is to resolve issues.

If you want to explain a numerical problem, you can do it quickly as long as you are of sound mind. With the inevitable differences in thought patterns, the chances of reaching an answer through various formulas are high. Simply put, we can carry out a similar task through different algorithms. The methods are a set of instructions that help an individual use the input to get the right output. In broad terms, a machine uses several methods to solve a problem. A change in its structure, data, or program makes it learn, leading to improvements in future performance. Machine learning is increasingly becoming a central aspect in information technology. With the massive amounts of data available, smart data analysis will be an inevitable phase of technological progress. But why should machines learn? Well, machine learning is proving to be an indispensable part of our society. A smart device can adjust its internal structures to produce the desired outputs after gathering a wide array of sample inputs. Besides, smart machines analyze large data piles to establish any correlations through the process of data mining. Humans can only encode specific amounts of data; with an intelligible machine, it becomes easy to capture large amounts of information. There is resurging interest in the concept of machine learning. With the growth of computational processing and significant data volumes, the popularity of machine learning can only increase. Machine learning is becoming a vast domain as technology continues to advance. Resultantly, ML has several classifications based on the learning tasks.

Through this chapter, you will understand the growth of machine learning, its application and related disciplines, and the broad category of artificial intelligence. The other chapters will delve more in-depth on the applications related to machine learning.

The Development of Machine Learning

While the 90s stand out as the golden era of the popularity of machine learning, the concept has a long history. Before the 1940s, most mathematical underpinnings used in modern day machine learning were available in statistical forms. One of the notable mathematicians was Thomas Bayes, who developed the concept of a theorem in 1812. The theorem is vital in data science, particularly the Bayesian inferences, which determines the probability of information's availability. In 1805, Andrien-Marie came up with the Least Squares method, mostly used in data fitting. Later in 1913, Andrey Markov developed the Markov Chains that described the different analysis techniques. Markov Chains compute probabilities of occurrence of events, which is a critical aspect in machine learning. During the late 1940s, the development revolved around stored-program computers. The computers stored programs and data collectively. The stored instructions in a computer's memory enabled it to perform different tasks, either intermittently or in a sequence. John Von Neumann introduced the idea in the late 1940s. He proposed the electronic storage of programs in a binary-number format to allow the computer to modify the instructions. Neumann worked with J. Presper Eckert and John W. Mauchly, a development that enhanced the power and flexibility of digital networks. Later in 1949, England Engineers built Manchester Mark 1, while the Americans came up with EDVAC. Both developments were stored-program computers that had increased functionalities. In 1950, Allan Turing had a query on the ability of machines to think. He developed a technical and philosophical approach to analyze the quagmire. Turing came up with the imitation game, which sought to ask questions to a machine and a human. Through the responses, the interrogator was to deduce the difference between a human and a computer. In conclusion, Turing believed that from an intellectual perspective, the digital machines could pass as humans.

In 1951, Dean Edmonds and Marvin Minsky developed the SNARC, which was an artificial neural network. Minsky had the idea of learning machines. Together with his colleague Dean, they used electromechanical and analog components to make 40 neurons. They wired the neurons into a network. After that, they installed a potentiometer and capacitor for long-term and short-term memory. Edmond and Minsky tested the machine's learning capability by navigating it through a virtual maze. A positive reward moved the potentiometer, which prompted learning that enabled it to solve future mazes. Minsky invented many other programs after becoming part of the MIT AI Laboratory.

Breakthroughs in artificial intelligence were bleak between the 1950s and 1960s. The previous enthusiasm in AI-related research reduced remarkably. Consequently, the funding was minimal, leading to an unanticipated stall in the field. In the 1980s, there were some changes. Researchers rediscovered old ideas and applied them in new settings. The use of terms such as computational intelligence and informatics came to play. The popularity of machine learning increased in 1996 when Deep Blue (an IBM computer) won against Garry Kasparov, the then world chess champion. The game was monumental, not only in the world of chess but also in the development of machine learning. In game one, Kasparov resigned after losing to the computer. Deep Blue relied heavily on brute computing power to score against the champion. From the encounter, it was clear that machine learning was taking the world by a storm. In 2006, back-propagation promoted machine learning by training deep neural networks. The concept grew in the early 1960s, but it gradually became unpopular. However, Geoff Hinton revived back-propagation through the introduction of highly effective modern processors around 2006. Deep learning has continually become central to machine learning. Later in 2014, DeepMind became prominent after the development of a neural network capable of playing videos. The technologies could analyze pixels of behavior on a screen. The Neural Turing Machine could also access a computer's external memory to complete the functions. The development was one of the notable advancements in the 21st century. Recent developments have seen the growth of speech recognition through the Long Short-Term Memory pioneered by Hochreiter and Schmidhuber. This neural network learns tasks necessitating memory. Creation of technologies such as Google speech recognition shows the extent LSTM has been impactful. Facial recognition is another program that depicts the utilization of machine learning. The evaluation of most of the face recognition algorithms shows that they are increasingly becoming more accurate.

What is Machine Learning?

One of the earliest definitions of machine learning was by Arthur Samuel in 1959. He stated that machine learning is the inherent capability of a computer to learn without undergoing programming. In simple terms, machine learning involves the study of techniques and algorithms for automating solutions to problems unsolvable through conventional programming. The two steps characterizing standard programming are receipt of specifications and implementing the design. The specifications give the commands on what to do, tasking the computer with the design and implementation. The traditional programming has been challenging because a machine might not detect the message in the intended way. Machine learning algorithms have a generic way of solving these problems. The algorithms learn from the labeled data and don't necessarily require an intricate and detailed design to execute a task. They learn from the data presented, and with more data sets, the level of accuracy is high. When a machine 'understands' the model of a labeled dataset, it can make precise predictions of information that is not within the set. Machine learning has a better outcome than human-created rules. ML algorithms incorporate the data points within a dataset leading to increased accuracy due to the absence of human bias. Data has an indispensable role in machine learning. The algorithms help to discover the data properties necessary towards solving a problem. The quantity and quality of data have significant implications on the prediction and learning performance. Machine learning has improved the global economy, health, and other areas of global concerns, making it a requisite in our daily lives.

Importance of Artificial Intelligence

The use of the terms Artificial Intelligence and machine learning interchangeably is evident in many scholarly articles. Nonetheless, the two terms are different. Artificial Intelligence is a broader field than machine learning, with the latter being one of the popular applications of AI. In simple terms, Artificial Intelligence is the computer's ability to perform tasks that necessitate human intelligence. The name was coined to describe the development of systems through an intellectual process akin to human reasoning, memorization, generalization, and discovering meaning. AI grew gradually after the development of computers. Despite the growing research in the memory capacity and processing speed of computers, the technology is yet to match with the highly intelligent human mind. However, some of the created programs have high performance levels that depict professionalism and expertise in executing diverse tasks.

The improved computing power, large data volumes, and advanced logarithms have increased the popularity of AI. In the 1950s, early research on Artificial Intelligence focused on topics such as symbolic methods and problem-solving. The concept gained precedence in the 1960s when the US Department of Defense started training computers to imitate human reasoning. In one of the street mapping projects, the Defense Advanced Researched Projects Agency developed personal assistants that foresaw the efficiency of the project. Following such advancements, computer automation became prevalent. AI is continuing to evolve, and the benefit it has to different industries is insurmountable. Artificial Intelligence is of utmost importance, particularly with the growing complexity of industries. AI adds an aspect of intelligence to products. While you don't buy AI as an application, the products you purchases have AI enhancements, which improves their capabilities. Features such as bots, automation, smart machines, and conversational platforms can develop several technologies, ranging from investment analysis to security intelligence. AI uses automation to perform high-volume and frequent tasks. This technology oversees a seamless completion of computerized tasks with no fatigue. Consequently, the level of accuracy is high. The concept of deep learning in neural networks, makes the machines perform exceptionally. In the case of medical fields, AI performs like trained radiologists. Through the diverse techniques in Artificial Intelligence such as image recognition, classification, and deep learning, MRIs are becoming more accurate. Contrary to conventional computer programs, AI can analyze more profound and more complex data. The new technology uses neural networks with numerous layers. With more data, the results are more accurate. AI also gathers enough information from the presented data. In this age of high competition in all industries, using AI to mine the best data can give you an edge of other firms. Artificial Intelligence has a broad scope. However, you can view it as part science, part engineering. The scientific goal of AI is to analyze ideas that represent knowledge, the use of that knowledge, and systems assembly.

Conversely, the engineering goal of AI is to use intelligence to solve some of the real-world issues. It is crucial to understand the role of Artificial Intelligence. Many people have the false impression that the ultimate goal of AI is to replace human workers in the commercial sector. While AI has dramatically reduced the labor cost, it is impossible to work solely with computers in the absence of humans. With the growth of Artificial intelligence, many industries are enjoying increased productivity and efficiency. Today, almost all industries are investing in artificial intelligence. The diverse capabilities in artificial intelligence have helped companies to automate and optimize their processes towards increasing profitability. One of the critical uses of AI is enabling businesses to know their customers. Such insights lead to accurate predictions on the customers' preferences and demands.Consequently, it becomes plausible to have personalized customer relationships. Another critical area of influence is on products and services. Consumers are ever eager to have intelligent products such as smartphones, home appliances, and cars. The automation of business processes is another great invention that has made AI gain precedence. The banking sector is one of the industries relying heavily on AI. Automatic learning, bots, adaptive intelligence, and automation have become an integral part of the industry. Some of the areas that automated data is relevant to include auditing and digitization. Feedback automation to customers' queries is also standard. In essence, artificial intelligence improves the effectiveness, precision, and speed of human efforts in the banking industry. American Express is one of the companies that have embraced artificial intelligence to improve customer service and detect fraud. Mastercard is another example of a firm using AI to reduce cases of false declines that lead to significant losses each year. In the manufacturing industry, the Internet of Things and artificial intelligence are enabling companies to remain competitive within the global economy. With the use of data analytics, artificial intelligence is providing advancements such as nanotechnology, Virtual Reality, Augmented Reality, and robotization. A company such as BMW has embraced AI in its recent car models. Tesla, on the other hand, is manufacturing smart cars; while Volvo is building the world's safest vehicles through machine learning.

The retail sector ranks highest in investment in artificial intelligence. The areas that are benefiting within the retail industry include operations involving multiple channels, purchases, and customer service. Alibaba Group is one of the multinationals using AI in its different business operations. The AI tools allow customers to navigate through the Alibaba online portals. Additionally, the company is using AI to create 'smart cities' that will promote a smooth flow of traffic, waste management, and lighting.

Artificial intelligence is reigniting the transport sector through advancements such as self-driving cars, route optimization, and radars that detect any road obstacles. The developments affect logistics directly. In the case of self-driving vehicles, operations can be 24 hours because they don't depend on the availability of a driver. The logistics sector have reduced costs and enjoy high profitability. The numerous AI applications in education are changing the academic world. Education is becoming more personalized and convenient following the increased accessibility of educational materials. Today, online classes are on the rise. You only need a computer and a stable internet connection. The invention has made it possible to undertake a course from any region without being physically present. In academic institutions, AI is promoting the automation of several administrative tasks. Resultantly, educators are focusing on students more than other operations within a school. With the exciting changes resulting from artificial intelligence, it is clear that technology will change a significant part of our daily lives. Recent improvements are making the advancement to be more adaptable. Further research and information are necessary so that the public can understand the significance of AI. As it stands, there are innumerable controversies because of the ethical dilemma created by artificial intelligence.

Applications of Machine Learning
Machine learning is an outgrowth of Statistics and Computer Science. While Computer science focuses primarily on manual programming, machine learning considers the 'how' of self-programming. On the other hand, statistics focus on conclusions that one can infer from specific data, while machine learning incorporates the idea of

computational algorithms and architecture that can help capture, index, store, merge, and retrieve the data. Early researchers established the existence of a close relationship between statistics and machine learning. Michael I. Jordan is one of the scholars who argued that machine learning ideas, including the theoretical to the methodological principles, have their basis in statistics. Over the years, some statisticians have significantly borrowed from machine learning to develop the field of statistical learning.

Machine learning and its related fields have several applications that are useful to our daily lives. One of the uses of ML is the virtual personal assistants, such as Google and Alexa. The virtual assistants have influenced most industries today because of improved convenience. They help find relevant information any time you ask. When you activate the virtual assistant, it can help answer different queries and act as alarms or reminders. The virtual assistants utilize your phone's different apps to collect information that can help you schedule better. Platforms such as mobile apps, smartphones, and smart speakers can incorporate virtual assistants. Video surveillance is another application powered by machine learning. It is difficult for one individual to monitor several video cameras. Training computers to control a video surveillance system is one of the surest ways to effectiveness. With this technology, it is possible to detect and deter crimes. The machine learning-enabled device can track any unusual occurrences and make timely alerts. It can detect motion, stumbling movement, or cases of standing motionless, which can signify an imminent attack. With the system's timely alerts, human attendants can act promptly to address any mishaps. In this case, machine learning improves different surveillance services. Machine learning helps to filter malware and email spam. The technology updates the spam filters continuously. Some of the available spam filtering technologies cannot detect the tricks used by spammers. Machine learning powers spam filtering techniques such as Decision Tree Induction. The services detect thousands of malware, which are mostly similar to previous versions. In-depth insights into the coding allow ML to power these security programs. It becomes easy to detect malware because they rarely vary from the previous ones.

The popularity of search engines has necessitated the use of machine learning to refine results. Search engines such as Google have improved their relay of search results because of incorporating machine learning. Each time you engage in an online search, the backup algorithms note your response to the presented results. Your activities on a webpage make the search engines interpret it as satisfaction with the displayed results. If you continue searching without opening specific pages, the search engines assume that your results did not match with the queries. Consequently, the algorithms try to improve the outcomes and might make extra suggestions. With the growing use of social networking services, using machine learning to improve social media experience is becoming popular. The advancement is personalizing news feed, making it possible to have ads targeting. The move is beneficial to users and businesses. The applications of machine learning are in our day-to-day social media use. In Facebook, the 'People You May Know' suggestion is the work of ML. The application collects information based on your connections, interests, the profiles you visit, or colleagues to suggest friends consider. Another intriguing invention that is attributable to machine learning is face recognition. When you upload a picture with a group of friends, Facebook is likely to recognize them if they are in your list of friends. You might get tagging suggestions. The precision concept is one of the core features of machine learning. Increased used of cyberspace has led to inevitable concerns of cybersecurity. Through machine learning, it is possible to detect online fraud. ML is securing cyberspaces, and financial entities such as PayPal are enjoying the anti-money laundering features. The company has several tools in place to analyze transactions and analyze its legitimacy. The techniques can detect fraudulent activities and limit the involved accounts. Commuting predictions is an area that machine learning has dramatically explored. The GPS navigation services stand out in traffic predictions. Using the service allows the traffic control technology to save our velocities and current locations. The data helps to map out the approximate traffic and execute a congestion analysis. The transport agencies in different regions can take advantage of this technology to address traffic snare in some streets. Online transportation networks have also enhanced commuting. When you book a cab, you get the estimated cost. Companies such as Uber have used machine learning to affect predictions and improve customer experience. When you visit a website, you are likely to get an active chat box, which allows you to chat with a company's customer support representative. Most companies cannot manage a live executive to attend to everyone who visits the website; chatbots have made the service plausible. When you ask a query, the chatbot gathers information from the company's website and gives you a response. The machine learning algorithms have made it easier for the bots to understand queries and respond appropriately.

Machine learning is making significant changes in almost every sector. More research on the field is necessary. With the right information, the public will know how to explore machine learning and make the most out of this technology.

Chapter 2: Types of Machine Learning

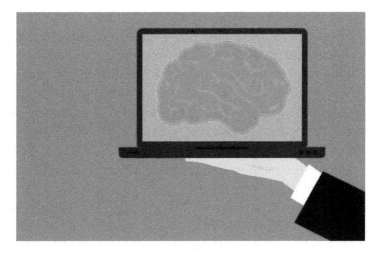

Computers have become an integral part of modern day operations in almost every sphere of life. Teaching computers how to operate and progressively improve on functionality takes different approaches. The types of machine learning are categorized into taxonomies depending on the underlying problems or the anticipated outcomes. These types of machine learning allow the computer to learn patterns and regularities that are useful across a variety of business and health related fields in the modern world. The following are some of the types of learning algorithms useful in the process of machine learning.

Supervised Learning
Supervised learning occurs where the algorithmscreate a function that maps raw data into desired outputs. Supervised learning is one of the most common paradigms for machine learning. It is easy to comprehend. The process of implementation of supervised learning may be achieved through systems from the training dataset. The training data or examples contain more than one input and the desired output. The output is also known as a regulatory signal, which is represented within the mathematical model. An array of vectors

represent the training example. When provided with data in the form of illustrations, the algorithms may be useful in the prediction of each name. Forecasting takes place in the process of giving a response on whether the answers were right or wrong. The approach allows the algorithms a chance to learn to make approximations over time that allow for the distinction between the labels and the examples. The method makes supervised learning a common option in the process of finding solutions.For instance, the use of digital recognition is a typical example of how supervised learning simplifies the process of problem-solving. The fact that classification is useful in deducing problems makes supervised machine learning a simplistic approach that may be useful when the inputs are undefined. As long as the data are unavailable, then supervised learning becomes a rather important paradigm. When using supervised learning, there is always the risk of leaving specific inputs undefined. The model is not useful when such data are available. However, when some of the inputs are unavailable, there will likely be a problem in the course of inferring any conclusions about the outputs. The use of supervised learning presents one of the easiest and most common approaches when training neural networks.

The most common supervised learning approaches include classification and regression. In the case of classification, the use of supervised learning occurs where the outputs may have restrictions to a fixed number of values. Classification typically deals with the identification in a given data set with a view to linking new observations into such categories. On the other hand, the use of regression occurs when the outputs have a wide range of numerical values within a given subset. The goal in both examples is to ensure that machine learning utilizes a fixed set of training examples to make the necessary comparisons on how similar or different a collection of data may be in a given subset. The optimal scenarios in such data sets ensure that the algorithms can determine the class labels for all the unseen occurrences within such a subgroup.

Unsupervised Learning

Machines learning may occur through unsupervised cluster analysis. The approach involves using a set of data that is made up of inputs, which is necessary in the development of a structure. The clustering of data points is an example of unsupervised learning. Unlike in the case of supervised learning, the test data in unsupervised learning does not have labels and is not within a specific classification. Unsupervised learning does not respond to feedback but instead focuses on the commonalities. The method seeks to identify the possibility of commonalities in a given set of data and use these commonalities to develop a pattern. Essentially, this means that the goal is to task a computer with learning how to do something without providing a logical approach to achieve this task. The unsupervised approach is, therefore, more complicated and more complex than the supervised process. This method means using a reward approach to affirm success in the achievement of the tasks without necessarily providing explicit instructions on how to achieve the set goals.

The purpose of the unsupervised approach is more aligned towards the decision making process as opposed to the mere classification of these data. Unsupervised learning trains the agent to act or respond to tasks based on the reward system or punishment built over time. A computer gradually learns how to navigate past commands without having prior information on the anticipated outcomes. This approach may be time-consuming and tedious. But, unsupervised learning can be powerful because it operates from the point of trial and error, which may produce discoveries. Unsupervised learning does not consider any pre-classified information and therefore works from an aspect of the invention. A typical example used to explain the use of unsupervised learning is the game backgammon, which is among the most complex chess games ever discovered. The original game format was outdone when a series of unsupervised programs gained more understanding of the game format and the structure than the best chess players globally by continually playing against themselves. What happened is that these programs eventually discovered new principles and approach to the game that would become a significant turning point in the game's set-up. Unsupervised learning may also take the form of clustering. In this approach, the underlying purpose is not to maximize a core utility function but to also find similarities in the set of data. The method allows for a process of developing meaning from a collection of data without necessarily having a set of pre-classified information. The assumption in the clustered approach is that the clusters set out will eventually show certain similarities that match an intuitive classification. The groups discovered may, therefore, be used to formulate examples that create meaning and develop new models based on these clusters. The unsupervised learning approach is critical in a world where most of the data sets in the world are unlabeled. This undisputable reality means that having intelligent algorithms that can utilize terabytes of unlabeled data and make sense of such information is critical. In the future, there will be different instances where unsupervised learning will become a crucial area of focus. Recommender systems will be a vital area where unsupervised learning will be applicable in the future. The recommender system allows for a distinct link to relationships, which makes it easy to categorize and suggest content based on shared likes. YouTube is an example of the application of unsupervised learning to support recommender systems. The approach allows the viewer to see the number of people who have viewed a specific video and offers suggestions on similar videos that these people have also watched in a bid to match shared likes. Social media platforms such as Facebook may also benefit from recommender systems as they seek to classify users within a specific cluster. Big corporate companies may also benefit from the unsupervised learning approach through the assessment of buying habits among the broad ranges of customers in the market. Unsupervised learning can assist in the group segmentation of such data to fit the product needs or the demands for services.

Reinforcement Learning
Reinforcement learning is useful when the exact models are unrealistic because they rarely assume knowledge of an accurate mathematical model. The approach focuses on how machines should operate to maximize some aspect of cumulative reward. In modern research, the application of reinforcement learning is observed from a

behavioral psychology point of view. The method thus functions through interacting with the immediate environment. As we noted earlier, supervised learning operates based on existing examples. The user of interaction with the situation in the case of reinforcement learning indicates a difference between the two approaches. The application of reinforcement learning in the field of Artificial Intelligence is an indication of the ability of the machines to learn and adjust to new tasks through interactions with the immediate environment. The algorithms adapt to taking specific action based on the observation of the contextual setting. The pattern of behavioral reaction to environmental stimuli is an indication of the process of learning that has become synonymous with artificial intelligence. Every action in reinforcement learning has a direct implication of the operational context, and this reaction provides an opportunity for the machine to receive feedback, which is critical in the process of learning. Reinforcement learning tends to rely on time-dependent sequences or labels. The results in the case of reinforcement learning depend on the connection between the agent and the environmental context. The agent is then given a set of tasks that have a direct implication on the environment. The method then approves a specific reinforcement signal, which provides negative or positive feedback depending on the job and the anticipated result. In a simplistic approach, if a reinforcement learning algorithm is set out in a particular context, it may make obvious mistakes at the beginning. The idea in the case of reinforcement learning is to ensure that this algorithm receives timely feedback on these mistakes by reinforcing good behavior and giving negative feedback to bad behavior. Consequently, the algorithm begins to understand that good practices attract reinforcement through direct input from the given environment. This process of machine learning allows the algorithm to make mistakes, then uses this approach to assist in unlearning the methods that may have led to these mistakes.

The reinforcement learning approach is behavior-driven, which means that there will be numerous instances where the method may be useful across a wide range of fields, including in the advancement of simulation-based optimization. The use of behavioral patterns to condition a machine as seen in reinforcement learning borrows significant insights from neuroscience and psychological research where behavioral learning has been an integral part of progressive advancements in game theory and other spheres such as in the development of autonomous vehicles. Most of the computer games such as Mario may be useful in assessing the link between the environment and agent. The game allows the agent to earn points and achieve new levels in a game where these points act as reinforcement strategies. Eventually, the use of reinforcement allows the algorithm to develop a pattern, where the levels or points work as a measure of reinforcement.

Semi-supervised Machine Learning

The use of semi-supervised learning algorithms is essential where there is a small amount of labeled data and enormous amounts of unlabeled data. The method utilizes the combination of both labeled and unlabeled data. The programmer, therefore, uses both data types to identify patterns. The deduced models become the basis on which relationships target variables, and the data examples become easy to identify and analyze. The approach refers to semi-supervised learning because it utilizes data from labeled and unlabeled examples and still makes sense out of this information. Semi-supervised learning is therefore a hybridization of supervised and unsupervised learning approaches. Semi-structured data is used in this case because it does not obey the formal structuring of data models. The tags and other indicators used in the semi-supervised approach aids in the separation of semantic elements. This is essential when there lacks enough examples to develop an accurate model. Semi-structured models often make critical sense when there is a lack of adequate resources and limited capacity to increase the available data examples. Scholars indicate that the semi-supervised learning approach presents a win-win situation in a wide range of functional fields that include the webpage classification and speech recognition fields of study. The use of this approach has been approved by scientists across the board, a more recent affirmation is within the field genetic sequencing. The use of semi-supervised methods allows for the recognition of the nature of specific webpages in a given context even when such labels are unspecified in the existing human-inputted labels. The fact that these approach allows for the inclusion of both labeled and unlabeled data increases the chance of effectiveness and utilization across a wide range of operational contexts and domains. The ability to increase the training data by utilizing both data sets is therefore a critical advantage in the use of this technique. The approach allows for the labeling process of the defined data, then it uses the trained model to classify the other data based on the specific model. In some instances, you may find situations where you have a wide range of data with a known outcome, yet also have another set of data that is unidentified. The use of semi-supervised machine learning allows the process to utilize the known data models to build a sequence that can be effective in the course of making labels for the rest of the data sets. As a result, when compared to other models, this approach provides the best option because it is time-saving and also reduces drastically the overall resources used towards achieving the intended outcome. The creation of an appropriate function when using semi-supervised approaches may be a critical solution in a modern setting where unlabeled data is likely to supersede labeled data in the process of classification. The use of semi-supervised methods in spam identification and detection from standard messages is the most realistic example in the modern world. The use of human knowledge to sieve through such messages would otherwise be impossible to achieve. Using semi-supervised techniques helps in resolving the high dimensionality concern that often affects the process of classification.

One of the most common methods in semi-supervised learning is the use of self-training approaches. The technique allows the class to undergo through a process of learning using a small labeled data set at the initial stages. The classifier obtained from the research is then used to classify a wide range of unlabeled data. Nonetheless, there is still a significant concern associated with the need to address the issue of deciding on highly consistent predictions. The second technique useful in the semi-supervised processes is the generative models. The model operates based on a repetitive approach where unlabeled samples are the heart of the process. The technique demonstrates a higher acceptable performance in the case of the models from this information as opposed to models that are a result of trained examples. Repetitive techniques conventional in the generative method include the interactive training approach.

The third common approach when applying the semi-supervised algorithm is the co-training method, where only a tiny percentage of the data is labeled. The context often has a considerable portion of unlabeled data, which may complicate the process of classification. The techniques allow for the running of a varying rating for each view using labeled samples. When applying the semi-skilled learning technique, one may also utilize the margin-based method. The method focuses on expanding the support vector machine, which may have a significant impact on the reduction of the overall margin costs. Semi-supervised learning can present a critical opportunity to cut on cost and reduce the time used up in the process of classification. An example of this progressive success is the recent discovery of deep learning, which will, in effect, address all the underlying problems associated with semi-supervised learning. The best approach when dealing with semi-supervised models would be to understand the faults in each option. The self-training method is the simplest because it may be useful in almost all of the classifications. Most of the semi-supervised hardliners opine that this iterative approach is virtually universally accepted when dealing with classifications. The only limitation to this approach is that it fails to offer much information when it comes to convergence. The reality is that self-training may strengthen errors, an issue that may affect the effectiveness of the option. Generative models can offer some of the most reliable predictions, which in most cases are notably closer to the solutions. The technique is also emerging as a critical source of solutions when addressing issues related to the knowledge of data systems and the problems that arise when dealing with such structures. However, this technique also has a question that is linked to the failure to address the inherent classification problems when undertaking research. The most common concern is the apparent limitation in genitive models when balancing unlabeled and labeled data where the latter is limited. Generative models may have an interest related to the risk of being prone to errors, especially when such errors are likely to damage the model.

Feature Learning

When performing a specific machine learning task, it is essential to identify and determine the various features that may affect the outcome. Feature learning is the set of methods that allow the identification of the requisite representation of data examples in the course of achieving the desired machine learning outcomes when given a task. A typical example is the need to identify the appropriate description of data when taking up the role of classification. The use of feature learning as a plausible machine learning option is especially critical when the data in question is linearly inseparable. Feature learning may be supervised or unsupervised, depending on the objective of the classification. The use of representative learning to describe feature learning is appropriate, given the interchangeable meaning in both cases. The approach seeks to maintain the information in the data examples while also transforming the data in a way that makes it valuable in the process of creating meaning. The technique allows for the machine to learn and also use the data in the accomplishment of various tasks and functionalities. Supervised feature learning occurs through the use of labeled data input. The use of supervised neural networks or the multilayer perception is indicative of the use of feature learning. For instance, supervised neural networks utilize computational convenience to achieve the intended ends. The use of unsupervised feature learning can be useful in finding the right representation in the process of performing machine learning tasks. The process involves the mapping of unprocessed data into a well-defined description of the same data, intending to actualize certain machine learning obligations. The most significant advantage that deep learning presents are that the algorithms focus on learning high-level characteristics from the data available in an incremental approach to such data. The procedure is always effective because it eliminates intransigent feature extraction. The use of feature learning in the course of achieving the set targets also has a critical advantage in that it reduces the need for domain expertise as this approach ensures that the machines can learn high levels of data mining and classification. The unsupervised feature learning approach focuses on learning from unlabeled data by developing an understanding of the low dimensional characteristics within such data sets. The model often incorporates the idea of semi-supervised data sets where learning occurs through unlabeled data sets, then the knowledge obtained from these data sets is applied to address the gaps in a supervised setting of labeled data. The feature learning technique introduces a variety of options. The K-means clustering is one of the approaches. The k-means is applied in the course of vector-quantization when considering a set of n vectors, K is the clustering of such vectors in clusters under k. The subsets ensure that each of the vectors fit into the groups that indicate a sense of having the closet mean. The approach is used in classifying the unlabeled sets of data examples into clusters. The procedure involves the addition of k binary to each sample where these samples have the k-means as the closest to the data examples. The use of feature learning may also incorporate the principal component analysis technique. The technique is useful when seeking to address the dimensional problem, which is a common problem. The problem is notable when subtracting the data example mean from the sample data vector. The p vectors in the case of PCA are linear functionalities, which may be obtained through simple algorithms.

While this approach is the most common feature learning technique, it encompasses several limitations that are likely to affect the outcomes of linear learning. The first limitation is that the approach takes the assumption that when observing variances the one with the most substantial forms the basis for mutual interest. The focus may be misplaced because this is not always the case where the direction with the broadest range of variances forms the most considerable attention. The approach has also been seen to have a problem associated with the fact that it only tends to exploit or focus on the first two moments of the data set. The focus on the first two may often have a direct implication on the predictability of the data distribution in a given data example. The use of the PCA may also be limited to instances where the different data vectors correlate with an aspect that may be overly limiting.

Further, it is possible to utilize local linear embedding in the course of undertaking the feature learning process. The technique involves the reconstruction of high-dimensional data through the use of low-dimensional variables forms the original data sets in the course of non-linear learning. The method seeks to capture the intrinsic geometric characteristics of a neighborhood in a given collection of input data. Compared to the PCA, the LLE is a more effective technique in the process of undertaking feature learning. The feature learning approach may also encompass the use of independent component analysis. The method uses separate non-Gaussian components to form a data representation that utilizes a weighted sum within the broader data set. Nonetheless, all these techniques serve to ensure that there is ease in the determined variables and attributes in a data set, which makes it possible to make predictions in a given data example. The role of feature learning in ML is, however, underscored by the fact that it allows for the classification and prediction of data even when such data is linearly inseparable.

Sparse Dictionary Learning

The representation of a training example in a data set as a combination of basic functionalities may be achievable through the use of sparse dictionary learning. The sparse coding technique attempts to find a sparse representation of the data set as a product of a linear combination of the elemental atoms in a given dictionary. The fragments do not necessarily represent an orthogonal pattern, which means that they may as well be over-complete spanning set. The technique ensures that the signal under-representation is higher than the one of the signals under observation. The approach tends to lead an aspect of improvement in sparsity and an obvious advantage when it comes to the flexibility in the representation of the data within these sets. The problem set in the case of a sparse dictionary allows for compressed sensing when dealing with a wide range of data. The signal recovery technique is among these changing methodologies in the course of dealing with the representation of learning outcomes. Sparse dictionary learning can be utilizable in the course of reducing the implications of multiple representations. The dictionary has to be inferred from the input data if the anticipated classification outcome will be achievable. The past approaches would involve a focus on the representation of input data using minimized components. The method has obvious limitations because it would often utilize predefined dictionaries. The modern context has, however, witnessed an emerging focus on trained dictionary approach to fit specific sparsity and flexibility needs in a given subset of data information. The use of data decomposition and compression may also be useful when applying the sparse dictionary approach to learning. Over the years, the use of image fusion and in-painting is an observable application of sparse dictionary learning in the process of machine learning. The dictionary learning approach has been used successfully in the linear decomposition that have been useful in the conclusion of the state of the art outcomes. The technique is critical towards addressing the classification problem that has been common when dealing with a broad range of data sets. The ability to create specific dictionaries for each class makes the process of classification and application of sparse dictionary learning easy. The classification based on sparsest representation may also be useful in the course of audio and video processing. Modern day data health care also uses a sparse dictionary learning approach as a means towards undertaking a review of medical signals. The MRI is within the conventional the medical context. The analysis of the message in the case of MRI may be more simplified when using the sparse dictionary approach. The ability to patch clean images when using the model may form the basis for the growing interest in developing machine learning techniques that embodies the abilities salient in sparse dictionary machine learning. The use of dictionary learning is favorable because it offers an opportunity to conduct a signal evaluation in detail across a wide range of tests such as ultrasound, which are essential in the medical health care context.

Anomaly Detection
One of the other critical modern day innovations in machine learning is anomaly detection. Anomaly detection relates to the ability to identify unusual patterns in data set that fail to conform to an expected trend within the broader analysis of data. The outlier detection allows the algorithms to identify events, actions, or activities

that may raise suspicion by having variances from the main data sets. The anomaly detection learning may fit into three broad categories, which are point anomalies, contextual anomalies, and common anomalies. The anomaly detection approach teaches the machines to detect rare events such as bank fraud or structural defects by comparing such events based on a wide range of other similar activities. The technique has been hailed as one of the most progressive steps in the field because of the ability to pinpoint potential gaps in such data as anomalies. The differentiation indicates a critical trait in machine learning where algorithms may be useful in the determination of the data items that may be defined as normal or abnormal in a given data set.

An example of such detection occurs in the case of two-dimensional data. The dimensions make it easy for the visual identification and determination of such anomalies by assessing the possible underlying differences within the distribution, between the common trends, and what may stand out as abnormal within such a data set. The combination of X and Y variable in such a subset of data allows the easy identification and determination of such anomalies especially when the algorithms can identify an underlying pattern that sets out a majority of the data set into a specific subset. The use of anomaly detection is in the health care, banking, and accounting sectors where an abnormal pattern in vast sets of data may mean a potential problem in the system.

Association Rule Learning
The association rule learning is a technique in machine learning that establishes a set of critical rules that apply in the documentation of exciting relationships between essential variables of a given data set. For instance, the transaction database seeks to identify an underlying connection between variables that are measurable based on the association between variables. The association then establishes the rules of engagement, which exist on the premise or assumption of (if) and (later). The relationship between variables often becomes the basis on which the rules of engagement exist in a defined machine learning context. The task in this machine learning technique is to

313

identify the relationship between variables then to use these variables as a basis on which to establish a rule book.

The association rule technique adopts two key basic types of algorithms. The first is theApriori intuition algorithm. The method is common in data mining and serves in the analysis of frequent itemsets and their relevance in the process of establishment of relevant association rules. The approach may be useful, especially in databases that contain a significant number of transactions. The authenticity of these association rules may be measurable using three standard metrics which are support, confidence, and lift. Support represents the frequency of appearance of an item in the whole subset. Confidence relates to the conditional probability that if this item is in the given subset, then the corresponding item will also appear. For instance, if one buys french fries, there is a chance that they may also buy a burger. Finally, the lift is the ratio of the confidence to the support. The following formula represents this relationship.

$$\text{support}(I) = \frac{\#\text{ transactions containing } I}{\#\text{ transactions}}$$

When developing an association rule, you need to identify a minimum support and confidence ration. The second step involves identifying all the subsets in a given data set that indicates less than minimum support. Then consider all the rules in a given subset, which indicate higher confidence than the minimum confidence. Then you can sort the rules by using the decreasing lift. The approach provides the relationship between the rules in such a subset of data.

Chapter 3: Models of Machine Learning

Machine learning models results from classification, which refers to the process of data class prediction. These classes are known as categories and targets. Classification, in this case, occurs within the supervised learning category, where the target also gets input data. Classification is applicable in several domains, including target marketing, medical diagnosis, and credit approval. The predictive modeling of classification involves approximating the mapping function from the provided input variables, which lead to output variables. Illustratively, email service providers seeking to detect spam can translate it to be a classification issue. The problem is a binary classification (s) considering the classes are either not spam or spam. The role of a classifier is to determine the relationship of input variables to a given level. In sorting emails, the non-spam and spam email act as the data for training. Accurate training of data helps in the detection of unknown emails in such a situation.

In classification, learners are either eager or lazy. Eager learners utilize the provided training data to construct a desirable classification model even in the absence of classification data. The category of eager learners works solely on a single hypothesis. The construction of the model makes eager learners spend a considerably long period in training. However, prediction takes less time. Some of the models under the category of eager learners include Artificial Neural Networks, Naïve Bayes, and Decision Tree. Conversely, lazy learners wait to utilize the stored training data once testing data is available. When this data appears, classification takes place based on the relevance of the stored data. Lazy learners have more prediction time but less time to train. Case-based reasoning and *k*-nearest neighbor are the main types of lazy learners.

The models of machine learning, irrespective of regression or classification, lead to different results. These supervised learning models utilize random simulation. Regardless of the approach taken, the machine learning models guarantee prediction accuracy when they use the provided data. This chapter will discuss in details the different models of machine learning and their applications.

Decision Trees

Decision trees create regression or classification to resemble a tree structure. The input data is broken down into small subsets, leading to the development of the decision tree. The tree follows a given direction and has a 'root,' which is a node with no edges. Such nodes are a test or internal nodes. The other terminal nodes have edges referred to as leaves. For a decision tree to play its intended purpose, the internal nodes split into sub-spaces based on the discrete functions of the data presented. Each of the internal nodes works with one attribute, leading to the partitioning of the instance space based on the value of the attributes. The leaves represent the target value. A leaf can work with a probability vector to show the probability of target attributes with specific values. To classify the instances, you navigate through to the leaf from the root.

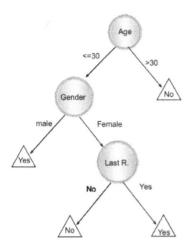

The diagram is a simple illustration of the way a decision tree works. The tree seeks to determine the probability of potential customer response to direct mailing. The circles represent internal nodes, and the triangles are leaves. The decision tree has incorporated numeric and nominal attributes. With this classifier, one can sort the tree to predict target customers' responses on mailing. Besides, the results lead to an increased understanding of the behaviors of potential customers. The nodes have labels to show the attributes they are testing, while the branches signify the corresponding values. When dealing with numerical attributes, you can interpret the decision trees geometrically. Decision-makers use the decision trees that are seemingly less complex to promote better comprehension. Interpreting the attributes through the geometrical approach is less common because of the inevitable complexities. A multifaceted tree can be undesirable because it increases the chances of inaccuracy. To measure the complexity of a decision tree, check the depth of the tree, the number of attributes, leaves, and nodes. The algorithms used for this model are the decision tree inducers, which utilizes the given dataset to build a tree. The main aim of these algorithms is to reduce the error resulting from generalization, leading to the creation of an optimal model. Getting a decision tree that is consistent with the dataset is hard. Decision-makers also face challenges in the construction of a binary tree with the required tests. In essence, the

317

algorithms are feasible when addressing small issues. The methods are either bottom-up or top-down. The standard used top-down inducers include the C4.5, ID3, and CART. Inducers such as CART and C4.5 are part of growth and pruning while others take part in the process of growing. For large datasets, the inducers for such decision trees are different. The Catlett method is one of the inventions that make it possible to analyze large sets of data. The approach works by reducing the level of computational complexity. In this case, the data is loaded in the primary memory for induction. The memory size is the determiner of the dataset that undergoes the induction. The ID3 algorithm suggested by Fifield can also be applicable because it focuses on fitting the dataset within the main memory. To increase the effectiveness, you have to partition the datasets into disjointed sets. Loading the dataset as a separate entity can induce clear decision trees. Combining the decision tree leads to the ultimate creation of a single classifier. One downside of this method is the reduction in classification accuracy. A single decision tree is preferable because it has minimal errors. SLIQ algorithm is another approach that is applicable when dealing with large datasets. The approach involves the use of a secondary disk as opposed to using the main memory. SLIQ uses the dataset to build a single decision tree. However, the approach has a limit on the size of data to undergo processing. In fact, the dataset size has to be consistent with the main memory. The SPRINT algorithm is similar to SLIQ. It analyzes the decision tree inducers and removes the restrictions. SPRINT addresses the impurities common in large datasets.

Decision trees have advantages and disadvantages that make it stand out from other models. The benefits have increased the use of decision trees as the preferable model. Firstly, the self-explanatory nature of decision trees makes them highly effective. Besides, it is easy to follow this model and deduce relevant information. You don't need professionalism in the field of computer science, especially in a case where the tree has a significant number of leaves. Secondly, decision trees are ideal for both numeric and nominal input attributes. You can use any form of data without having to change the approach. Thirdly, the model can handle erroneous datasets and ensure optimal classification. In a situation where some values are missing, a decision tree can analyze the available data, and the outcome will be useful. Conversely, decision making trees have several disadvantages. One of the notable methods of divide and rule utilized by decision trees limits its efficiency. The model performs well when there are relevant attributes. However, the presence of complex interactions reduces the performance of a decision tree. The second disadvantage relates to the characteristic of a decision tree, often termed as greedy. This feature makes the model to underperform in extreme situations. The approach is oversensitive to several attributes and specific training sets. The third disadvantage related to decision trees is the tendency to create complex trees unable to generalize.

Furthermore, the trees are somehow unstable, and slight data variations lead to the generation of a different tree. The fourth weakness of a decision tree is that it is impossible to update it incrementally. You have to retrain each arriving data, rendering the existing tree useless. Complementing the decision tree with ensemble methods such as boosting trees and random forests can address some of these limitations.

Neural Networks
Neural networks refer to a set of algorithms that are changing the field of machine learning. The approximate general functions apply to most of the problems related to machine learning, such as complex mapping. The biological neural networks have been significant determinants of ML neural networks development. Research on artificial neural networks recognizes the resemblance between the functioning of a digital computer and that of a human brain. However, the brain has considerable differences because its information-processing network is non-linear, parallel, and complex. A neural network models the performance of the brain in implementing specific tasks. Developers use electronic components or simulate a digital computer's software. Neural networks use multiple interconnections known as processing units or neurons to promote optimal performance. From this description, one can define the neural network as a processor with several processing units that store

experiential knowledge and retrieving it when necessary. A neural network is similar to the brain on matters of knowledge acquisition, which is from the environment. Another similarity is the presence of synaptic weights, which are interneuron connections that store knowledge. Several neural networks are gaining considerable attention today. Perceptrons are the first type of neural network considered the first generation of the model. Perceptrons refer to computational models emanating from one neuron. Frank Rosenblatt coined the term perceptron in his early work when researching on the brain and information storage. Back-propagation is essential in training the perceptrons. The process involves providing the network with datasets paired as input or output. The neurons process data and convey it as output. Hidden neurons within a system correlate the input and the output. The figure below is a pictorial illustration of Rosenblatt's perceptron.

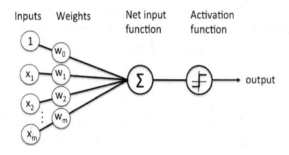

The recurrent neural network is another category of neural networks that differ from perceptrons because of the connections found between passes. The recurrent neural networks are robust because of the existence of non-linear dynamics, allowing them complex updates of hidden states. Secondly, they can store a significant amount of information on past events with the utmost efficiency. Neurons have a similar function to a computer, especially when endowed with adequate neurons. These RNNs can implement multiple small programs that run parallel to bring forth complex results. One of the major cons related to the recurrent neural network is the issue of vanishing gradient problem. The situation leads to loss of information based on the activation functions. Principally, RNNs can prove useful in several fields that require data in a sequence. The recurrent networks play a critical role in tasks such as auto-completion because they complete or advance the presented information. A convolutional neural network is a modification of LeNet, developed by Yann LeCun in 1998. The system utilized back-propagation that had multiple hidden layers, replicated units, and a wide net capable of coping with substantial characters within a single function. Convolutional neural networks possess different features from other networks. One of the central roles of these networks is image processing. When you present the system with a clear image, you get classified data. CNN's have a scanner where data passes through for analysis. When you 'feed' your network with data, it passes through a series of convolutional layers that have interconnected nodes. The deepening of the layers causes them to shrink. Pooling, which is a form of filtering takes place to produce the final information. Auto-encoders present another class of neural networks intended to complement unsupervised learning. The auto-encoders work as models for data compression and can encode an input into smaller dimensions. Consequently, one can use a decoder on the encoded data to have a meaningful reconstruction. The network functions by presenting the data in few numbers than its original presentation. In a case where you have 100 numbers, you can have the representation in 10 numbers or fewer. However, there is a fear of information loss, which is inevitable when limiting the input data.Nonetheless, it is easy to visualize such data based on the ability to plot the dimensions on a graph. Auto-encoders can prove useful in pre-training neural networks, data generation, and dimension reduction. This neural network is advantageous because of its flexibility in mapping. Besides, the resultant encoding model is fast and compact. The challenge mostly emanates from the difficulty in using back-propagation in optimizing the auto-encoders. Today, auto-encoders are rarely available for practical applications because of their downside.

But why neural networks? Well, if you are wondering the importance of these programming paradigms, these outlined capabilities and properties show the extent in which neural networks are useful.

- **Adaptability**

One of the notable features of a neural network is the ability to adapt its synaptic weight to the environment. Exposure of a neural network to a different setting does not disrupt its functionality; instead, it can be retrained to accommodate any changes within its operating environment. The adaptive capability makes the neural networks to perform exemplary in signal processing, control functions, and classification of patterns. The adaptability of this system results in a robust performance.

- **Nonlinearity**

A neural network is mostly non-linear because the interconnections involve non-linear neurons. Nonlinearity enhances the neural networks' robustness in capacity recognition during the process of augmenting data. Additionally, the nonlinearity plays a central role in generating input signals such as speech signal.

- **Fault Tolerance**

Neural networks have an inherent nature to tolerate faults. In simple terms, the network has a robust computation that is incapable of degradation when the operating conditions are adverse. In a case where there is damage to the connecting links or the actual neurons, the quality of the stored data becomes poor.

Nonetheless, the distribution nature of neural networks reduces network degradation unless the damage is highly extensive. As such, it is rare for a neural network to experience a catastrophic failure. It is crucial to train the neural network to be fault-tolerant in case of damage.

- **Input and Output Mapping**

In supervised learning, the neural networks modify their synaptic weights by using training examples. Each of these examples has exclusive input signals, with an equivalent desired response. The examples help the system to learn, leading to the construction of an input and output mapping.

- **Uniformity in Design and Analysis**

One of the features that characterize neural networks is the universality of information processors. The aspect of uniformity is evident when neurons represent a common ingredient that relates to all the neural networks. The commonality further enables the sharing of learning algorithms and theories in neural networks applications. More importantly, modules can integrate seamlessly to build modular networks.

The properties of artificial neural networks make them advantageous and highly applicable in the real world. Programmers can choose the type of neural network with multiples capabilities.

Bayesian Networks

The growth of the Bayesian network is attributable to Thomas Bayes, who invented the Bayes rule in the 1700s. He came up with the law of probability that facilitates the update of changing probabilities. The concept of Bayesian Network in the 1980s was by Judea Pearl, who considered the differentiation of causal and evidential reasoning.

Bayesian networks have been gaining significant attention in different domains. Broadly, Bayesian Model refers to a framework that enables reasoning during uncertainty with the use of probabilities. It utilizes a probabilistic graphical language that promotes reasoning and knowledge representation. A BN has directed acrylic graph structure. The graph has different nodes corresponding to random variables. The edges are a representation of conditional dependencies. Unconnected nodes represent conditionally independent variables. Each of the nodes relates to a CP Table and provides specifications on the state of the nodes. Bayesian networks use principles from statistics, computer science, graph theory, and probability theory. The diagram below is an illustration of the Bayesian network as a graphical model.

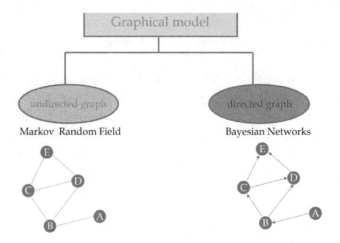

Besides the model's qualitative part encompassing the DAG, it is crucial to highlight the quantitative parameters of BN. The parameters build on the Markovian property in which the CPD within each of the nodes is solely dependent on the parents. A table represents the conditional probability of a discrete random variable. A CPT determines any joint distribution of variables. Bayesian networks are useful because they provide relevant knowledge in causal learning. They have probabilistic and causal semantics that facilitate a combination of prior data and knowledge. BN allows encoding dependency among variables. Bayesian networks are in different types, and each of the categories addresses specific situations that might not be possible when using the model as a whole. The dynamic Bayesian network is a unique structure that models a temporal process. The DBNs provide indispensable representations because they go beyond the description of probabilistic relationships. The DBNs are in two parts; the prior BN and the transition BN. The first part is a general network, while the second part differs slightly because of the available structure. The latter has several arcs and nodes that are not present in the first network. The causal interaction network is a distinct Bayesian network where the parents are independent. The noisy-OR model is one of the common types of causal interaction models. The decision networks, also known as influence diagrams, are special BNs that enhance decision making in uncertain situations.

Applications of Bayesian networks are diverse. Originally, BN was mostly applicable in medicine, which continues to be dominant today. However, the aspect of predictions has made Bayesian network stand out in different fields. In forecasting, Bayesian networks make accurate predictions based on available knowledge. The HailFinder network is one of the BN applications that have been forecasting weather. In economics, the Bayesian network has been forecasting oil prices to determine market trends. In medicine, BN plays several central roles. One of the most notable applications is the quick medical reference, which is a diagnosis system. The system considers the disease, background, and symptoms. With the numerous arcs and nodes within the system, developing algorithms to make inferences was inevitable. The Pathfinder project is another diagnostic system used in diagnosing the lymph-node disease. On the other hand, the MUNIN network has been useful in the diagnosis of neuromuscular conditions. The ALARM network developed in 1989 has been essential in monitoring patients receiving intensive care. The Bayesian network is an easily implementable algorithm with a guaranteed accuracy of results in most cases. Its ability to take linear time makes it scalable to big datasets. One of the primary advantages of Naïve Bayes is that the algorithm doesn't need a large amount of training dataset to make an accurate estimation of the parameters. Additionally, the classifiers are faster than most of the other methods. The issue of zero probability in the Bayesian network is of concern to many users. When an attribute has zero conditional probability, the prediction is hardly valid. The use of a Laplacian estimator is necessary in such instances.

Support Vector Machine

Support Vector Machine is a recent development when compared with other models of machine learning. Vapnik, Guyon, and Bosser coined the term Support Vector Machine in 1992. SVM refers to a set of interrelated methods of supervised learning, mostly used for regression and classification. SVMs are in the category of linear classifiers. Support Vector Machine is a regression and classification prediction tool utilizing the theory of machine learning to enhance predictive accuracy. Initially, SVM was common in the NIPS community; today, it has become a critical part of machine learning research. The popularity of SVM results from the accuracy of outcomes when the input is in pixel maps. The figure below shows the classes defining support vectors.

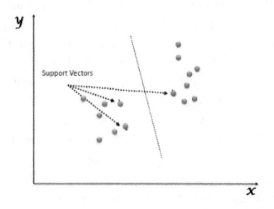

How does the SVM work? For non-professionals in the field, understanding SVM might seem complicated. You can follow a more straightforward approach to understand the concept. The first stage is the identification of hyper-planes, A, B, or C. The hyper-plane that you choose should have the ability to segregate classes. In the second scenario, you will need to increase the distances between the data points. With a high margin, the robustness of classification increases. Low margins lead to misclassification. In the third scenario, you already have the hyper-plane with the most upper margin. SVM considers the issue of classification errors and selects a hyper-plane that seems more accurate. Support Vector Machine is applicable in several domains, including face and handwriting analysis for application based on regression and classification. The basis of SVM formulation is the principle of Structural Risk Minimization, which is more effective as compared to the conventional principle of Empirical Risk Minimization utilized by neural networks. SRM reduces the risk expected in upper bound, increasing the ability of a Support Vector Machine to generalize. The intended role of SVM was addressing classification problems; however, it is gaining popularity in solving regression problems. The types of Support Vector Machines are classified based on their roles. The least-squares SVM is one of the versions developed by Vandewalle and Suykens. Its primary function is to recognize patterns and analyze data for regression analysis and classification. To find the solution when using this method, you have to solve several linear equations. The structured SVM is another version that enhances classifiers' training to promote labels with structured outputs. The Support Vector Clustering is a type of SVM mostly involved in cluster analysis. The process involves partitioning of data to group it into a meaningful form. In Support Vector Clustering, one maps the data points from the data space through the kernel function. Transductive SVM is a type of reasoning based on observed training and test cases. The method is applicable in supervised learning. One-class SVM, developed by Scholkopf is a type of SVM that helps in anomaly detection.

All the Support Vector Machines have their advantages and disadvantages. One of the pros is that SVM is significantly effective, especially in spaces with high dimensions. When there is a clear separation margin, the accuracy level of SVM is desirable. Besides, it produces quality results even when the samples are fewer than the dimensions. SVM is memory efficient following its use of support vectors within the decision function. Conversely, SVM has the shortcomings that might make it less common as compared to other ML models. SVM underperforms in cases where the dataset is significant because of the high training time. In instances where there is overlapping of target classes, the performance is poor. When using SVM, you will have to use the fivefold cross-validation because the model does not give probability estimates. With the mentioned pros and cons, it is easier to work with SVM and other complementing approaches towards enhancing accuracy.

Model Optimization

One of the recent developments in the field of computer science is the interplay between machine learning and optimization. The different formulations in optimization have been essential in the design of algorithms that extract relevant knowledge from large data volumes. Machine learning is increasingly generating new ideas on optimization. The approaches are prominent because of their attractive theoretical properties and broad applicability. Optimization models are in two categories; constrained and unconstrained. The strategies in unconstrained optimization include Gradient descent, Stochastic Gradient Descent, and Newton's method. Gradient Descent is a popular algorithm that trains several models of machine learning. This approach is one of the iterative models that analyze biases and weights. Gradient Descent minimizes the cost function. The process is sequential, with the first step being the random initialization of weights (W). The second step is the calculation of the gradients, which is through a partial differentiation $G = \partial J(W)/\partial W$. G is the gradient's value, which depends mostly on current values, the input, and cost function. The next step involves updating the weight, in which the amount should be proportional to the gradient. Repeat the process until you reach the cost stability of $J(W)$. Stochastic is one of the common types of optimization's Gradient Descent. Stochastic refers to a process or a system linked to a random probability. This approach involves a random selection of samples for each of the iteration. While using the entire dataset can enable one to get absolute minima, batches are highly effective when the dataset is huge. The Newton method of optimization, also referred to as Newton-Raphson utilizes two derivatives. The first step involves having a guess closely related to the root. The next step is the use of calculus for approximation and in finality, uses the elementary algebra for x-intercept computation. The method has several limitations that make it difficult to use. One, it is hard to calculate a function's derivative. Besides the high cost of evaluating an analytical expression, getting the derivative is not easy. The method may fail to converge to the root because of unmet assumptions. Another issue is poor initial estimation, which leads to the algorithm's non-convergence. Regardless of the flaws, optimization algorithms remain ideal because they reduce the error function resulting from the internal parameters of a model.

Further research on machine learning is vital to deconstruct the existing myth on this vast growing technology. Within the next few years, machine learning will be a central part of our daily activities. Learning the models and applications of this field will give you an edge especially in business.

Chapter 4: Probabilistic Models

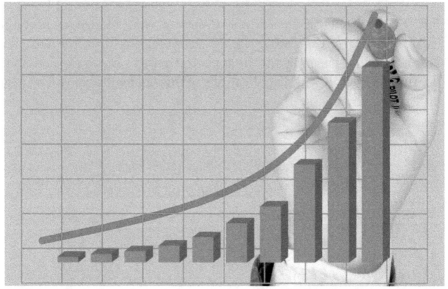

Machine learning algorithms can be classified in many ways. This chapter looks at the models briefly before discussing the probabilistic models of machine learning in-depth. The mode of explanation reflects the comparative analysis approach. While the book strives to give an understanding of the probabilistic models, it essential to note that the other models are equally worth a mention in this chapter.

Logical models

There are two categories of logical models. The types are tree models and rule models. The two groups make use of logical functions to split the instance spaces, creating classes. A rational function can be said to be one that gives a different value such a yes or no result.

In a logical expression, once the data has been categorized, it is then divided into homogeneous categories for the problem to be solved. For instance, in classification problems, all the example in a given type are said to belong to a single class. Logical models are grouped into two categories. The categories are; tree models and rule models.Rule models are comprised of a pool of suggestions. Sometimes the rule model is called the WHAT IF-THEN rule. For a tree-based rule, the IF part describes a section and the THEN part defines how the section behaves.

The tree models can be considered as part of the rule model where the IF and THEN segments are structured in the form of a tree. Both the tree model and the rule model works in the same way as supervised learning. The approach taken by the two models can be summarized as follows.

The first method is finding the concept of the rule (its body) that deals with adequately standardized sets then find a label that represents the concept. The second method is targeting a specific study class and then determining the rules that cover the features in that class.

Geometric models

In the previous section on logical models, we have seen that rational expressions are used to divide the instance space. In this section, we will take into account designs that explain comparisons by making an allowance for the geometry of the instance space. Geometric models represent features in two or three dimensions (the x and y-axis or the x, y, and z-axis). Geometric models have both linear and distance-based models. In linear models, the features are represented in direct arrangements of the inputs in the element. In the range-based model, functions are described based on the difference of distance between two points within the task. The charts below represent the two model used in the geometric representation of functions.

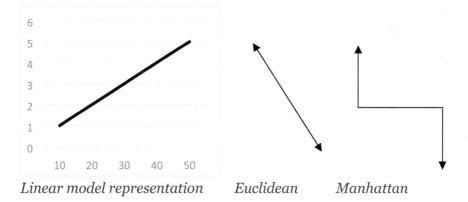

Linear model representation   *Euclidean*   *Manhattan*

Probabilistic models

In understanding probabilistic models, I will try to elaborate on the concept by breaking it down. The first section will explain the term probabilistic while the second section will go straight in detailing the models.

A probabilistic technique or model is based on the theory of uncertainty (probability) or the notion that chance can play a role in forecasting future events. The opposite of this model is deterministic, which entails the accurate determination of events through facts and not chance.

Probabilistic models integraterandom variables and prospect arrangement into the model of an incident or an occurrence. The probabilistic model offerslikelihooddissemination as a result. On the other hand, deterministic models that give a single solution to a given problem. The two models work by because a situation may not present all the factors needed to analyze it. Therefore, there is always a provision for random selection.For example, we can explain the situation using a life insurance policy. The policy takes into account the fact we will die. What is unknown is the date and the circumstances of death.

Probabilistic models can also be partly deterministic or entirely random. Random values from standarddispersal, binomial dissemination and Bernoulli distribution create the basis for probabilistic designs.

Probabilistic Method

The probabilistic methods are ways to verify the presence of structures with definite characteristics in groupings. The concept entails the creation of probability space, proving that the elements within the area have the qualities studied. Probabilistic methods are applied in various fields such as statistics, computer science, and quantum physics.

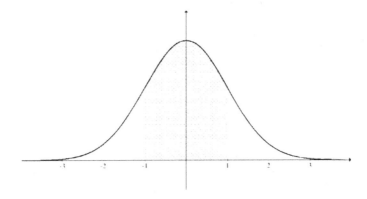

A standard distribution curve, (also called a bell curve) is one of the elements that create a probabilistic model

Probabilistic models can be subdivided into two units, graphical models and stochastic models.

Graphical models

In general, probabilistic graphical models utilize representation based on graphs as the groundwork for encrypting a dispersal over a multi-dimensional space. The models also use diagrams, which are condensed illustration of variables found in the limited distribution. There are two known types of graphs used probabilistic models. The two methods are Bayesian networks and Markov random fields. The techniques incorporate the functionalities of factorization and unconventionality. However, they are different in the way they prompt factorization and translate fairness.

Bayesian Networks

The Bayesian networks are a category of probabilistic graphical replicas, which are sometimes used to construct a different model from data or expert opinions. Bayesian networks can be used for many tasks. In machine learning, the Bayesian networks are used for estimation, detection of a fault in a set of data, diagnostic reasons, computerized intuition, and reasoning, calculating time series, and making decisions that fall under undefined circumstances. The table below is a representation of the aptitudes in four significant analytical terms. The terms are Graphic analytics, Problem-solving analytics, projecting analytics, and Dogmatic analytics.

Graphic analytics	Problem-solving analytics	Projecting analytics	Dogmatic analytic
Computerized insight	Information value	Supervised or unsupervised	Decision automation
Large patterns	Reasoning	Anomaly detection	Decision making based on cost
Anomalous patterns	Troubleshooting	Time series	Decision support
multivariate	Anomaly detection	Latent variations	Decision making under uncertainty

The representations are sometimes called the Bayes nets, Belief Networks, or Causal networks.

Characteristics of Bayesian networks

Probabilistic: Bayesian networks are predictive. The Bayesian networks are structured from distributions that are based on likelihood/chance. The Bayesian networks also follow the rule of probability to make forecast and detect faults for reasoning and problem solving, making decisions under uncertain conditions, and calculating time series.

Graphical: as shown in the image below, Bayesian networks are represented in graphical forms. The best way of learning the Bayesian network is through graphical representation. However, this method is optional.

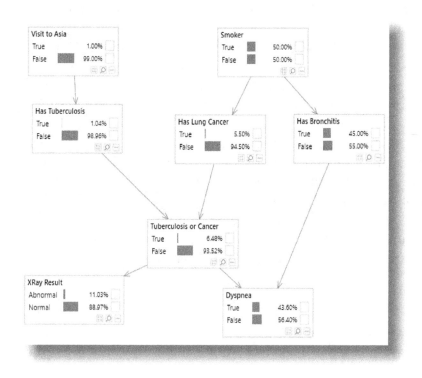

A simple Bayesian network, (called the Asia network)

A Bayesian network can be represented by a graph with nodes consisting of directed links in between them.

Nodes: in a Bayesian network, the node represents a known variable; for example, the age of a person. The feature can either be distinct, for instance, the size of a building (large or small) or continuous, for example, the age of a person.

In a Bayes server, the nodes consist of numerous parameters. Nodes that include multiple parameters (more than one setting) are called multi-variable nodes.

The nodes and links infuse to create the structure of the Bayesian network. This infusion is called the structural specification. Bayes structures are built to support both distinct and continuous parameters.

Distinct variables: a discrete or separate variable is a parameter that contains a jointly exclusive state, for instance, complexity (light or dark)

Continuous variable: a continuous variable is one that can depend on each other. A Bayes server is built to sustain constant parameters with the Conditional Linear Gaussian distributions (CLG). CGL process means that the sparsity of the feature in a continuous form is in such a way that the variables rely on each other (hence considered to be multivariate). Additionally, constant variables can also rely on one or more distinct variables.

The conditional linear Gaussian distribution can mould a multifaceted non-linear and hierarchical relationship in a set of data. This ability comes in play even though Gaussians are perceived to be limiting. The Bayes servers are also capable of sustaining latent variables that can mould concealed relationships of data. The ability to model such a structure is called Programmed feature extraction, which is comparable to hidden layers in an artificial neural network.

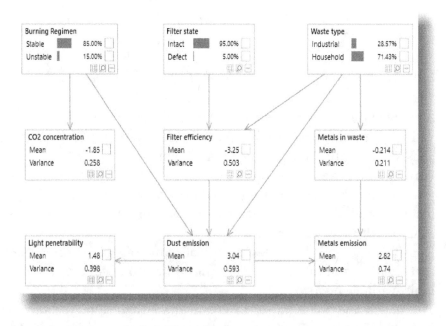

Links: links are add-ins that are infused between nodes to show the effect of a node on the other node. In some cases, a node may be connected by other nodes, which means that a link may not be available. In such a circumstance, the node is not considered independent. However, the node can become independent or dependent on the others as long as there is visible evidence of its relationship with other nodes. Information in a Bayesian structure can flow in either direction even though the links within the structure are directed. The flow, however, follows strict rules not discussed in this book.

Structural learning: a Bayes network consists of a necessary learning algorithm within the Bayes server. The first learning algorithm is capable of robotically determining the needed links from a given set of data. It is worth noting that there are various methods of solving different problems within the scope of a Bayes network. For this reason, structural learning may not be required.

Feature selection: a Bayes server is configured in a way that supports feature selection. The feature selection algorithm helps determine the variables that are most likely to have an impact on others. This method is advantageous in studying the structure of a specific model. Using latent variables is another method that can prove convenient in automatic extraction of features as part of the larger model.

Directed acyclic graphs (DAG): A simple Bayesian network is producing a type of chart known as the directed acyclic graph, abbreviated as DAG. A directed acyclic graph is a type of diagram with no directed cycles but contains directed links.

Directed cycles: A directed period in a Bayesian represented graph is a track beginning and ending at the same node. In this type of chart, the track taken can only lead through the direction of links.

Other categories of probabilistic graphical models

Other probabilistic models include;

Tree-augmented classifier or the TAN model

Naive Bayes classifiers

Naive Bayes classifiers are centred on the Bayes' hypothesis. The theory of classification by Bayes assumes independence among crucial variables in a set of data. Shortly put, the Naïve Bayes classification mechanism believes that a particular aspect in a class of data is not related to the next level. The application of the Naïve Bayes classifiers is suitable in the classification of widespread sets of data.

Decision Tree Classifiers

The decision tree prototype makes a classification in the structure of a tree. The decision tree is built to spread and break down data into smaller division, taking the form of branches of the tree. The result is, therefore, in the way of decision bulges and leaf bulges. A decision bulge, say the root grows to produce more than one branch. The leaf bulge signifies a classified class (in this case a decision). The first class/decision is the tree corresponding to the best predictive value (root). The decision tree classifiers can solve arithmetical and clear-cut problems.

Deep Deterministic Policy Gradient

The DDPG is a type of reinforcement learning that banks on the actor vs critic model. The actor component is applied to adjust the feature θ for the program function. In essence, for each state, the algorithm has to decide the best course of action to take. The algorithm also borrows a leaf from deep Q-learning, especially on the concepts of the separate target network and capability reiteration. Occasionally, the system performs a survey for the actions. However, this is neutralized by the addition of noise to the functionality space.

Types of graphs

Factor graph

This is an undirected split graph which joins variables and metrics. Each factor is a representation of a specific function over the variable it is linked to. This type of graph is useful in understanding and instigating belief transmission.

Chain graph

A chain is a type that is both directed and undirected. However, the figure lacks a directed cycle. Good examples of chain graphs include directed acyclic graphs and undirected graphs. These graphs can provide ways of joining and simplifyingtheBayesian and Markov networks.

Ancestral graph

An ancestral graph is one with further extensions consisting of undirected, a bi-directed, and directed ends.

Random Field Techniques

Markov Decision Processes

MDP is an algorithm of reinforcement learning. The algorithm consists of real value reward functions, model sets, a collection of probable actions, a pool of likely world states, and a policy. For effectiveness, the Markov Decision Processes uses an open framing method to study the relationship of variables. The component here selects an action that corresponds to the natural effects within the environment. The two steps are then made to correlate to present new situations to the element

A Markov random field (also called the Markov network), is a model over a graph that is not directed. In Markov Network, a graphical prototype with numerousrecurrent sub-divisions can be exemplified with plate representation.

Stochastic Models

A stochastic model is a type of probabilistic model that exemplifies condition where uncertainty is present. In simple words, it is a model for processes that possess unpredictability. In the real world, improbability forms part of our daily life. For this reason, a stochastic model can represent everything. The reverse of this model is a deterministic model, which forecastsresults with 100% conclusion. As opposed to deterministic models, stochastic models gives a different outcome every time the model is run.

All stochastic models have the following standard features.

1. All models reflect all the given features of the studied element.
2. Chances are allocated to measures within the model.
3. The changes within the model can be utilized to predict or give further information about the element of study.

Chapter 5: Soft Computing

As the term suggests, soft computing is the concept of figuring out problems in a smooth way. The methods involved in soft computing tend to work out problems the way human beings would. Lofti Zadeh first visualized the idea. Zadeh pioneered the mathematical concept of Fuzzy sets. The Fuzzy sets have enabled developments in various fields of computation. Such areas include fuzzy graph theory, fuzzy control system etc. In his argument, he observed that people think softly as opposed to computers which are hard thinkers. The difference in the concept can be drawn from the terms that people used as opposed to what machines use.

Expression of people	Computers expressions
Quantitative terms like most, some, etc.	Precise terms like 3, 499, etc.
General terms like warm, cold, etc.	Exact terms like 100 degrees Celsius

In general comparison, human beings learn, find patterns, adapt to changes in the environment and are very unpredictable. On the other hand, machines learn to be precise, use metrics, are fragile to changes, From the above inclination, we can understand soft computing as developing the model that is not so much organized or programmed to fit one course. The computers must be flexible. These are neural models which are highly bendable. There is, however, no single method that allows computers to compute like humans. For this reason, soft computing revolves around the use of a collection of ways that bend towards achieving flexibility.Machine learning is one of the main components that underline the concept of soft computing.

Soft computing has continued to be a necessary scope of study in computer science and IT since the 90s. The traditional approaches of computation could replicate andaccuratelyexploresimple patterns alone. More complex problems in fields such as biology and mathematics became challenging to solve using the conventional methods of analysis. For these purposes, soft computing was introduced to solve the grey areas of imprecision, improbability, fractional truth, and estimations to make computability possible and at a lower cost. In this sense, soft computing forms the basis of a substantial amount of machine learning methods. New inventions and development s tend to reflect evolutionary and cloud intelligence that is based on algorithms that are inspired by biological processes, such as artificial neural networks.

In general terms, soft computing methods bear a resemblance to biological procedures. The arrangements are not inclined to formal logic techniques and do not depend heavily on computer-supported arithmetical analysis. Contrary to hard computing formats that go all-out for exactitude and precision, soft computing techniques make use of certain forbearance of vagueness, fractional truth, and improbability for a meticulous hitch. Another general distinction can be drawn from the significance of roles played in the two methods.

Components of Soft Computing

There are several components of soft computing. The major ones include:

1. Machine learning (Neural networks, which encompass Perceptron and support vector machines)
2. Fuzzy logic
3. Evolutionary computation
4. Metaheuristic and cloud Intelligence

5. Probabilistic ideas(including the Bayesian network)

Of all the components, this book will dwell mostly on the machine learning front. The direction taken by this book is generally based on the scope and context of the book. Other components will be discussed in the next issue. The machine learning component of soft computing primarily focuses on ANN and SVM. As discussed in the opening chapters of the book, the two will be addressed in a slightly different angle.

Support vector machines in soft computing
At this point in learning, I suppose the reader is familiar with both linear regression and logistic regression algorithms. The knowledge in the areas is very vital in understanding SVMs. The support vector machine is a simple algorithm recommended for anyone wishing to dive in the field of machine learning. Machine learning experts mostly use the SVM model due to its ability to give results with striking accuracy will less calculation power. Support vector machine, otherwise abbreviated as SVM can be applied in both classification and regression tasks. However, SVM is broadly used for classification purposes.

Understanding a support vector machine in soft computing
The support vector machine is usually purposed to find a hyperplane in an N-Dimension space. This statement can be summarized in a formulation where N is the number of parameters that categorize the data points.

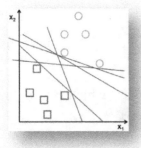 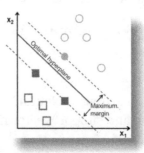

Probable hyperplanes

Various possible hyperplanes can be used to sort out the two classes of data points. The end goal is finding the plane with the highest margin; in essence, the thoroughgoing distance between the two data points in the classes. Getting the best out of the margin distance would allow for future reinforcement such that the following data points are easy to classify.

Relationship between hyperplanes and support vectors

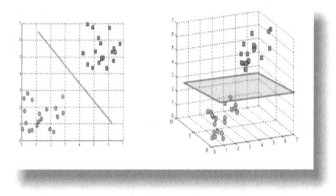

Two-dimensional and three-dimensional hyperplanes

Hyperplanes can be defined as the decision borders that are used in classifying the data points. The data points that stray on either side of the hyperplane can be classified in different classes. The dimension quality of the hyperplane is exclusively reliant on the number of parameters/metrics within the set of data. If there are only two features in the input data, then the hyperplane will assume a line dividing the features. If the number of elements in the input data is three, then the hyperplane will consider a two-dimensional plane. Functionality beyond three in the input data become hard to solve using the hyperplane.

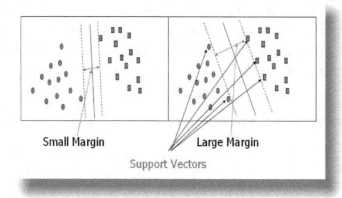

Small Margin   Large Margin

Support Vectors

Support Vectors

Support vectors are data points that stray closer to the hyperplane (as shown in the image above). The support vector impacts the location and the alignment of the hyperplane. The use the support vectors can maximize the margin of the classifier. When the support vectors are deleted, the position of the hyperplane changes. In general, the points within the hyperplane are useful in structuring a support vector machine.

The awareness of the large margin

In logistic regression, the output value of the linear function is taken and compressed within the range of 0-1 by the use of the sigmoid function. If the compressed amount is more significant than a threshold value of 0.5, it is assigned a mark (1). If the value is smaller than the threshold value, it is assigned the score (0).

In support vector machines, the output value of the linear function is taken, and if that output is more significant than 1, the cost is identified with a single class. In cases where the output value is lesser than 1, the value is determined with another type. Since the threshold values are changed to 1 and -1 (value below 1) in support vector machine, the reinforcement range of benefits (-1 and 1) that performs as the margin is obtained.

344

Neural networks as a component of soft computing

Sometimes referred to as artificial neural networks, these models have been defined in broad context by major players in the field. Deriving from Dr Robert Hecht-Nielsen, I want my readers to digest this component as;

A model of computation that is made of modest, largely intersected features that extract usefulness from data through their active reaction to outward inputs.

Artificial neural networks are devices (software devices, i.e., algorithms or hardware) that process information and are roughly molded to resemble the components of the human brain, but on lower levels. More extensive neural networks consist of many units that process data. In contrast, the human brain is made up billions of neurons that correspond with a rise in the extent of general relations and evolving conduct.

The Basics of Neural Networks in soft computing

Artificial neural networks are characteristically grouped in layers. The layers are completed with numerous intersected nodes containing specific performance feature. Different designs are infused I the layers by the use of an input layer. The input layer interconnects to other layers within the network. The layers in the network perform the actual processing through a system of subjective associates. The segments that are connected with the input layer link with the output layer.

Many artificial neural networks have different forms of training rules which refine the connections within the layers in the system, per the input data design. As a child learns to identify objects in the environment by seeing and interacting with the item, so does neural network learn?

This book will explore the delta rule learning method as used by neural networks. Note that the neural networks can use other rules. In most cases, the delta rule is applied by collective classes of ANN known as the 'backpropagation neural networks.' Backpropagation is an acronym for the backward transmission of fault.

Similar to other types of backpropagation, the delta rule training method is a supervised process. The process occurs in epochs (the

345

cycle of presenting new data input in the network) by a forward flowing functional output. The flow of the production corresponds with the backward propagation of error. The neural network predicts the type of data each time it is infused in the network. The prediction is followed by the interpretation of the deviation of the answer given from the actual answer. The system then makes correct adjustments. It is worth noting that every layer connected to the input layer consist of a sigmoidal functional unit, which separates the activities of the network hence creating stability.

Backpropagation achieves an inclined pedigree within the solution's vector space concerning a 'universal minimum' end to end with the vector of the error function. The universal minimum is the hypothetical explanation with the least probable fault. The error surface can be looked at as a hyper-paraboloid. It is, however, even as illustrated in most graphical representations. For most problems, the answer is always contained in an irregular answer space. The irregularity of the area makes the network to settle on the local minimum, which may not be the most suitable solution.

How the delta rule finds the correct answer

The nature of the error space is sometimes hard to establish before the study. For this reason, the neural network analysis, in most cases, require several trials to produce the most suitable answer. Most learning rules have arithmetic terms as extensions to help in controlling the beta-coefficient and the momentum of the process of learning. The beta-coefficient is always the rate of merging between the real answer and the universal minimum. The Momentum of the learning process supports the network to overcome snags and settle for a value that is the global minimum of the value closet to it.

The neural network is often used as a tool to analyze other sets of data once the network if fully trained. At this level, the user may not require to specify any testing procedures. Instead, the user lets the system to perform in a headfirst propagation approach alone. New data inputs are infused in the responsive design. The data is then filtered into the plan and are sort out by the mid-layers in a manner that resembles the training process. Retention of the input data happens at this point while no backpropagation happens. The resultant output (in a headfirst propagation) becomes the forecast model for the data. The output data can be used for auxiliary breakdown and clarification.

In some instances, the neural network gets trained to answer back to a single type of data input accurately. This situation is considered as an over-training of the neural network. The process works more like a routine memorization process. Such circumstance requires the learning process of the system to cut shot and is therefore referred to as a grand-mothered network within the neural network redundancy. The application of this method is, however, not common in real life.

As a component of soft computing, neural networks can be broken down to focus on perceptron.

What is a Perceptron?

A perceptron canbe defined as a simple unit of a neural network. The group is capable of doing the following.

1. Taking arithmetical values along with its weight as input in the centre.
2. Calculating the weighted sum and gives a return of 1 if the summation is positive.

A perceptron can also be considered a model for computation that draws a boundary (a line in two-dimensional cases) to isolate two classes in a given space.

Initially, the weights and the bias which represents the classification hyperplane is usually unknown. In this case, random weights and partiality are allocated to the model. The random assignment leads to misclassification of points.

The Perceptron trick

The objective of the perception trick is decreasing the amount of misclassified points. The reduction can be made by sliding the line over the space. In other words, it is altering the expression of the hyperplane. For all the wrongly categorized points, we adjust the weights and bias to move the hyperplane closer to the points that are improperly classified. After some time, the algorithm will rectify the problem to classify the points correctly.

347

Chapter 6: Data Mining

Data mining is a trendy field in machine technology. The concept was first generated in the 90s. The idea of data mining has been, in broad perspective, referred to as big data or data science. The definition of this concept varies depending on the application and scope. In this book, I will look at data mining as the process of extracting raw sets of data for analysis and discovery of more knowledge about the collection. Thanks to the advancement in computer networks, data can now be stored effectively and cheaply. Additionally, the transfer of data has been enhanced due to the availability of electronic sources. These reasons and many more have enabled the spread of data mining techniques. Many organizations are thereby able to store massive amounts of data in databases without the fear of losing sensitive information. The ability to store vast amounts of data in databases is excellent. However, it is also essential to know how to analyze and interpret the sets of data at your disposal. Possessing larges sets of data that we cannot explain and draw meaningful information from is as good as having no data at all. That brings the question on how to analyze data stored in various databases. Traditional methods of analyzing data included the manual hand analysis process. However, conventional methods have proved to be time-consuming, tedious, and the result may not reflect accurate outcomes. The traditional ways missed critical information in datasets making the analysis processes a miss.

Additionally, the emergence of massive sets of data have made conventional techniques irrelevant and unrealistic. To mitigate the problems, automated methods have been designed to help sort data and extract useful information, trends and patterns that may be desirable. The field is where data mining methods and techniques come in handy. In clear terms, data mining processes aim at explaining the outcome of an event, forecasting future results, and helping in understanding complex data. The science of data mining have been used to describe phenomena such as why a ship sank or plane crushed. In aeroplanes, data mining is done through black boxes fit with datasets and information about every flight. This way, it easy to tell the circumstances that led to a crush. As opposed to other machine learning methods of predicting outcomes, data mining techniques are used to foretell the possible outcome based on facts and not instinct.

The process for analyzing data

For an efficient means of data mining, there must be an observance of seven steps called the knowledge discovery in databases. The seven stages of knowledge discovery in databases are illustrated below.

Data cleaning. This is the first step in analyzing data. In this phase, data is cleaned to remove noise and other variations that may hamper proper analysis.

Data integration. The second step following data cleaning is data integration. This process involving linking, infusing and incorporating data from various sources to prepare the data that is to be analyzed. For instance, if the information is stored in different databases, integration is done to put the data together in one database.

Data selection. After data is put together in a single file, the relevant set is chosen for analysis. This is a process called data selection.

Data transformation. Having done all the procedures above, the data is now ready to be converted into a fitting format. The conversion is done to make analysis easy. For instance, some techniques of mining data may require that all arithmetic values be standardized.

Data mining. This step involves the application of data mining algorithms to analyze the data and extract meaningful patterns and information from the analyzed sets of data.

Assessment of the extracted patterns and knowledge. This step in data mining involves the study and evaluation of the derived patterns and information from the analyzed data. The review of results can be done in subjective or objective terms.

Visualization of data. The last step in the data mining process is the conception of the extracted information from the analyzed data. This step is when we try to understand the outcome.

It is essential to know that the steps above may vary depending on the technique and the algorithms used. For instance, some algorithms of data mining may perform the steps concurrently or continuously.

Application of data mining in related fields

Several data mining algorithms can be used in the various sectors and domains where data analysis is vital. Some of these applications are listed below.

1. Detection of fraud
2. Prediction of stock market valuations
3. Analyzing the purchasing patterns of clients

In a broad sense, the techniques of data mining are chosen based on the following metrics.

1. The type of data to be analyzed
2. The form in which the information extracted from datasets is required.
3. The application of extracted knowledge (how the information is used).

Relationship between data mining and other research areas

Data mining is an inter-categorical field of study that overlaps and corresponds to different segments such as machine learning, computer science, soft computing, etc. The relationship between data mining and these fields overlay the fundamental notion of supplementing artificial intelligence. This notion holds that each subsect and area in artificial intelligence complement each other and work both dependently and independently.

Data mining and statistics

There are striking differences between data mining and statistics. However, the two fields of research have many components and concepts in common.

In the past, descriptive statistics concentrated on labelling data using metrics, while inferential statistics put more weight on theoryanalysis to draw noteworthyinference from the data or generateprototypes. On the contrary, data mining techniques are more concerned about the outcome of the study as opposed toarithmeticalimplication. Many methods of data mining do not focus on the arithmetic test or connotation, as long as given metrics likeviability and precisionare met to the maximum. Additionally, data mining is usually concentrated on automated analysis of datasets, and in most cases by machinery that can scale to a massive amount of data. The proximity in scope is realized by mathematicians, who sometimes refer to data mining in statistics as "statistical learning."

Main data mining software

To successfully perform the process of data mining, there are some software and algorithmic computer program available. The software varies in model and use. Some software is all-purposeimplements that offer algorithms of different kinds. Other software is more specified. It is important to note that some software is developed for commercial purposes, while others are free to access and configure (open-source). The various software can perform data mining onseveral data types.

Data mining software and algorithms are specifically developed to be used on different types of data. Below, I offer a summary of the countless examples of data generallybumped into, and which can be analyzed using the methods of data mining.

Relational databases: relational databases are the classic type of database that is mostly found in institutions and firms. In this form, data is categorically structured in tables. Conventional methods, like SQL, are used to query the database when trying to find faster information in the database. However, data mining enables the finding of sophisticated patterns within the database.

351

Customer transaction databases: another commonly used type of database is the customer transaction database. This type is mostly used in retail stores. The database is made up of all dealings made by the clients. The study of this database is essential in understanding the patterns of purchase and sales. It allows the retailers to understand the changes in the market, thus helping in planning sales and marketing strategy.

Temporal data: Another prevalent form of data is temporal data. The mundane type considers the time dimension in the data. Here, arrangements are created in many realms such as a sequence of items purchased by a customer, a chain of part of the population that is vegan, etc. The temporal data is further divided into time series. The series is a systematic list of arithmetic values like the price of shares in the stock market.

Spatial data: another set of data that can be easily analyzed is spatial data. This type of data consists of aggregate information like environmental data, forestry data, and data about substructures such as railway lines and air distribution channels.

Spatio-temporal data: this is a type of data that has both characteristics of spatial and temporal data. For instance, the data can be about climatic conditions, the movement of the wilder beast in crowds, etc.

Text data: the text type of data has become a widely studied area in data mining. The utilization spreads even though text data is mostly amorphous. Text documents are mostly disorganized and lack a definite form. Examples of text data are in feeling analysis and composition acknowledgement (predicting the author of a given text).

Web data: this a type of data that originates from websites. The data is mainly sets of a document, e.g. journals from the web with attached links. The sets are bound to form a graph. Some specific examples of data mining activities in the internet include predicting the possible next page in the website, grouping the webpages according to subjects automatically, and evaluating the time taken on every webpage.

Graph data:graphs is also another type of database. Charts are found in social networks (for instance, the list of Facebook friends) and chemistry (for example a graph of biochemical molecules and atoms).

Assorted data. Different or miscellaneous type of data is a collection of many kinds of data. The classes are linked and can be sorted into a specific arrangement.

Data streams: A data stream is said to be a continuous and high-speed torrent of data that is theoretically boundless. For instance, the data stream can be ecological data, data from video cameras, or digital television data). The limitation of this type of data is that it cannot be adequately stored in the computer. Therefore, the data should be evaluated regularly using suitable methods of data mining. Everyday data mining tasks in stream data are usually the detection of variations and tendencies.

Patterns found in data

As previously deliberated, the objective of data mining is to mine desirable patterns of information from data. The leading types of designs that can be extracted from data are as follows (take note that this list is not the finished product):

Clusters

Algorithms used I clustering are always applied in a situation where the sets of data are supposed to be sort in groups of similar instances (clusters). The main aim of these algorithms is condensing data to make it easy to understand and make an inference. Clustering modus operandi likes K-Means can be utilized to robotically group student showing similar performance.

Classification models

The algorithms used for classification tasks are purposed to extract models, which can be used to group objects and new instances into classes. For example, classification algorithms such as Naive Bayes, decision trees, and the neural networks can be used to create designs capable of predicting the trends in customer behaviors or the possibility of individual students to pass an examination. These models can also be hauled out to execute a forecast about the future.

Patterns and associations

Some methods are designed to study the relationship between data and frequently occurring patterns. For instance, the frequency of an item set can be analyzed, using data mining algorithms, to determine the most purchased items in particular retail outlets. Additional types of patterns are temporal patterns, progressive rules, irregular patterns, and recurrent subgraphs.

Anomaly detection

The AD is a method of machine learning that seeks to detect glitches and variances within a given set of data.

Simple Statistical Methods

The simplest way to detect anomalies within a set is to ensign the data points that strays from the mutual arithmetical properties of the distribution of the class of data. The features may take in the mean, median, mode, or quantiles. In simple terms the most variable data is one with the highest deviation from the central distribution unit, say the mean.

Anomaly detection approaches based on machine learning

There are a host of machine learning-based methods of anomaly detection. A brief overview of these methods is given below.

Density-Based Anomaly Detection

This technique is based on the concept of the K-nearest neighbor algorithm. In this process, an underlying assumption that standard data points ensue around a compressed neighborhood and deviations are far away is made. The classes of data point that occur closest are calculated using a score. The score can be a Euclidian space or an analogous measure depending on whether the data is categorical or numerical. This approach can further be classified into two;

1. K-Nearest Neighbor algorithm: this is a simple, non-feature based learning procedure used to categorize data based on matches in distance metrics.

2. Local outlier factor: this approach is also called the relative density tactic. The method is entirely based on the reachability distance metric.

Clustering-Based Anomaly Detection

As discussed earlier in this book, clustering is a fundamental concept in the domain of unsupervised learning. In the clustering-based approach of anomaly detection, the assumption that similar data points tend to fall in the same classes/clusters (as determined by the distance from the core of the class) is made. The most used algorithm in this approach is the K—Means. The K-Means creates data points with similar "k" function in a cluster. Any data that finds itself out of the group is perceived to be irregular.

Support Vector Machine-Based Anomaly Detection

Another instrumental technique to detect an anomaly is by the use of the support vector machine. The support vector machine is typically associated with supervised earning. However, some add-ins can be used to detect irregularities in an unsupervised model. For the training set of data, the algorithm studies a soft boundary to group the standard data. On the other hand, the machine fine-tunes itself to recognize the irregularities that stray out of the learned region in the testing phase. The output of an anomaly indicator can be a numeric scalar value for clarifying on particular domain onsets or textual markers depending on the use.

Association rules

Association Rules is a very critical theory of machine learning. The concept is widely used in the market product pool analysis. For instance, in a shopping mall, you will find that utensils are placed on the same shelf, and all electronics are arranged in a similar rack. This type of product arrangement is meant to help the customers locate what they want in the shortest time possible. The layout is also usually appealing, which may remind a customer of the relevant kinds of stuff they might be fascinated with purchasing. The method thus allows the outlets cross-sell in the process.

Association rules make it possible to unearth the relationships between objects within a massive set of data. It is important to note that:

Association rules do not mine the inclinations of an individual. However, the law learns the relationship between the items in different purchase records. This essential trait differentiates association rules from the collaborative filtering.

In association rules, the IDs of items purchased by customers are studied to identify the relationship between the elements. Details with similar traits are then considered separately in one group.

The diagram below can illustrate how an association rule looksooooo. The layout consists of original data and the resultant item. All the details are on a list. It is worth noting that inference here is co-occurrence and not connection. For any given rule, *item-set* is the list of all the items in the original set and the resultant set.

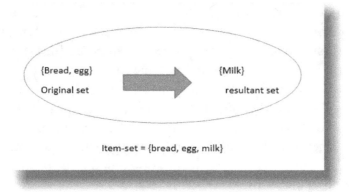

Item-set = {bread, egg, milk}

Numerous metrics can help in understanding the strength of the association between the two items.

1. Support

This metric helps by showing the frequency of the item-set in all purchase records. For instance, let us consider the first item-set to be {bread} and the second item-set to be {shoe polish}. In all purchase records, there will be more bread than shoe polish. For this reason, the first item-set will have more support than the second. The same treatment applies to item-sets that have more than one item. Arithmetically, support is the portion of the total purchase record in which the item-set occurs. Formulated as:-

Support ({A} => {B}) = (Total appearance of A and B in purchase record) / (Total number of purchases)

The value of support helps identify the rules to consider for additional scrutiny.

Confidence

This metric shows the probability of occurrence of the resultant set when the basket already has an original set. For instance, the metric will tend to explain the probability of milk appearing in a basket that already has bread and butter. For this case, we will find that {bread, butter} => {milk} have a higher confidence rule. Theoretically, confidence is the uncertain likelihood of occurrence of resultant given the original set.

Confidence ({A} => {B}) = (Purchase record with both A and B) / (Occurrence of A)

Lift
Lift controls the frequency (support) of the resultant in computing the uncertain likelihood of occurrence of item {B} given item {A}. Lift is considered a precise term for this process. Consider this example. Lift that {A} gives the possibility of the {B} occurring in the same basket. In other words, a lift is the increase in the likelihood of item {B} appearing in a basket when we know that the same basket contains item {A} over the likelihood of issue {B} appearing in a basket when we do not understand that the bucket has item {A}.

Lift ({A} => {B}) = (Transactions with A and B) (Transactions with A alone)/ (A section of transactions with B)

Trends and regularities
Data mining methods can be applied to study trends and uniformities in databases. Some applications of these patterns are forms that study the changes in the market valuation of shares and stock prices and make predictions on investments. Other applications are capable of findingsequences in the ways a system performs, and determine the order of events leading to system failure.

As mentioned previously, the aim of data mining is finding patterns in data and extracting useful information from the designs. Such occurrences like frequency and trends are essential components that underline the concept of data mining. As I have always said, it is crucial to find a balance that is suitable for yourself. The listed examples are only meant to give a brief overview of the concepts.

Chapter 7: Machine Learning Datasets

Numerous concepts underpin the general knowledge of machine learning. These components lay the foundation for understanding the field as well as making the processes a go.

In this chapter, my readers will get comprehensive information about the catalogue (standard terms) used to refer to data and datasets in machine learning. Additionally, I have availed a comprehensive analysis of the concepts and conditions that are used to build the literature on machine learning and datasets.

Data

As we have seen earlier, machine learning algorithms learn from examples. The most crucial element to note in this section is the input data and various terms used to describe these sets of data.

In this chapter, I would like to explain data in terms of rows and columns, similar to an excel spreadsheet. Data analyzed in this method reflects the traditional structure that is commonly used in machine learning. Unstructured data sets like images have not to be discussed here. The image below is a representation of sets of data used in machine learning algorithms.

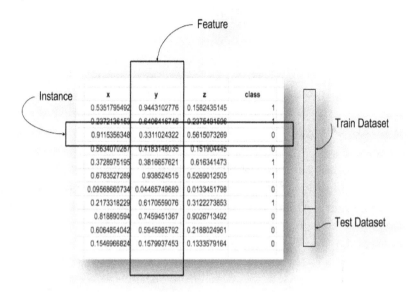

Feature

	x	y	z	class
Instance	0.5351795492	0.9443102776	0.1582435145	1
	0.2372136152	0.6406416746	0.2375491596	1
	0.9115356348	0.3311024322	0.5615073269	0
	0.5634070287	0.4183148035	0.151904445	0
	0.3728975195	0.3816657621	0.616341473	1
	0.6783527289	0.938524515	0.5269012505	1
	0.09568660734	0.04465749689	0.0133451798	0
	0.2173318229	0.6170559076	0.3122273853	1
	0.818890594	0.7459451367	0.9026713492	0
	0.6064854042	0.5945985792	0.2188024961	0
	0.1546966824	0.1579937453	0.1333579164	0

Train Dataset

Test Dataset

An image of data sets

Defining the terms

Instance: an instance is a single line (row) of data in a machine learning algorithm. A case is an inference from the realm.

Feature: a feature is a single column of data. An element is a constituent of observation and is also known as the attribute of a data instance. A function may also be called a metric or a parameter. Some of these metrics may be data inputs to an algorithm (the training data, also called the predictors) while others may be outputs (the parameters to be determined or predicted).

Data Type: metrics have different forms of data. Types of data may be actual or integer-valued. In other instances, the type of data may have a clear-cut or standard value. Additional classes may be in the form of strings, times, lengths, etc. When traditional machine learning techniques are used, the various types of data are reduced to real values.

359

Datasets: a dataset can be defined as a group of instances. Machine learning models usually require a few sets of data for various functions.

Training Dataset: a set of data that is fed into the system to help guide the algorithm is called a training dataset. As the name suggests, they train the system.

Testing Dataset:

After training the machine learning model, it is essential to test their performance. The sets of data that are used to evaluate the accuracy of the algorithm are called testing datasets. In other terms, they are called validation or evaluation datasets.

Learning

The focus here is based on machine learning. As seen, machine learning is all about training algorithms to perform tasks. In this perspective, we will take a look at some concept of learning

Induction: the algorithms in various models of machine learning are trained through a process known as induction or inductive learning. Induction is a process of deciding sweeping statements (generalization) from detailed information (training datasets).

Generalization: The notion is also called sweeping statements. The process is vital because the representation set by a machine learning algorithm is required to make forecasts. Such findings are based on specific data instances not present at the training phase.

Over-Learning: over-learning is described as the situation where an algorithm of machine learning observes the features in the training data too much but still fails to perform generalization. This situation is broughtabout by poor performance on data other than the training dataset. This instance is also known as over-fitting.

Under-Learning: under-learning is a situation whereby machine learning algorithms do not observe the training datasets to completion. The process may be caused by early termination f the training process — under-learning results in good generalization but poor performance on all data, not excluding the training dataset. The situation is also described as under-fitting.

Online Learning: online learning methods are instances when the data instance form a domain is used to update the system as the data become available.in online learning, robust processes that are not affected by noisy data are used. These methods can produce models that correspond to the current state domain.

Offline Learning: Offline learning is when a technique is produced on data that is pre-prepared to be used operationally on unlearned data. The process of training the system can be carefully tuned since the training dataset is known. After the preparation of the model, no further updates are made. This scenario may lower the performance in case there is a change in domain.

Supervised Learning: This is a method of machine learning that is used to generalize problems where a forecast is necessary. A "training process" compares predictions by the model to known answers and makes corrections in the model.

Unsupervised Learning: as discussed earlier, unsupervised learning is the process of generalization without any training data set being fed to the system. In this technique, naturally occurring structures are observed and utilized to interpret the relationship between the instances.

Modeling
A structure that is created by the process of machine learning is considered a model. The method of producing models is modeling.
Model Selection: the process of model selection can be described as the process in which configuration and training of a model of machine learning are done. In every given time, the system should present different models to modify, use, or discard. The choice of which algorithm to install in machine learning is also a part of model

selection. For a given problem, the algorithms of machine learning will pick a model in which it operates.

Inductive Bias: a bias is an impartial input in a given model of machine learning. All machine learning models are biased to induce an error in the model. The failure caused is usually used to test the model or to act as a control set of data. Bias can be produced in a model during the configuration phase of the training phase. A machine learning algorithm can have a low or high preference depending on the input data. There are methods to remove high bias in algorithms.

Model Variance: variance the sensitivity of a model towards a training data set. Generally put, a variation is how a model responds to data input for training. A machine learning model can show high or low variance to training datasets. The best way to reduce the difference is by running the machine on a dataset over and over again. This process is done under different parameters and conditions. When variance has diminished the accuracy of the model is enhanced.

Bias-Variance Tradeoff: a model selection process can be regarded as a trade-off of the bias and the variance. The relationship between bias and variance is inverse proportionality. A model with low bias will possess high variation and will require longtime and continuous training to get a usable model. On the other hand, a model with high bias will maintain low variance, which makes it learn faster, but realizes adverse and limited performance.

Chapter 8: Machine Learning Vs Deep Learning

Both machine learning and deep learning are branches of artificial intelligence. The two areas have attracted a lot of focus over the years. This chapter offers the best place to understand the differences in these two areas in the most straightforward manner possible. In this chapter, I will explain the striking areas that differentiate the two models and help you point out the best way of incorporating the two.

Before I commence, I would wish to give you an overview of what the two terms mean (even though you are now familiar with the concept of machine learning).

Machine Learning

As explained earlier, machine learning is a subdivision of artificial intelligence. Machine learning involves the development of intelligent machines. These machines operate by the use of algorithms that are capable of mimicking human actions. In machine learning, the algorithms are built in a way that they perform tasks without too much interference.

Deep Learning

Deep learning is also a subsect of artificial intelligence. In deep learning, the algorithms are built in the same way as those of machine learning. The difference is that in deep learning, there are many layers of algorithms. Each layer provides a different outcome of the input data. The layers are joined to form a network of algorithms. The systems are known as artificial neural networks (ANN). The artificial neural networks work in a way that imitates the functioning of the neural networks in the human brain.

To make the definitions simpler and point out the differences, we will take a look at an example.

Taking an example of images of boys and girls, we will go step by step in analyzing how machine learning ad deep learning would analyze the information.

Image an image of a boy and a girl. Now let us try to identify the images separately using machine learning algorithms and deep learning algorithms.

Solving the problem through Machine Learning

To enable categorization of images by machine learning algorithms, we have to feed the algorithm with the data (feature present) in both pictures. The feature, in this case, becomes the data input.

In line with the definition given above, the data must be structured. We have to mark the datasets with the features of both boys and girls. The input should be able to reflect the distinguishing features in both boys and girls. The data provided will aid the learning process of the algorithm. After that, the algorithm will be able to work based on the interpretation of the data input, thereby classifying more images of people into boys and girls.

Solving the same problem using Deep Learning

In addressing the same issue, deep learning will assume a different approach. The main hi in deep learning is that the networks do not require structured data (labelled) to classify images of people. The neural networks in deep learning interpret the images through layers of algorithms. Each layer in the interface defines a different feature on the image. The human brain works in the same way. The networks in deep learning will solve this problem by establishing question marks through an assortment of hierarchies of feature and other related components. The system determines the appropriate features that can classify the images following the processing of data in the algorithm layers.

Points to note

The best way to differentiate machine learning from deep learning is the mode in which information (input data) is presented to the systems. In machine learning, the algorithms mostly require labelled data (apart from unsupervised learning). On the other hand, deep learning relies on artificial neural networks to make simulations.

The algorithms of machine learning are deployed to "learn" how to perform specific tasks by interpreting marked data and then using it to process outcomes. However, the system needs to be trained again in case the findings do not meet the required standards. On the other hand, deep learning networks do not require a lot of training. The algorithmic layers in the neural networks pass data through hierarchies of diverse models. The models learn through the trial and error approach.

The quality of data impacts the quality of output. In other words, the systems try to work on the GIGO (garbage in garbage out) approach, which implies that the machine gives result according to the feed it receives. The quality of input is the governing factor in both systems.

Machine learning algorithms are not appropriate for solving problems that require a massive amount of data.

When to apply deep learning:

Deep learning techniques are essential when the load of data required to solve a problem is massive. The artificial neural networks also come in handy when the issue at hand is very complicated. Lastly, you can use deep learning if you have the computational funds and operating cost to configure hardware and programs for training networks.

Chapter 9: Pros and Cons

This chapter focuses on the pros and cons of machine learning drawing analysis from both sides of the coin. The reader and potential users must take note of the bits that make machine learning a win and the feature that need review. This way, the balance is established to ensure proper incorporation of intelligent machines in our daily lives.

As shown, the advantages of machine learning do not rest solely on the ability to mine large sets of data and transform it into useful information. Many organizations have turned to machine learning to automate the functions of computer programs. This way, other methods of analyzing data are complemented

The first section will look at the benefits of machine learning that have not been mentioned in the above chapters. The advantages create massive openings that transform the game into many applications. I want my readers to note the benefits listed below. And as said before, the interests are looked at at a different perspective.

1. Enhancing Data mining

Data mining is the extraction of massive sets of data for analysis and transformation into valuable information. The frequent use of digital information calls for a reliable and competent method of retrieving data from its raw source and state. These methods must generate a large amount of data in the shortest time possible. How fast data analysis and the results are required makes manual processes challenging; thus, machine learning comes in hand.

The functionality of machine learning in the field of data mining is crucial. When incorporated, the method allows for analysis of the large volume of data while providing accurate assumptions that give weight to the outcome at the same time. A point to note is that data mining is the extraction of data, while machine learning is the analysis of the extracted data to make predictions and get accurate results. The two go hand in hand and supplement each other for best outcomes.

2. Enabling continuous improvements and innovation

The term 'learning' from machine learning indicates the ability to improve in knowledge and performance. The general context of learning shows that experience is used to improve future outcomes. In machine learning, the software and algorithmic functions act as agents that will enhance the performance of individual computer systems. I have shown that the algorithm learns sets of data inputs to refine the system they operate in. When a prediction is made, the outcome is stored. If the result is not fitting the users' needs, the algorithms learn to improve their performance the next time such a task is performed.

The ability of machine learning to enable improvements and further innovations can be applied in various fields. For instance, let us take a look at a machine learning algorithm that analyzes the changing patterns of stock prices. The algorithm will not only take into account the past results and data but also look at the newly input features. Such features may include all the factors affecting the market. These factors are analyzed within a specified duration. Machine learning systems are thereby able to make accurate predictions and recommendations.

3. Computerization of tasks

The widely known advantage of machine learning is the automation of tasks. The development of intelligent machine has seen a change in methods of operation. Software and other computer programs are trained to perform the functions that are instead deemed tiresome to human beings. Automation of these processes is made possible by supplementing both data mining and machine learning through constant improvements. Machine learning has undisputedly been developed to perform tasks on their own without any programming commands.

Human functions are complemented well with machine learning systems. It is my take to mention that incorporating machine learning algorithms in one or more tasks would free up humans to focus on more critical issues. There are notable instances of automating human tasks that are worth a mention. I want to refer you to the applications and uses of machine learning in the chapters above to get a glimpse of the automated tasks. However, I will take a peek on another area in this chapter.

Technology has evolved to the extent that driving and piloting functions can be automated. As an area that did not get massive back up in my opening chapters, I would like to focus a bit here. Drones and crewless planes are an example of automated functions. Human is no longer required to pilot aeroplanes. However, the processes remain controlled by humans on the ground. Nevertheless, a wide range of production sectors and industries are at present, reaping the benefits of machine learning systems. The companies are using the methods to introduce innovations, advance their service delivery mechanisms, and encourage effectiveness in operations. These functions have created an opportunity to use fewer people in handling the processes. On the contrary, automation can also be seen as a miss. Many people argue that machines have taken human chances of employment. A human cannot outperform machine in some areas, thereby falling victims of computerization processes. It is, however, important to use devices sparingly and only in fields that human performance is deemed irrelevant.

Limitations of Machine Learning

The wins of machine learning, as discussed above the point at the innovation of systems capable of improving the way processes and tasks are accomplished. However, regardless of the numerous benefits, machine learning processes do not fall short of limitations. The limitations of machine learning are outlined below.

1. The algorithms of Machine Learning are bulky

One of the most notable aspects of machine learning algorithms is bulk. These algorithms require large storage spaces for the training data. It is worth noting that machine learning algorithms and systems are trained and not programmed. The training phases need a lot of data input to train and test the system. The complexity of the tasks makes it even more bulky in terms of the sets of data required to complete the processes.

Contrary to the fact that data is generated at fascinating speed, robust computing power for this performance means that a lot of information is used. In return, the data requires a lot of input space. Large amounts of data are challenging to mine, analyze, and transform into meaningful information. For this reason, deep learning is used to utilize backpropagation. This algorithmic function enables adjustment of the weights between nodes, thus ensuring that data input corresponds to the right output.

The main limitation with these processes is that machine learning algorithms need too much 'applied features' to perform at the same level as the intelligence level of humans.

However, this limitation can be mitigated by infusing deep learning and unsupervised learning methods. As discussed earlier, we can note that unsupervised learning does not require massive labelled data input for training algorithms. A case in point is that reinforcement learning algorithms are trained through trial and error instead of input data. Using this method would ensure that the massive sets of data are checked.

2. The process of labelling training data is time-consuming

Supervised learning is a fundamental component of machine learning. In supervised learning, the algorithms require labelled datasets for training. The method works efficiently when datasets from previous functions are infused into the system. The process of data labelling entails cleaning up raw data and sorting it out for machines to gulp down. Machine learning functions, especially in supervised and semi-supervised learning, require large amounts of training data. The process of labelling these sets of training data is not only tiresome but also time-consuming. On the contrary, when unlabeled data is fed in the system, the performance of the machine is lowered. This is down to the fact that algorithms can make decisions, recognize, and behave intelligently only if mapped targets are made available. A time-wasting and tedious process of identifying and labelling training data are required to establish the targets. A point of relief is that developers are coming up with new means of identifying and labelling training data that may not be as time-consuming as the existing methods. The developments in this area include adding features to the system that would naturally develop the training data. The innovation not only promises to upgrade the quality of data collection but also save the users time and energy required to do so.

3. Machines do not offer explanations

The human brain has an insightful physics engine. This means that the human brain is capable of collect information in all sorts of environment and makes conclusions of the outcome of the collected data. Well, thought explanations can back the findings. One of the most limiting factors of machine learning is the inability of the machine to give insights about the outcome generated. In other terms, computers are not capable of backing up their decisions with explanations. For ages now, devices have continued to exhibit a lack of common sense. Many models of machine learning depend on the availability of training data. Such circumstances have primarily resulted in a lack of receptiveness in machine learning in fields that require explanations. Social processes have the right to descriptions. Whether the results are bad or good, we at time demand to know why and how the decisions are made. The understanding of the outcome is very crucial in knowing how the systems operate. The knowledge can be used to understand mechanical machines and their models as well as the modes of operation.

4. Machine Learning algorithms are prone to bias

Any system that relies on the deployment of information by a human is usually likely to prejudice. Partiality comes in the order at the point of feeding input data for training. Humans may tend to shift the machine operations to fit their need. In some cases, systems that seem to perform effectively manage to operate on "noisy data. "The reliability of machine learning processes is dependent on the data input. This means that when the information is bias, the result may not reflect the actual value on the ground. The best way to overcome bias is by collecting data randomly from numerous sources. An assortment of data limits the exposure of the data to prejudice, thus ensuring accurate outcomes.

5. Machine Learning Algorithms do not collaborate

Despite numerous improvements in machine learning, the systems continue to show an inability to generalize factors within their environment. That is to say that those machines fail to apply the knowledge in different cases. The models of machine learning find transferring experience from one problem to the other a challenge. Machine learning algorithms can only perform a task they have trained to do. As a result of this limitation, many users are forced to put their resources in training different algorithms to perform various tasks. A situation that requires a lot of investments.

To solve this problem, users and developers need to learn how to transfer training. Transfer learning means that a model is fed with input data that reflects a possible problem and other related problems. From this process, the know-how acquired from solving one problem can be used for a similar problem without further training.

Points to note on the benefits and limitations of Machine Learning

The above-mentioned hits and misses of machine learning do not portray the general scope of the process. It is worth noting that different methods are used to build and train the algorithms. The pros and cons all depend on the techniques in which the models are developed, deployed and trained. Additionally, the limitations of machine learning rely on the problems to be solved and the software that they are built-in. Lastly, it is essential to note that the wins and losses are dependent on the quality of input data.

Conclusion

The last couples of years have witnessed amazing breakthroughs in the field of artificial intelligence and its branch; machine learning. In this era, machines can learn and act like humans while performing various tasks. The innovations in machine learning have enabled experts to build tools that can mimic multi-dimensional functions such as making decisions, reasoning deductively and making inferences. Robotics is no longer considered science fiction. The reality in the ground is that the concept of machine learning has evolved to an unimaginable extent. Today, human society is more dependent on the complement of machines in making decisions and solving their daily problems. Multiple industries have embraced the incorporations of intelligent machines in their production practices. As indicated in the chapters above, machine learning application has become a part of human life. And as Sundar Pichai would put it, the use of machine learning in human life is more intense than electricity and fire.

However, it is good to understand that these uses have evolved to cover deep learning and other areas of artificial intelligence completely. The coverage has enabled algorithms to perform complex tasks with noteworthy inferences for the way production methods are run, giving results in the least possible time. In all the buildup that surrounds this fantastic field of technological study, the integrity that gets lost is that machine learning, like any other field, has its limitations. Machine learning technology requires considerable effort to overcome the hurdles and advance in scope. My opinion, therefore, is that my readers should try the different models and note the ones suitable for their course. For academic purposes, learners should juggle books that touch on basics of all branches of artificial intelligence.

Python Machine Learning

A Hands-On Beginner's Guide to Effectively Understand Artificial Neural Networks and Machine Learning Using Python (With Tips and Tricks)

Introduction

We are living in a world where technology has become a primary preoccupation every day. Many industries and organizations across the universe are trying what they can so that they end up improving their production. It is because of this and other reasons that they decided to employ new techniques within the industries. New technologies, such as the introduction of Machine Learning, usage of robots, deploying of drones among others came into being. However, for many years, the rate of production in terms of data input and information output was still low. Going by this, they would look for that type of machine that could enable them to predict their outcome using the features variables that they had by then. Remember, being in a position to know the result of a specific task within the organization even before they could perform a particular task motivated them. Sadly, some types of methods used in data prediction proved to be wrong while few gave out the expected results. At one point, their data lacked enough accuracy, and some were vague, while others you could not read and interpret. Due to all these, many scientists thronged the internet and technological libraries so that they could come up with something tangible to solve the current predicament of solving the workload within the industries.

Therefore, you need to understand or comprehend why Machine Learning was the most convenient way to solve many burning issues within their labor sectors. There are several cases where human beings were only dealing with the mathematical concept of the companies' accounts in a manual way. However, this was inconvenient since many organization or industries involved huge workload that could not be done by human beings. Cases of tiredness and lack of enough knowledge to perform every task of prediction became rampant.

Therefore, Machine Learning which was fully deployed refers to a situation where some specific tasks were solved using simple algorithms and some statistical models. Machine Learning relies mostly on the inference and some patterns. To some, this is artificial intelligence while others based their belief on the mathematical models that had sample data which they later refer to as "training data." The process became more manageable as this machine could make some decisions within the organization using the data available. Later on, the organization used the algorithms from machine learning to cater to the needs of the company. Up-to-date, computer vision, and even issues to do with email filtering uses algorithms from machine learning. As a result, several organizations had to realize the improved work rate, which led to high output at the end.

Many studies show that machine learning relates to some sorts of statistics, especially those from the computer. That's computational statistics. However, it is good to note that this focuses only on using computers to make much--needed decisions and predictions. Some aspects of machine learning enable it to perform its function accordingly. Examples of these are mathematical optimization which only involves application domains, uses of theory, and even different methods that make the machine learning work better. Another aspect is data mining. Many studies show that data mining relates to field study work, mainly within machine learning. Its main objective is to help in the analysis of data. In most cases, many businesses employ machine learning for predictive analytics purposes.

Chapter 1: Introduction: A Historical Overview of Machine Learning

Machine Learning came into limelight in 1959, and this happened with the help of American pioneers. Arthur Samuel, who spent much of his time in computer gaming, came up with the initial term of machine learning. During this time, machine learning became part and parcel of scientific endeavour. Later on, it widespread as the need for artificial intelligence grew. Many people, especially the researchers, got much interest in it to the extent of deploying machine learning in getting some data. At this point, the researchers had no option but to fully implement all the means at their disposal to get the required results. They ended up using perceptrons even though this was later seen as an application of linear models. Still, on this, they also deployed the probabilistic reasoning, especially in the automation of the medical diagnosis. Fortunately, this automated technique seemed to work better, thus improving their work in medical sectors.

However, issues with increased logical and an approach which depended much on knowledge caused a technological war between the Machine Learning and AI. In this juncture, you realize that the probabilistic system could not perform it's tasking as intended. That's, they had problematic issues about practical and theoretical, especially when it came to data representation and even acquisitions.

As the AI came into a great halt, the industry was left with nothing to solve their workload and heavy tasks. As a result, machine learning started flourishing again. That's, in the 1990s. It then changed its objective or goal from achieving intelligence deemed to be artificial to tackling problems mainly from practical nature. Its focus shifted. In that, the symbolic approaches came to cease. It acquired the probability theory and use of statistical models. Machine learning, later on, benefited from the digitized information and the easy way of internet distribution. Therefore, internet distribution created a transferable mode through which many scientists could use to get the machine learning. Remember, with the partial death of the AI, and Machine Learning became part and parcel of every industry. In that, many scientists and several organizations could not afford to miss it. Its usage increased as many people involved it in all kinds of data predictions.

The Evolutionary Perspective of Machine Learning

Machine learning passed through several stages to reach where it is today. The steps marked with improved technology and natural problem solving. In addition to this, the level of accuracy in output predictions increases. However, this was still below what the scientists and most organizations required. Also, the rate of solving and acquiring data became much more manageable but with few cases of inaccuracy within the output data. It is because of this that the urge to improve on the features of machine learning came to be. Therefore, all these lead to the ultimate birth of evolution.

The first stage was a game of checkers and machine learning. Here, Arthur Samuel came up with a computer program which he could use to play checkers. He induced alpha-beta pruning to cater for the less memory within the gadget. This knowledge could predict which chances of winning in the game of checkers. In the end, this resulted in a minimax algorithm. He, later on, went with his designation to improve his machine.

The next phase of evolution was the Perceptron. Frank Rosenblatt came up with this model. It was a combination of machine learning and brain cells model. It is good to note that brain cell model was the work of Donald Hebb. Frank, who used to work in the laboratory of

Cornell Aeronautical, came up with this Perceptron at a time when industries were lacking ways to solve some statistical data and analysis. He planned to do his work, that's, Perceptron a machine and not anything to do with a program. Perceptron uses Mark 1 perceptron for recognition of the image. As a result, the transferring of the software and the machine became even more accessible. According to him, this was the most successful machine. Also, though this was successful, some aspects lacked solutions. That's, the device was unable to recognize visual patterns. As a result, many scientists and computers programmers went into another research. However, their struggle continues until the 1990s where they managed to come up with another problem-solving machine.

Therefore, the continued research led to the birth of another algorithm called The Nearest Neighbor.

In his work, Marcello Pelillo realized that he could easily recognize the patterns. Another main objective of this algorithm was to map routes. The usage of this program was beneficial as salespersons could use it to enter into different cities. They also used it to find the best efficient way during their day to day travel. Even though this discovery was helpful, there are some situations that it failed to tackle. As a result, it was leading to the ultimate birth of multilayers. Multilayers came into limelight in the 1960s and went ahead to improve that research of neural network. The double usage of layers increased the processing power of Perceptron, thus making it more efficient. Again, the introduction of multilayers led to the development of backpropagation. The main task of backpropagation was to solve any errors within the system. It used a principle of spreading these errors backward so that solving them may not be difficult. It is now being applied in many sectors of industry such as a neural network. It is also good to note that this system came to be in the 1970s.

Backpropagation led to the development of the Artificial Neural Network. Here, this machine could solve more complex tasks that Perceptron couldn't undertake. It involves the usage of input data which transformed into output information. The jobs here are complex, and human beings could find them difficult to tackle.

In the 1970s and some parts of 1980s, algorithms came to cease. Artificial intelligence started using logical approaches in solving its tasks. Again, there was an abandonment of some research, such as a neural network. In the end, a schism evolved between the two large bodies. That's machine learning and artificial intelligence leading to their separation. Later on, the machine learning struggled for almost ten years after its reorganization. Here, its goals moved from artificial intelligence training to provisions of services. Again, its focus led to the development of probability theories and some elements of statistics. The flourishing of machine learning came to being in the 1990s, where it was able to concentrate on the neural network. However, internet growth played a significant role in the success of this.

The next evolution involves boosting and boosting reduced bias within the data used. It deployed the use of machine learning algorithm where the transformation of weak learners into strong learners occurs. In his finding, he deduced that a set of weak learners could make one stronger learner. Machine learning has undergone many evolutions.

Examples of these evolutions may include speech recognition and much more. Therefore, it is also good to note the benefits of the machine in our daily lives.

- It helps in analyzing data, especially sales data, within the industry.

- It promotes mobile personalization

- It helps in detecting fraud

- It helps in making a recommendation about a specific product.

- It leads to proper learning management.

- It promotes dynamic pricing, thus increasing flexibility in pricing.

- It also helps in the processing of natural language. That's, you can speak with humans.

Chapter 2: Types Of Machine Learning

In a world soaked in artificial intelligence, it is interesting to understand machine learning in depth. This is a concept that allows an algorithm to perform specific tasks without relying on any explicit instructions. Instead, the machine relies on inference and patterns such that the user feeds data to a generic algorithm rather than writing the code. In response, the machine constructs the logic based on the input data. Usually, the accuracy of the prediction made by the algorithm is evaluated and the algorithm only gets deployed when the precision is acceptable.

Types of Machine Learning

There are three broad categories of machine learning. We will discuss each of them in detail below.

1. *Supervised Learning*

    This paradigm happens to be the most popular, probably because it is easy to comprehend and execute. Here, the algorithm creates a mathematical concept from a labeled dataset, i.e a dataset containing both the input and output parameters. This dataset acts as a trainer to the model. Taking an example, we may decide to use the algorithm to determine whether a particular image contains a certain object. In this case, the dataset would comprise images with and without the input (that object), with every image having the output designating whether or not it contains the particular object. The algorithm is likely to predict any answer; whether right or wrong. However, after several attempts it gets trained on picking only the images containing the said object. Once it gets totally trained, the algorithm starts making right predictions even when new data is input. A perfect example of a supervised learning model is a support vector machine. On the diagram below, the support vector machine divides data into sections separated by a linear boundary. You realize the boundary separates the white circles from the black.

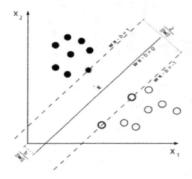

Types of Supervised Learning

- **Classification**: These algorithms are used in instances where the outputs are limited to discrete values. In the case of filtering emails for example, an incoming mail would be classified as the input, whereas the output would be the folder name.
- **Regression**: This is the algorithm under which the output has a continuous value, which means they many pick on any value within a given range. Perfect examples include; temperature, wind speed, price of a commodity etc.

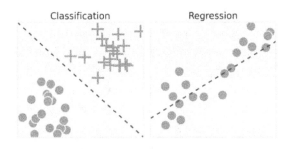

Supervised machine learning is exhibited in many common applications, some of which we have discussed below.

- ➤ **Advertisement Status**: Most of the ads that you encounter when browsing the internet are positioned there because a supervised learning algorithm vouched for their clickability and popularity.
- ➤ **Face Recognition**: This one is quite common on Facebook. It is very likely that your face has been used in a supervised algorithm that is trained to recognize it. When Facebook is suggesting a tag you must have noted that the system guesses the persons on the photo, which is a supervised process.
- ➤ **Spam Classification**: The spam filter that you find on your modern email system is a supervised learning concept. Apart from preemptively filtering spiteful emails, the system also allows the user to provide new labels and express their preference. See the illustration on the figure below.

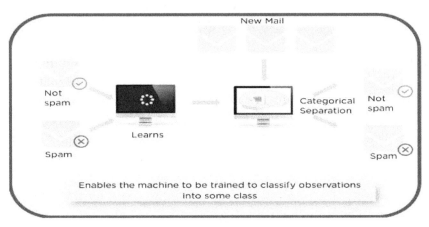

2. *Unsupervised Learning*

As the name suggests, unsupervised machine learning is the exact opposite of supervised learning. The model finds structures in the data and also learns through observation. When given a dataset, the model automatically finds relationships and patterns by creating clusters in the dataset. The paradigm cannot add labels to the created cluster, but it does the creation perfectly. This means that if we have a set of apples and oranges, the model will separate the apples from the oranges, but will not say that this is a set of oranges or apples.

Now, suppose we had more than two sets, say we present images of grapes, oranges, and apples. As explained above, the model, based on some relationships and patterns, will create clusters and separate the datasets into those clusters. Whenever new data is input, the model adds it to one of the already built clusters as shown in the figure below. You realize the output is grouped perfectly even without addition of labels.

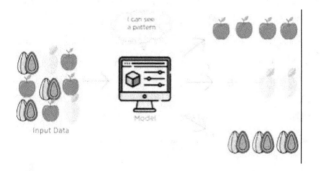

Input Data   Model

Let us take another classical example for better understanding. Think of a little baby and his family dog. He very well identifies its features. When a family friend brings along another dog to try play with the baby, the baby will identify that as a dog even without anyone telling them. They will easily classify it because it has the features like two eyes, ears, walks on four, among other details. This falls under unsupervised learning because you classify the input data without being taught. If it were supervised learning, the family friend would have to tell the baby that it's a dog.

Types of Unsupervised Learning

- **Clustering:** This concept identifies a pattern in an assortment of unclassified data. Clustering algorithms categorize any existing natural groups in the data. The user is also at liberty to adjust the number of cluster they want their algorithms to identify. Under clustering there are more types that you can utilize;
  - ❖ **Exclusive (partitioning)**
    Under this type, classification of data is done such that one data can only belong to a single only. K-means serves as a perfect example.
  - ❖ **Agglomerative**
    This is the technique where every data is in itself a group. The number of clusters is reduced by the iterative mergers between the two closest groups. An example is the hierarchical clustering.
  - ❖ **Overlapping**
    Under this technique, data is associated with a suitable association value. Fuzzy sets are used in grouping data and each point could fit into two or more groups with different membership degrees. Fuzzy C-Means is a suitable example under this type.
  - ❖ **Probabilistic**
    This concept creates clusters using probability distribution. See the example below given some keywords;
    - o "Men's pants"
    - o "Ladies' pants"
    - o "Men's wallets"
    - o "Ladies' wallets"

    The given keywords could be grouped into two; "pants" and "wallets" or "Men" and "Ladies".

385

- **Association**

  The rules under association allow the user to institute associations in the midst of data objects inside big databases. As the name suggests, the technique seeks to discover unique relations between variables contained in large databases. For instance, shoppers could be grouped based on their search and purchase histories.

Applications of Unsupervised Machine Learning

Unsupervised ML is based on data and its attributes, and Therefore, we can conclude that it is data-driven. The results from a task are controlled by the nature in which the data is formatted. Some of the common areas that rely on unsupervised learning include but are not limited to;

- ➤ **Buying Habits:** It is not surprising to find your purchasing habits stored in a database somewhere. The information could be used by marketers to group clients into similar shopping segments so that they can reach out to them easily. The clustering is easy to do under unsupervised learning algorithms.
- ➤ **Recommender Systems:** If you are a Netflix or YouTube user you might have encountered a video recommendation severally. Often times these systems are contained in the unsupervised domain. The system knows the watch history of its users. The model uses the history to identify relationships between users who enjoy watching videos of certain genres, length, etc, and prompt them with a suggestion of related videos that they may not have watched.
- ➤ **Identification of Fraudulent transactions:** Anomaly detection is the technique used in discovery of abnormal data points. The algorithm picks out any unusual points within the data set, hence sending an alarm.

Supervised Vs. Unsupervised ML Techniques

Data specialists employ an array of machine algorithms in their discovery operations. Below are some insights on the classification of supervised and unsupervised learning techniques, which will help you to judge when to use either of the techniques.

Parameters	Supervised machine learning	Unsupervised machine learning
Data usage	Employs training data to study the link between the input and output.	Does not use output data.
Accuracy of the outcome	Highly accurate reliable.	Less accurate and Therefore, not trustworthy
Input data	Labeled data is used in training the algorithms.	Algorithms are used against unlabeled data.
Number of classes	Known number of classes.	Unknown number of classes.
Major drawback	Classification of big data.	Failure to get precise information concerning output and data sorting due to use of labeled and unknown data.
Real time learning	Learning takes place offline.	Learning happens in real time.
Process	Both input and output variables are given.	Only the input data is given.
Computational complexity	Relatively simple; less complex.	Complex in terms of computation.

Deciding to employ a supervised or unsupervised machine learning algorithm classically depends on your data volume and structure.

Essentially, a well-formed data science plan will employ both algorithm types to come up with predictive data models. Now, these models are more advanced and help the stakeholders in decision-making across a variety of business hold ups.

3. *Reinforcement Learning*

This is a neural network learning technique that trains machine learning concepts how to make a progression of decisions. The agent is trained how to attain their objective in an indecisive, potentially complex environment. In this technique, an artificial intelligence engages into a game-like situation and the computer tries to solve the problem using trial and error method. For the programmer to get the machine to do what they want, the artificial intelligence gets penalized or rewarded for the actions performed. The idea is to fully exploit the total reward.

Usually there is a reward policy in form of game rules, but the designer does not give any hints on how the model should solve the puzzle. The model starts from completely random trials and advances to sophisticated approaches and even superhuman skills. In the process, this technique leverages the full power of search, hence qualifying to be the most effectual in hinting machine's creativity. As opposed to humans, artificial intelligence can employ a reinforcement algorithm to collect experience from thousands parallel gameplays as long as it is run on an adequately powerful computer infrastructure.

Let us look at a practical example that will perfectly illustrate the reinforcement learning technique. However, before then we need to understand some terms that we will use in the illustration.

- **Agent:** This is an implicit entity that seeks to gain a reward by performing actions in an environment.
- **Environment (e):** A situation that an agent must face.
- **Reward (R):** An instant response given to an agent on performing a specific action.
- **State (s):** The current scenario returned by the environment.

388

- **Policy (π):** An approach employed by the agent to determine their next action based on the prevailing state.
- **Value (V):** The projected long-term return, which is discounted comparing with the short-lived reward.
- **Value Function:** This one stipulates the total reward, i.e, the value of a state.
- **Model based methods:** Handles the reinforcement learning-based problems that apply model-based techniques.
- **Model of the environment:** It imitates the behavior of the environment, helping you draw conclusions regarding environment behavior.
- **Action value / Q value (Q):** This is not very different from value. In fact, the only variation is that this one takes an extra parameter as a current action.

Illustration

Think of trying to teach your dog some new tricks. This dog does not understand human language so you need to devise a strategy that will help you achieve your goal. You will initiate a situation and observe the various reactions by your dog. If the dog responds in the desired way, you give him some beef. You will realize that every time you expose the dog to a similar condition, they will tend to respond with greater enthusiasm hoping to get a reward (the beef). It means that the positive experiences inspire the responses your dog gives. As well, there are the negative experiences that teach the dog what not to do because should they do it, then they will certainly miss their share of beef.

In the given paradigm, your dog is an agent exposed to the environment. You may decide to have your situation as requiring your sitting dog to walk when you utter a particular word. This agent responds by performing an action where they transition from one state to another, like transitioning from sitting to walking. In this case, the policy is a process of choosing an action given a state with the expectation of better results. After transitioning, the agent may get a penalty or a reward in response.

Reinforcement Learning Algorithms
There are three techniques in implementation of a reinforcement learning algorithm.

i. **Value-based:** here, the agent is anticipating a long-term return of the prevailing states under policy and so you ought to maximize the value function.

ii. **Policy-based:** under this RL scheme you endeavor to find a policy such that the action executed in each state leads to maximal reward in the future.

Policy-based method is further classified into deterministic, where the policy produces the same action for any state, and stochastic, where every action has a definite probability determined by the stochastic policy. The stochastic policy is n{a\s} = P\A, = a\S, =S]

iii. **Model-based:** in this case you are expected to generate a virtual model for every environment, where the agent learns how to perform in that very environment.

Types of Reinforcement Learning

i. Positive
This is an event triggered by specific behavior. It positively influences the action taken by the agent. This happens through enhancing the frequency and strength of the behavior. This method helps you to capitalize on performance and sustain change for a longer period. Even so, you have to be careful as over-reinforcement may cause state over-optimization and impinge on the results.

ii. Negative
It involves strengthening behavior prompted by a negative condition which should have been dodged or stopped. Although it helps define the least stand performance, this method provides adequate to meet up the minimum behavior, which is a drawback.

Applications of RL in Real Life

- ➢ Data processing and machine learning.
- ➢ Planning of business strategy.
- ➢ Robotics for industrial computerization.
- ➢ Aircraft and robot motion management.
- ➢ Helps in creation of customized training systems for students.

Summary

- Data used in unsupervised learning is labeled and unknown, and Therefore, you cannot get accurate information concerning data sorting.
- When moving from image to image you will have varied information because the spectral properties of classes are also likely to change over time.
- Unsupervised machine learning locates all unknown types of unidentified patterns in the data.
- The user has to dedicate time to label and interpret the classes which follow a particular classification.
- The major downside of unsupervised learning is the failure to get accurate information in regard to data sorting.
- Reinforcement learning is a machine learning method with three algorithms; 1) value-based, 2) policy-based and 3) model based.
- The two types of reinforcement learning are 1) positive and 2) negative.
- RL should not be used for problem-solving when you have adequate data.
- The major RL method drawback is that learning speed may be affected by parameters.

Chapter 3: Use of Python in Machine Learning

Machine learning and associated technologies such as artificial intelligence (AI) are the technologies for the present and future. In a world that is increasingly aggregated towards more personalized gadgets and machines with improved and technical functionalities, tech companies and innovators are on the overdrive, researching, developing and testing the innovative technologies of the future. These technologies are aimed at revolutionizing the human experience while also cementing the place of machines especially computers as the primary drivers of all spheres of human life. While seemingly dedicated to meeting the ever-changing human demand technology and hence, user experience, these companies and individuals are also seeking to develop technologies that can increase their bottom line. These new technologies not only use huge of data to execute complex processes that cannot be accomplished manually, they are also come with increased accuracy and efficiency. They can also analyze data patterns to make predictions and come with solutions to problems beforehand. Essentially, machine learning and AI are premised on turning the numerous scientific fictions of the past decades into reality.

However, AI technology comes with the added disadvantage of collecting and analyzing large volume of data to process in order to execute these complex processes. Additionally, bringing science fiction to life also require skill sets in programming, creativity, conceptualization, ideation, and analysis. But most importantly, it requires the right programming language that is easier to understand and flexible to work with. The last thing you need as a programmer writing the algorithms for the next game changer technology that would transform human experiences is being stack with a programming language that is inflexible and incapable of handling data complexity. This can easily lead to error in the coding of the machine's program or applications. A code error can lead to embarrassing situations for developers as exemplified in the 2016 case involving Microsoft's chat box which malfunctioned and resorted to communicating misogynistic messages to the millennials instead of the intended happy and positive themed messages. Amazon, the world's leading online retailer also suffered a reputational damage in 2014 when its AI machine designed for talent recruitment turned in a discriminative tool that singled out female applicants. These are just a few cases involving well-established tech giants whose Machine Learning and AI algorithms were erratic due programming issues.

Python and AI and ML
Training a computer to possess human-like ability of learning and making predictions without continuous specific process-based programming can be daunting task without the right programming language. By eliminating the need for explicit programming, a program developer would then need to feed the computer the right training data what the computer will use as a point of reference, more like a library to learn from. This is one of the primary points of departures between traditional and non-traditional programming projects such as IA or machine learning. Using the training data, a programmer will be able to develop a software using numerous lines of codes to create the desired algorithms for the machine. However, such complex project require a mastery of statistics and mathematical optimization to achieve the best result: an algorithm free of coding errors which can lead to machine malfunctioning. Additionally, a

393

programmer should also understand the concept of probability to ensure that the developed algorithms are capable of making predictions which one of the primary functional capabilities of machines equipped with AI capabilities.

To facilitate the execution of such complex programming tasks, Python, a programming language conceived by the software engineering guru Guido van Rossum, is equipped with various libraries or modules. These modules come in handy for programmers when coding as they have inbuilt code pieces that are already written. Programmers can use these pre-written codes as the backbone of the algorithms they are aiming to write for a specific project. With a pre-existing code, a programmer has the jumpstart to develop even complex algorithms that artificial intelligence-based technologies require. This is because the codes that comes with the programming language modules have level items that support basic functionalities. They also act as launch pads for the next set of coding actions thereby eliminating the need for starting afresh any programming project.

Python's extensive library ecosystem includes: Scikit-learn, Seaborn, NumPy, and Pandas. Others include Keras and SciPy. These sets of library are specialized for different tasks during the development of algorithms for AI and machine learning. For example, Seaborn module is primarily used for coding tasks involving visualization of training data to be used in machine learning. This includes exploration of data with the view of plotting statistical patterns. It is from these patterns that machines use their AI to project scenarios.

On the other hand, Pandas is readily the most popular set of library among programmers using Python language because of its functional versatility. The module is suitable for all forms of coding-related data analysis. As an object-oriented language, Python relies heavily on analysis and interpretation of these data during coding to develop algorithms that the machine can learn from and use the knowledge to make predictions. This is why SciPy and NumPy are the most important Python libraries. The bulk of Python programming-related projects use these two libraries. NumPy lacks the general-purpose nature of Pandas even though it is also used for analyzing coding data. However, it is most suitable in analyzing high-performance data.

Scikit-learn library is the most flexible of all these modules and plays an important role in the overall simplicity, flexibility, and versatility of Python as a programming language. It can be easily integrated with other modules such as NumPy and SciPy to achieve greater coding success. Programmers using Scikit-learn library will find it easy to implement tasks during coding as this will take only a few lines to accomplish. Such functional simplicity in task implementation is because Scikit-learn is compatible with unsupervised and supervised algorithms, a variety in algorithms that machine learning and AI rely on to achieve functional autonomy. Therefore, coding that involves probability testing, mathematical optimization and statistics such as regressions, decision trees, and k-means are easily executed using Scikit-learn library set.

Basics of Using Python Modules in Machine Learning Projects

The first step towards developing algorithms for your machine learning project using Python programming language is problem identification. Programming for machine learning is a targeted undertaking aimed at tackling a specific problem. Therefore, when fully defined, a problem will help the programmer in developing the parameters of the algorithm and the data set to be collected. Defining a problem directs the whole coding process. It will determine what kind of predictions that machine will be able to make as well as identifying its functional integrity. That is, identifying the integrity of the algorithm and the program used by the machine.

Secondly, determine whether your version comes with or without prebundled modules. Python's anaconda and miniconda packages usually come with the fundamental module: SciPy Libraries. Upon installation, SciPy libraries come with preinstalled modules such as NumPy, Scikit-learn, Pandas and SciPy among others. In case the Python package does not come with SciPy libraries, download the library and instill it. For prebundled packages, use the cmd command and type the specific name of the module to install. Always make sure that your versions of the bundles are updated. Using the latest version of modules will allow the programmer to access new and better features that improves the integrity of their software or applications.

After installing and updating Python and the modules, import all the relevant objects and modules that will be required during the coding process. The type of libraries imported is dependent on the dataset and the functional capability that the algorithms are projected to achieve. This should be followed by loading the dataset to be used for machine learning from the relevant source suing the Pandas modules. The loaded training data should be prepared appropriately to meet the project needs. It should be large enough to improve the accuracy of the predictions of the machine. Adding randomness links to your training dataset will improve the machine's ability to make predictions. In case you are using a hosted version of the dataset due unreliability issues, it is always advisable to include a link to it. This will reduce cases of coding errors as a result of using redundant dataset.

A dataset summary will give the programmer insights on his or her dataset dimensions including classes and attributes such as number of data columns. Additionally, it shows a brief overview of the dataset. A programmer also has the chance to discern the various statistical attributes associated with the data they are using for coding. After summarizing, it is advisable to visualize the dataset using either univariate or multivariate plots. Plotting allows a programmer to have a greater understating of the relationships between the various variables within the dataset to be used in developing algorithms for the machine. Data visualization is done using Pandas libraries which has different options for visualization including scatterplots and distribution graphs. Testing the dataset using models and a validation dataset before developing the final algorithms for machine learning is very important. Validation dataset will act as your point of references whenever you are using the algorithms to predict unseen dataset. Moreover, it also act as a starting for any further changes and improvements you will need to make on the algorithms; it eliminates the need to start all over again in case of coding error.

Benefits of Using Python in M.L. and A.I.

One of the reasons behind Python's growing popularity as a programming language of choice for many programmers is its relatively large library ecosystem. Python's library ecosystem is comprised of numerous modules and extensions that support the implementation of a wide range of coding tasks including data analysis and visualization among others. From Pandas to SciPy, NumPy and Keras, Python has a wide range of libraries that gives it the versatility needed to code even for complex algorithms.

It also boasts of simple syntaxes and semantics that are easy to follow and use. They have a math-like characters which make them easier to familiarize with when coding. This makes coding with Python easier and less technical. Mastering basic coding using Python does not require technical knowhow. This makes coding preferable among basic users as opposed to other mainstream programming languages such as Java and C. It is also a general-purpose language that makes it easy to use to developing a wide range of algorithms for machine learning.

Summary

The past few decades has been marked by a radical transformation in the tech world with new inventions being churned out from production conveyor belts of individual and corporate entities. The dawn of a new era marked by complex machines and megadata is upon us. Machines equipped with artificial intelligence are increasingly being incorporated into almost all spheres of human life. These machines are capable of high performance and execution of very technical and complex tasks that are impossible to complete manually. They also achieve such performances with a high level of accuracy and autonomy from human. This is the era of artificial intelligence and machine learning. Despite the apparent maturity and age of machine learning, it's perhaps the best time to learn it, primarily because of its practical uses. And Python is probably the best programming language that can help you excel in your career in this field. With a robust understanding of fundamental machine learning and Python skills, you should be all set to dive deeper. Just remember the fact that as with learning any skill, the more you work with it, the better you become. Practicing with diverse types of algorithms and trying to work with different datasets obtains a solid understanding of machine learning using Python, and enhances your overall problem-solving skills in event space.

Chapter 4: Essential Libraries For ML In Python

Many developers nowadays prefer the usage of python in their data analysis. Python is not only applied in data analysis but also statistical techniques. Scientists, especially the ones dealing with data, also prefer using python in data integration. That's the integration of Webb apps and other environment productions.

The features of python have helped scientists to use it in machine learning. Examples of these qualities include consistent syntax, being flexible and even having a shorter time in development. It also has that ability to develop sophisticated models and has engines that could help in predictions.

As a result, python boasts of having a series or set of very extensive libraries. Remember, libraries refer to a series of routines and sorts of functions with different languages. Therefore, a robust library can lead to tackling of more complex tasks. However, this is possible without writing several code lines again. It is good to note that machine learning relies majorly on mathematics. That's mathematical optimization, elements of probability and also statistical data. Therefore, python comes in with a rich knowledge of performing complex tasks without much involvement.

The following are examples of essential libraries being used in our present.

Scikit – Learn

Scikit learn is one of the best and a trendy library in machine learning. It has that ability to supporting learning algorithms, especially the unsupervised and supervised ones.

Examples of Scikit learn include the following.

❖ k-means
❖ decision trees
❖ linear and logistic regressions and also
❖ clustering

This kind of library has major components from NumPy and SciPy. Scikit learn has the power to add algorithms sets which are useful in machine learning and also tasks related to data mining. That's, it helps in classification, clustering, and even regression analysis. There are also other tasks that this library can efficiently deliver. A good example includes ensemble methods, feature selection, and more so, data transformation. It is good to understand that the pioneers or experts can easily apply this if at all, they can be able to implement the complex and sophisticated parts of the algorithms.

TensorFlow

It is a form of algorithm which involves deep learning. They are not always necessary, but one good thing about them is their ability to give out correct results when done right. It will also enable you to run your data in a CPU or GPU. That's, you can write data in the python program, compile it then run it on your central processing unit. Therefore, this gives you an easy time in performing your analysis. Again, there is no need for having these pieces of information written at C++ or instead of other levels such as CUDA.

TensorFlow uses nodes, especially the multi-layered ones. The nodes perform several tasks within the system, which include employing networks such as artificial neutral, training, and even set up a high volume of datasets. Several search engines such as Google depend on this type of library. One main application of this is the identification of objects. Again, it helps in different Apps which deal with the recognition of voice.

Theano

Theano too forms a significant part of python library. Its vital tasks here are to help with anything related to numerical computation. We can also relate it to NumPy. It plays other roles such as;

- ❖ Definition of mathematical expressions
- ❖ Assists in the optimization of mathematical calculation
- ❖ Promotes the evaluation of expressions related to numerical analysis.

The main objective of Theano is to give out efficient results. It is a more fast python library as it can perform calculations of intensive data up to 100 times. Therefore, it is good to note that Theano works best with GPU as compared to the CPU of a computer. In most industries, the CEO and other personnel use theano for deep learning. Also, they use it for computing complex and sophisticated tasks. All these became possible due to its processing speed. Due to the expansion of industries with a high demand for data computation techniques, many people are opting for the latest version of this library. Remember, the latest one came to limelight some years back. The new version of Theano, that's, version 1.0.0, had several improvements, interface changes and composed of new features.

Pandas

Pandas is a library which is very popular and helps in the provisions of data structures which are of high level and quality. The data provided here is simple and easy to use. Again, it's intuitive. It is composed of various sophisticated inbuilt methods which make it capable of performing tasks such as grouping and timing analysis. Another function is that it helps in a combination of data and also offering filtering options. Pandas can collect data from other sources such as Excel, CSV, and even SQL databases. It also can manipulate the collected data to undertake its operational roles within the industries.

Pandas consist of two structures that enable it to perform its functions correctly. That's Series which has only one dimensional and data frames which boast of two dimensional. Pandas has been regarded as the most strong and powerful python library over the time being. Its main function is to help in data manipulation. Also, it has the power to export or import a wide range of data. It is applicable in various sectors, such as in the field of data science.

Pandas is effective in the following areas:

- ❖ Splitting of data
- ❖ Merging of two or more types of data
- ❖ Aggregating of data
- ❖ Selecting or subsetting of data and
- ❖ Data reshaping.

Diagrammatic explanations
Series Dimensional
SERIES

A	7
B	8
C	9
D	3
E	6
F	9

Data Frames dimensional
DATA FRAME

	A	B	C	D
*0	0	0	0	0
*1	7	8	9	3
*2	14	16	18	6
*3	21	24	27	9
*4	28	32	36	12
*5	35	40	45	15

Applications of pandas in a real-life situation will enable you to perform the following:

- ❖ You can quickly delete some columns or even add some texts found within the Dataframe
- ❖ It will help you in data conversion
- ❖ Pandas can reassure you of getting the misplaced or missing data
- ❖ It has a powerful ability, especially in the grouping of other programs according to their functionality.

Matplotlib

This is another sophisticated and helpful data analysis technique that helps in data visualization. Its main objective is to advise the industry where it stands using the various inputs. You will realize that your production goals are meaningless when you fail to share them with different stakeholders. To perform this, Matplotlib comes in handy with the types of computation analysis required. Therefore, it is the only python library that every scientist, especially the ones dealing with data prefers. This type of library has good looks when it comes to graphics and images. More so, many prefer using it in creating various graphs for data analyzation. However, the technological world has completely changed with new advanced libraries flooding the industry. It is also flexible, and due to this, you are capable of making several graphs that you may need. It only requires a few commands to perform this.

In this python library, you can create various diverse graphs, charts of all kinds, several histograms, and even scatterplots. You can also make non- Cartesian charts too using the same principle.

Diagrammatic explanations

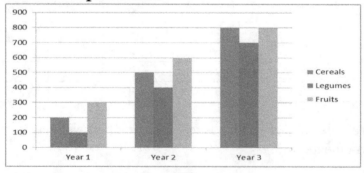

The above graph highlights the overall production of a company within three years. It specifically demonstrates the usage of Matplotlib in data analysis. By looking at the diagram, you will realize that the production was high as compared to the other two years. Again, the company tends to perform in the production of fruits since it was leading in both year 1 and 2 with a tie in year 3. From the figure, you realize that your work of presentation, representation and even analyzation has been made easier as a result of using this library. This python library will eventually enable you to come up with good graphics images, accurate data and much more. With the help of this python library, you will be able to note down the year your production was high, thus, being in a position to maintain the high productivity season.

It is good to note that this library can export graphics and can change these graphics into PDF, GIF, and so on. In summary on this library, the following tasks can be undertaken with much ease. They include:

- ❖ Formation of line plots
- ❖ Scattering of plots
- ❖ Creations of beautiful bar charts and building up of histograms
- ❖ Application of various pie charts within the industry
- ❖ Stemming the schemes for data analysis and computations
- ❖ Being bin a position to follow up contours plots
- ❖ Usage of spectrograms and lastly
- ❖ Quiver plots creation.

Seaborn

Seaborn is also among the popular libraries within the python category. Its main objective here is to help in visualization. It is important to note that this library borrows its foundation from Matplotlib. Due to its higher level, it is capable in various plots generation such as the production of heat maps, processing of violin plots and also helping in generation of time series plots.

403

Diagrammatic Illustrations

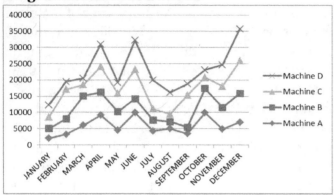

The above line graph clearly shows the performance of different machines the company is using. Following the diagram above, you can eventually deduce and make a conclusion on which machines the company can keep using to get the maximum yield. In most occasions, this evaluation method by the help of seaborn library will enable you to predict the exact abilities of your different inputs. Again, this information can actually help for future reference in the case of purchasing more machines. Seaborn library also has the power to detect the performance of other variable inputs within the company. For example, the number of workers within the company can be easily identified with their corresponding working rate.

NumPy

This is a very widely used python library. Its features enable it to perform multidimensional array processing. Also, it helps in the matrix processing. However, these are only possible with the help of an extensive collection of mathematical functions. It is important to note that this python library is highly useful in solving the most significant computations within the scientific sector. Again, NumPy is also applicable in areas such as linear algebra, derivation of random number abilities used within industries and more so Fourier transformation. NumPy is also used by other high-end python libraries such as TensorFlow for Tensors manipulation. In short, NumPy is mainly for calculations and data storage. You can also export or load data to Python since it has those features that enable it to perform these functions. It is also good to note that this python library is also known as numerical python.

SciPy

This is among the most popular library used in our industries today. It boasts of comprising of different modules which are applicable in the optimization sector of data analysis. It also plays a significant role in integration, linear algebra, and other forms of mathematical statistics. In many cases, it plays a vital role in image manipulation. Manipulation of the image is a process that's widely applicable in day to day activities. Cases of photoshops and much more are examples of SciPy. Again, many organizations prefer SciPy in their image manipulation, especially the pictures used for presentation. For instance, wildlife society can come up with the description of a cat then manipulate it using different colours to suit their project. Below is an example that can help you understand this in a more straightforward way.

The first picture above is an original image of a cat which the wildlife society took.

The above refers to the second picture, which has undergone manipulation. It is a tinted image of a cat. When you resize this image according to your preference, you will come up with the picture below.

Keras

This is also part and parcel of python library, especially within machine learning. It's also joining the group of networks with high level neural. It is significant to note that Keras has the capability of working over other libraries, especially TensorFlow and even Theano. Also, it can operate nonstop without mechanical failure. In addition to this, it seems to work better on both the GPU and CPU. For most beginners in the python programming, Keras offers a secure pathway towards their ultimate understanding. They will be in a position to design the network and even to build it. Its ability to prototype faster and more quickly makes it the best python library among the learners.

PyTorch

This is another accessible but open source kind of python library. As a result of its name, it boasts of having extensive choices when it comes to tools. It is also applicable in areas where we have computer vision. Computer vision and visual display play an essential role in several types of research. Again, it aids in the processing of Natural Language. More so, PyTorch has the abilities to undertake some technical tasks that are for developers. That's enormous calculations and data analysis using computations. It can also help in graph creation which mainly used for computational purposes. Since it is an open-source python library, it can work or perform tasks on other libraries such as Tensors. In combination with Tensors GPU, its acceleration will increase.

Scrapy

Scrapy is another library used for creating crawling programs. That's spider bots and much more. The spider bots frequently help in the data retrieval purposes and also applicable in the formation of URLs used in the web. From the beginning, it was to assist in data scrapping. However, this has undergone several evolutions and led to the expansions of its general purpose. Therefore, the main task of the scrappy library in our present-day is to act as crawlers for general use. The library led to the promotion of general usage, application of universal codes, and so on.

Statsmodels

Statsmodel is a library with the aim of data exploration using several methods of statistical computations and data assertions. It has many features such as result statistics and even characteristic feature. It can undertake this role by the help of the various models such as linear regression, multiple estimators, and analysis involving time series, and even using more linear models. Also, other models, such as discrete choice are applicable here.

Chapter 5: Regression Analysis (Linear Regression and Logistic Regression)

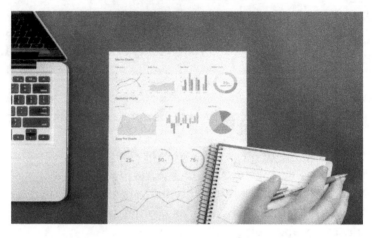

Several industries across the globe are struggling with the best way to come up with the correct data or information that will eventually enable them to solve their incurring prediction problems. Several banks have made some losses, especially within their credit section as they could not correctly predict the trustfulness of the defaulters. In the health sector, you realize many have lost their lives because of poor planning and risk management, which come as a result of the lack of modeling to tool for more straightforward prediction. We also have other sectors such as weather forecasting where farmers were not advised on the occurrence of rain, as a result leading to more losses. Another area involved the payment of mortgage by homeowners. Due to all these, everyone across the universe went on a rampage looking for the best possible way to handle the prediction roles of the organizations. Later on, all these gave birth to what is termed as regression analysis. Therefore, regression analysis refers to statistical processes for prediction analysis using variables. In that, it helps in identifying the variables relationships. This analysis consists of both independent and dependent variables. In other words, regression analysis aids in understanding the effect of one independent variable on the dependent variable when other independent variables are kept constant. In most cases, regression analysis will try hard to predict the conditional expectation, especially of the variable which is dependent. Regression analysis is applied in several areas such as weather forecasting and prediction. Here, it helps predict the outcome of the rain within a specific period. It is also applicable in other fields such as medical sectors for predicting chances of diseases. Regression analysis comprises of the following: linear regression, logistic regression, polynomial, stepwise, ridge, lasso, and elastic net regression. All in all, this chapter will only tackle the most widely used regression analysis, such as linear regression and logistic regression. It is good to note that ElasticNet regression is a combination of the Lasso and Ridge regression.

Logistics Regression

Logistic regression comprises of logistic model, logistic function, statistics model, and much more. Therefore, many organizations apply logistic regression in their day to day activities which mainly composed of data predictions and analysis. You can always conduct this regression analysis, especially when the dependent variable is binary. That's dichotomous.

Just like other types of regression analyses, logistic regression is entirely applied in any analysis dealing with prediction. Its primary function, in this case, is to describe data. Also, logistic regression can be used to explain or illustrate the kind of relationship between the binary variable, which is dependent and the rest variables which are independent. In some occasion, this regression might look challenging to interpret, but by the help of the logistic tools such as Intellectus Statistics, you can easily undertake your data analysis.

Logistic regression knowledge can be easily applied in statistics by the help of the logistic model. In this case, the primary function of the logistic model is actually to come up with the correct results of certain predictions or class by the help of probability. For example, probability works best in areas where you are only required to predict the outcome of the existing events. These events include: healthy or sick, win or lose, alive or dead, or even in places where you are making your analysis about the test where someone either fails or pass. Still, in this model, you will be able to fine-tune your result primarily through probability. In the case of an image, you will be able to extend your model to cover up various classes. You will be able to detect whether the image in your analysis is for a lion or a cat, and so on. In this case, the individual variable within the image will have their probability number between 0 and 1. However, the sum here should be adding up to one.

Therefore, logistic regression refers to a basic statistical model which makes greater use of the available logistic function regardless of the complexity of more extensions that might exist. Logistic regression is part and parcel of the regression analysis, and on many occasions, it is applied in various analyses where logistic model parameters are estimated. Remember, the logistic model is like a form or a type of binary regression. Therefore, a binary regression consists of a binary logistic model. This model is composed of a dependent variable which includes of two possible values of events. These values can be represented as pass/fail, alive/dead, good/bad, and much more. You need to note that the indicator variable actually denotes these possible values and always they have labeled 0 and 1. Within this logistic model, the odds logarithm that's log-odds, for the values of 1 represents a linear combination. In that, this combination has got one or more variables which are entirely independent. In this case, they are called predictors here.

Moreover, in logistic regression analysis, independent variables sometimes may each form a binary variable or sometimes a continuous variable. In the case of a binary variable, there must be the presence of two classes or event, and they have to be coded by the indicator variables. However, on the other hand, continuous variable represents real value. In the logistic regression analysis, the corresponding probability of these values always varies between 0 and 1 as has been denoted previously above. In this analysis, these log-odds, that's, algorithms of odds will be converted by logistic function into probability. Log odds are measured in logit which also a derivative of its name (logistic unit). Again, you can also use a probit model with a different sigmoid function to convert the log odds into a probability for easy analysis. You need to note that the probit model is an example of an analogous model which comprises of the sigmoid function.

All in all, you will realize that the logistic model is the most preferred in this conversion due to its defining attributes or characteristics. One such feature of the logistic model is its ability to increase the multiplicatively scales of each of the independent variables. As a result of this, it produces an outcome with parameters assigned to each independent variable at a constant rate. However, this will generalize the odd ratio if at all, it is part of a variable which is a binary dependent. It is also good to note that there are extensions when it comes to dependent variables, especially in some regression such as binary logistic. However, this extension is only applicable where two or more levels are used. These two extensions include multinomial logistic regression which works best with categorical outputs, especially the one having several values that's, two values and above. The next type of logistic regression extension is the ordinal logistic regression which deals with a huge collection of multiple categories. A good example here is the ordinal logistic model dealing with the proportional odds. However, this system only does modeling and not performing any classifications dealing with the statistics since it is not a classifier. Therefore, it will only convert the probability input into an output. Following this, let us discuss the applications of logistic regression in a real-life situation.

Now that we have had a chance to take a look at what this logistic regression is all about, we are going to take a look at some of the steps that we can take to write one of our own in the Python language. There are other languages that we can use with data analysis and these algorithms, but we are going to focus on the Python language because it comes with the libraries that we talked about earlier, and it is an easy one to work with.

In general, a binary logistic regression is going to help us to describe what relationship, if any, is going to be present between our dependent variable, which should be binary, and one or more of the independent variables. When we work with the binary dependent, there are two outcomes that are possible for the dependent variable. 1 is going to be used for success or true, and then 0 will be for failure or false. There are a few steps that need to happen here in order to get the process to work in the manner that we want. We will look at the code in a moment, but first, let's talk about a few of the parts that are there. We need to gather the data that we want. There is usually a dataset that will help us with this. You can create your own, or you can import one that is already created to help.

Then we need to import some of the packages that are needed to make this code work. For this code, we are going to make sure that we have seaborn, sklearn, and pandas on our computer. If these are not already installed on your system, then take the time to do this because we need them. When the libraries and packages are all ready to go, it is time for us to build up our data frame, This is usually going to be something that we are able to do with the Pandas library, but you can choose the method that works the best. And that is where we are going to move on to creating the logistic regression with the Python language.

When we are ready to bring all of these parts together, we can then write out the code. The code to help us with this is below:

import pandas as pd

from sklearn.model_selection import train_test_split

from sklearn.linear_model import LogisticRegression

candidates = {'gmat':
[780,750,690,710,680,730,690,720,740,690,610,690,710,680,770,61
0,580,650,540,590,620,600,550,550,570,670,660,580,650,660,640,
620,660,660,680,650,670,580,590,690],

'gpa':
[4,3.9,3.3,3.7,3.9,3.7,2.3,3.3,3.3,3,1.7,2.7,3.7,3.7,3.3,3.3,3,2.7,3.7,2.7,2.3,
3.3,2,2.3,2.7,3,3.3,3.7,2.3,3.7,3.3,3,2.7,4,3.3,3.3,3,2.3,2.7,3.3,1.7,3.7],

'work_experience':
[3,4,3,5,4,6,1,4,5,1,3,5,6,4,3,1,4,6,2,3,2,1,4,1,2,6,4,2,6,5,1,2,4,6,5,1,2,1,
4,5],

'admitted':
[1,1,1,1,1,1,0,1,1,0,0,1,1,1,1,0,0,1,0,0,0,0,0,0,0,1,1,0,1,1,0,0,1,1,1,0,0,0,0,
1]

}

df = pd.DataFrame(candidates,columns= ['gmat',
'gpa','work_experience','admitted'])

X = df[['gmat', 'gpa','work_experience']]

y = df['admitted']

X_train,X_test,y_train,y_test =
train_test_split(X,y,test_size=0.25,random_state=0) #in this case,
you may choose to set the test_size=0. You should get the same
prediction here

logistic_regression= LogisticRegression()

logistic_regression.fit(X_train,y_train)

new_candidates = {'gmat': [590,740,680,610,710],

        'gpa': [2,3.7,3.3,2.3,3],

        'work_experience': [3,4,6,1,5]

        }

df2 = pd.DataFrame(new_candidates,columns= ['gmat',
'gpa','work_experience'])

413

y_pred=logistic_regression.predict(df2)

print (df2)

print (y_pred)

Applications of Logistic Regression

Logistic regression is applied in metrological and other forecasting stations which consist of meteorologists. The algorithm here is used to predict the probability of rain. This information is vital as it helps in many sectors such as agricultural, transport and so on. Time of planting can efficiently be planned for, and the right arrangement can be put into place. This analysis is also applied in some risk management systems such as credit control system. Here, the analysis will predict whether the account holder is a defaulter when it comes to payment or not. Still, on this, the regression analysis will predict the exact amount that someone can be given by using the previous records. This always enables many organizations to run, as they are able to control everything when it comes to risk management. All accounts will undergo a critical analysis before any credit is appended. Logistic regression is also applied in political sectors, especially during an election. Here, it gives out the probability of winning and losing each candidate owing to their strengths and resources they used. Again, this regression analysis will be able to predict the number of people who might fail to vote and who will vote at the end and to which particular candidate. Some factors help determine the prediction outcome here such as the age of the candidate, sex, the incomes of both the candidate and the voters, state of the residence of both and more so, total number of votes in the last elections.

Logistic regression is also applied in various medical fields. It is applied in epidemiology. Here, the analysis is used to identify all those risk factors that may eventually result in diseases. As a result, precautions and other preventive measures may be put into place. Its knowledge is usable in the Trauma and Injury Severity Score(TRISS) where predictions of mortality, especially in injured patients, are done. We have several medical scales which have been designed to check on the severity of patients across the globe.

All these medical scales have been developed or managed using logistic regression. In most cases, especially within the health sector, you can use this knowledge to predict the risk of acquiring some dangerous diseases. For examples, diseases such as coronary heart disease, diabetes, and other forms of health-related complications can be easily controlled. These predictions are based on the day to day observable characteristics of the individual patient. The traits or characteristics here include the body mass index, sex, age, and even different results of their blood tests. This will eventually help in proper planning and risk management in the medical sector.

Again, this knowledge can be applied in the engineering sector. Here, it is used to predict the failure probability of a particular system, a new product, or even any kind of process. In the field of marketing, logistic regression analysis helps to determine the buyers' purchasing power, their propensity to purchase, and also this knowledge can be used to stop the various subscriptions of the companies. The technique is also applied in economics. Here, knowledge is used to predict the outcome of being involved in the public labor sector. We also have this technique in the issues to do with the probability of homeownersnot paying a mortgage. Natural language processing uses conditional random fields which is also an extension of logistic regression, especially to sequential data.

Logistic Regression vs. Linear Regression

You may be wondering about the main difference between these two examples of regressions. In terms of the outcome, linear regression is responsible for the continuous prediction while there is a discrete outcome in logistic regression. A model predicting the price of a car will depend on various parameters like color, year of make, and so on. Therefore, this value will always be different, indicating the continuous outcome. However, a discrete outcome is always one thing. That's, in case of sickness, you can either be sick or not.

Advantages of logistic regression

> It is very effective and efficient

> You can get an outcome without large computational resources

➤ You can easily interpret it

➤ No input features required for scaling process

➤ No tuning required

➤ You can easily regularize logistic regression

Linear Regression

Linear regression refers to a statistical approach used for modeling a relationship between various variables in a particular set of different independent variables. In this chapter, you'll learn more about dependent variables such as response as well as independent variables, including features of simplicity. To be able to offer extensive search results and have a clear understanding regarding linear regression in python, you need to be keen on the primary basis. We begin with the primary version of the subject. For instance, what it is a simple linear regression?

By definition, simple linear regression refers to a significant approach that's used in predicting a significant response by utilizing a single feature. Therefore, it's assumed that the main two variables, in this case, are directly related. That's why it's vital to determine the linear function since it often predicts the main response value of the equation accurately. There are different regression models utilized in showing as well as predicting the main relationship between two different variables as well as factors. As such, it's important to note that the main factor that's being predicted is known as the dependent variable. But the factors utilized in predicting the main value of the dependent variable is identified as the independent variable. With that said, it's also vital to note that good data doesn't always narrate the entire story as it may be. Therefore, regression analysis is often used in the research as well as the establishment of the correlation of variables. However, correlation isn't the same as the subject of causation. Therefore, a line found in a simple linear regression which may be fitting into the data points appropriately may not indicate a definitive element regarding a major cause and effect relationship. When it comes to linear regression, every observation has two values.

Therefore, one of the values is specifically for the dependent variable. The other is certainly for the independent variable.

Linear Regression in Python

Linear regression refers to a statistical approach used for modeling relationship between various variables in a particular set of different independent variables. In this chapter, you'll learn more about dependent variables such as response as well as independent variables including features of simplicity. To be able to offer extensive search results and have a clear understanding regarding linear regression in python, you need to be keen on the primary basics. Linear regression is also defined as linearity found in algebra. It often refers to a unique linear relationship found between two as well as more variables. Drawing from the said relationship, the result becomes a straight line. For that reason, we begin with the primary version of the subject. For instance what is simple linear regression?

By definition, simple linear regression refers to a major approach that's used in predicting a significant response by utilizing a single feature. Therefore, it's assumed that the main two variables in this case are directly related. That's why it's vital to determine the linear function since it often predicts the main response value of the equation accurately. There are different regression models utilized in showing as well as predicting the main relationship between two different variables as well as factors. As such, it's important to note that the main factor that's being predicted is known as the dependent variable. But the factors utilized in predicting the main value of the dependent variable is identified as the independent variable. With that said, it's also vital to note that good data doesn't always narrate the entire story as it may be. Therefore, regression analysis is often used in the research as well as establishment of the correlation of variables. However, correlation isn't the same as the subject of causation.

Therefore, a line found in a simple linear regression which may be fitting into the data points appropriately may not indicate a definitive element regarding a major cause and effect relationship. When it comes to linear regression, every observation has two values. Therefore, one of the values is specifically for the dependent variable. The other is certainly for the independent variable. When discussing

417

the simple linear regression analysis, we are looking at some of the simplest forms of regression analysis that are used on various independent variables as well as one independent variable.

Consequently, in such a model, a straight line is often used in approximating the main relationship between an independent as well as dependent variable. Multiple regression analysis occurs when there are 2 major independent variables applied in regression analysis. As a result, the model is not going to be a slightly simple linear one. Usually, this model ($y = \beta 0 + \beta 1 + E.$) *represents simple linear regression.* By applying the relevant mathematical convention, two main factors are herein involved. They include x and y which are the main designations. Also, the equation often provides a description on how y correlates with x. This is what is defined as the regression model. Apart from that, the linear regression model has an error term which is often represented by E. It can also be termed as the Greek letter epsilon. Usually, this error term is applied to mainly account for the variability found in y. However, this element cannot be explained in terms of the linear relationship found between x as well as y. It's also important to note that there are parameters representing the major population being studied. Some of these parameters represent the main population that is being studied. Usually, a regression line can easily show how a unique positive linear relationship, no relationship, as well as a negative relationship.

With that said, if the line that has been graphed appears to be in a simple linear regression that's flat in any way, there is no relationship that will be found in the two variables. On the other hand, if the regression line slopes upwards with the line's lower end located at y, on the graph, then there will be a positive linear relationship within the graph. But if the regression line tends to slope downward where the upper end of y that intercepts at the graph's axis. In the case where the parameters are well identified and known, the equation of the simple linear regression can utilize the computed meaning of the value of y. But in real practice, there are various parameter values that aren't known. Therefore, they have to be estimated using some form of data sample from the actual population. Therefore, the parameters of these populations are often estimated using sample statistics. These statistics can be represented using bo + b1.

It's evident that we are living a world that requires us to use tons of data coupled with powerful computers as well as artificial intelligence. While this may only be the beginning, there is a rise in use of data science in various sectors across the world. Machine learning is also driving image recognition as well as autonomous vehicles development and decisions based in the sector of finance as well as energy industry. As such, linear regression in python is still a fundamental statistical as well as machine learning technique. Therefore, for those who aspire to do statistics or scientific computing, there are high chances that this will be a requirement in the course work. Not only is it advisable to indulge in the learning process but also proceed to various complex methods appended to the studies.

It's important to understand the different types of linear regression. One of them includes multiple linear regressions which involves a unique case of the linear regression that has two to more independent variables. As such, in a case where there are two independent variables, it happens that the probable regression function is going to represent a major regression plane situated in a three-dimensional space. As such, the objective of the regression appears to be the value that will determine different weights. This also happens to be as close to the actual response as possible. In a different scenario, the case that exceeds two independent variables is often similar.

However, it's general more general as well. In a similar case, you may regard polynomial regression as a major generalized issue of linear regression in python. With that said, you can easily assume the polynomial dependence found between the output as well as inputs. In that case, your regression function may also be f which can include other non-linear terms. Usually, linear regression is the initial machine learning algorithm that data scientists encounter in their practice. It's a vital model that everyone in the sector should master. This is because it helps in laying a strong foundation for different machine learning algorithms. Since this is a powerful technique that can be applied in different sectors as discussed in the earlier chapters, it becomes important for professionals in scientific sectors to grasp the basis of using the subject. For starters, it may be utilized in forecasting sales by analyzing sales data for initial months. Also, it may be used in gaining important insight regarding consumer behavior.

Now that we have had some time to talk about how we can work with the linear regression and how it is going to work, we need to take this a bit further and look at some of the coding that we can write out to work with this. Again, we are going to stick with the Python language. And since we are looking at a graph to see how things are going to work and where our points will end up, we need to work with not only the NumPy library, but also the matplotlib library as well. The code that we need to use in order to make our own linear regression work includes the following:

```
import numpy as np

import matplotlib.pyplot as plt

def estimate_coef(x, y):


  # number of observations/points

  n = np.size(x)


  # mean of x and y vector

  m_x, m_y = np.mean(x), np.mean(y)


 # calculating cross-deviation and deviation about x

  SS_xy = np.sum(y*x) - n*m_y*m_x
```

```python
    SS_xx = np.sum(x*x) - n*m_x*m_x

    # calculating regression coefficients
    b_1 = SS_xy / SS_xx
    b_0 = m_y - b_1*m_x

    return(b_0, b_1)
def plot_regression_line(x, y, b):

    # plotting the actual points as scatter plot
    plt.scatter(x, y, color = "m",
            marker = "o", s = 30)


    # predicted response vector
    y_pred = b[0] + b[1]*x


    # plotting the regression line
    plt.plot(x, y_pred, color = "g")


    # putting labels
    plt.xlabel('x')
```

```python
plt.ylabel('y')

# function to show plot
plt.show()

def main():

    # observations
    x = np.array([0, 1, 2, 3, 4, 5, 6, 7, 8, 9])
    y = np.array([1, 3, 2, 5, 7, 8, 8, 9, 10, 12])

    # estimating coefficients
    b = estimate_coef(x, y)
    print("Estimated coefficients:\nb_0 = {} \
        \nb_1 = {}".format(b[0], b[1]))

    # plotting regression line
    plot_regression_line(x, y, b)

if __name__ == "__main__":
    main()
```

Take some time to look through this code, and add it to your compiler to see how it is going to work for your needs. You may be surprised at how well it works and all of the neat things that you are able to do with this code along the way. And with that, you are done creating your first linear regression!

Chapter 6: The Perceptron

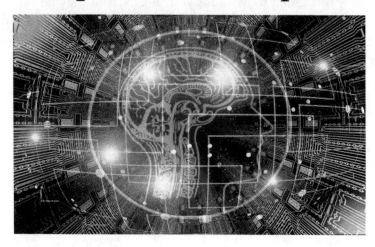

This chapter is set to look at the perceptron learning algorithm, which was first applied and propose by Minsky. This chapter offers explicit coverage of perceptron as an algorithm rather than the model. I would advise my readers to find reference material for the same topic in my book *MACHINE LEARNING FOR BEGINNERS*. In the book, the coverage of this topic is limited in scope. However, in this one, I offer an in-depth analysis of perceptron based on the content, structure, and applicability.

Defining Perceptron

A perceptron is a layer of the neural network that is capable of doing the following.

Configuring arithmetic values to the core of the data pool and estimating the sum of the positive return to the value of 1 for positive (+) outcomes.

In a different point of view, a perceptron can also be considered as a model for computation that draws a boundary (a line in two-dimensional cases) to isolate two classes in a given space.

Initially, the weights and the bias which represents the classification hyperplane is usually unknown. In this case, unsystematic weights and bias are allocated to the model. The random assignment leads to misclassification of points.

The Perceptron Trick

The objective of the perception trick is decreasing the amount of misclassified points. The reduction can be made by sliding the line over the space. In other words, it is altering the expression of the hyperplane. For all the wrongly categorized points, we adjust the weights and prejudice to move the hyperplane closer to the points that are improperly classified. After some time, the algorithm will rectify the problem to classify the points correctly. However, in this chapter, I choose to look at the perceptron differently. The approach taken is to identify perceptron in the context of the machine learning algorithm. Here, the perceptron is defined as an algorithm that predicts whether a given feature belongs to a specific class or not. From this angle, the algorithm is considered a binary classifier that is used for supervised machine learning. In most cases, the feature to be studied is always represented by a number with both magnitude and direction. As a classifier, the perceptron is used for linear classification and representation of data in graphical forms.

The graphical representation model can take either two-dimension or the multi-dimension way. The perceptron identifies a feature, weighs its sum, and give an outcome of value that is 1 if the weighted summation is higher than the result from other function. The equation supports this statement in the image below

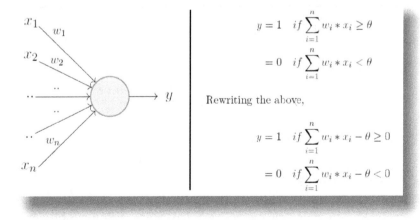

$$y = 1 \quad if \sum_{i=1}^{n} w_i * x_i \geq \theta$$

$$= 0 \quad if \sum_{i=1}^{n} w_i * x_i < \theta$$

Rewriting the above,

$$y = 1 \quad if \sum_{i=1}^{n} w_i * x_i - \theta \geq 0$$

$$= 0 \quad if \sum_{i=1}^{n} w_i * x_i - \theta < 0$$

When the equation edge is substituted (second equation in the image above) and made to be constant with the weight of a given parameter, the equation in the image below is arrived at.

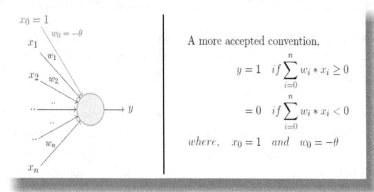

A more accepted convention,

$$y = 1 \quad if \sum_{i=0}^{n} w_i * x_i \geq 0$$

$$= 0 \quad if \sum_{i=0}^{n} w_i * x_i < 0$$

$$where, \quad x_0 = 1 \quad and \quad w_0 = -\theta$$

A single unit of a perceptron algorithm can be used to perform a divisible linear equation. The only group works by weighting or assigning a weight to both Boolean and positive metrics, with a corresponding partiality.

Using a Perceptron to Perform an OR Function

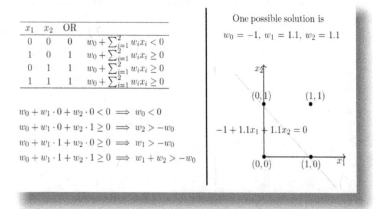

x_1	x_2	OR	
0	0	0	$w_0 + \sum_{i=1}^{2} w_i x_i < 0$
1	0	1	$w_0 + \sum_{i=1}^{2} w_i x_i \geq 0$
0	1	1	$w_0 + \sum_{i=1}^{2} w_i x_i \geq 0$
1	1	1	$w_0 + \sum_{i=1}^{2} w_i x_i \geq 0$

$$w_0 + w_1 \cdot 0 + w_2 \cdot 0 < 0 \implies w_0 < 0$$
$$w_0 + w_1 \cdot 0 + w_2 \cdot 1 \geq 0 \implies w_2 > -w_0$$
$$w_0 + w_1 \cdot 1 + w_2 \cdot 0 \geq 0 \implies w_1 > -w_0$$
$$w_0 + w_1 \cdot 1 + w_2 \cdot 1 \geq 0 \implies w_1 + w_2 > -w_0$$

One possible solution is

$$w_0 = -1, \ w_1 = 1.1, \ w_2 = 1.1$$

$$-1 + 1.1x_1 + 1.1x_2 = 0$$

In the image above, conditions have been defined in line with the OR function. Such terms are meant to meet the optimum model, which requires the summation of weighted data to be zero (0) or more than

426

it, for a given outcome of value one (1). The summations of the weights have been done a straight line that separates the positive (+) values from negative (-) values established.

The Minsky proposal set out the standards of learning the features by the use of sample data. The proposed models have been described below.

Basic Components of Linear Algebra

Vector

The vector value can represent a lot of things depending on the type of data and the user. Thus, there is more than one way of describing a vector. It may be a feature in space with both directing and magnitude, a structure or a database used to keep large amounts of data, etc. for this study; we will look at a vector as a line with an arrow being the head and the other point without an arrow as the origin. This is not the best definition. However, I want you to just grab the end. The images used in this presentation are mined from 3Blue1Brown.

Representing a Vector

A vector can be expressed in a two-dimension and a three-dimension plane, depending on the choice of the user and the function. Below is a two-dimensionally described vector(the first image) and a 3-D one (the second image.

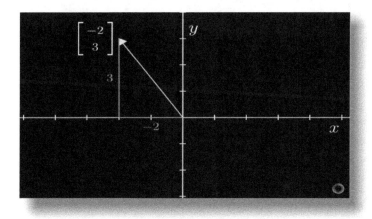

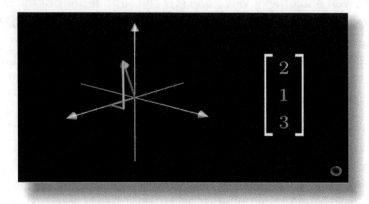

Calculating the Dot Product of Two Vectors

Given two vectors (n+1, w) and (n+1, x), their dot product is calculated using the formula below. For substitution of value, the formula I written in a matrix form.

$$\mathbf{w} = [w_0, w_1, w_2, ..., w_n]$$
$$\mathbf{x} = [1, x_1, x_2, ..., x_n]$$
$$\mathbf{w} \cdot \mathbf{x} = \mathbf{w}^T \mathbf{x} = \sum_{i=0}^{n} w_i * x_i$$

From the equation, the vectors /w/ and /x/ are represented by a line with an arrow. The dimension of the vectors is the (n+1) value. The outcome of the computation represents the dot product of vectors /w/ and /x/. This result shows the extent to which a single vector goes to the direction of the other vector. A perceptron creates a line that separates the positive value from the negative ones. This line is called the separating boundary. For the function in our example, this is represented as, w. x = 0.

The Angle Between Two Vectors

The dot product mentioned above can be calculated using a different method. However, certain conditions must be met

    I.   The angle between the vectors must be known.

    II.   The magnitude of the vectors must be known.

When conditions are met, the computation of the dot product is done by substituting in the formula in the image below.

$$\mathbf{w}^T\mathbf{x} = \|\mathbf{w}\|\|\mathbf{x}\|\cos\alpha$$

The reverse method can be used to determine the angle between the two vectors. This can be done by first identifying the vector, getting its magnitude and the dot product.

The image below can guide in the substitution of values into the equation.

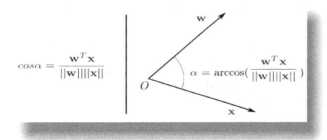

From the equation and a mathematical point of view, we know that when the cosine of an angle is 0, then the lines making the angle are perpendicular to each other. Taking from this, we can conclude that when the dot product of vectors /w/ and /x/ is 0, then line w is perpendicular to line x. that is the relationship between the dot product and the angle between two vectors.

Problem Representation Using the Perceptron

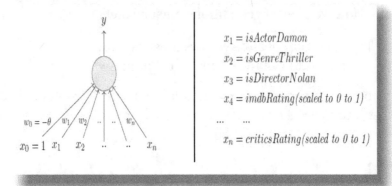

$$x_1 = isActorDamon$$
$$x_2 = isGenreThriller$$
$$x_3 = isDirectorNolan$$
$$x_4 = imdbRating(scaled\ to\ 0\ to\ 1)$$
$$\vdots$$
$$x_n = criticsRating(scaled\ to\ 0\ to\ 1)$$

The set example is going to be used to determine if a person will settle on a movie, basing on previous data and inputs that are indicated on the diagram. The input data provided in this diagram have both real (+) and negative values (-). The actual values represent the movies watched by the person in question. We will use the data to see how the perceptron learning algorithm estimates weight in a dataset. For simplicity and clear visualization, we are going to use a 2-D representation.

Using the Perceptron Learning Algorithm
The main objective here is identifying the vector that can separate the real (+) from the negative (-) inputs, say vector (w), as used in the example.
We will use the set algorithm below.

```
Algorithm: Perceptron Learning Algorithm
P ← inputs   with   label   1;
N ← inputs   with   label   0;
Initialize w randomly;
while !convergence do
    Pick random x ∈ P ∪ N ;
    if x ∈ P   and   w.x < 0 then
    |   w = w + x ;
    end
    if x ∈ N   and   w.x ≥ 0 then
    |   w = w − x ;
    end
end
//the algorithm converges when all the
  inputs are classified correctly
```

The first step is adjusting the vector (w) with any other vector. After the initialization, we restate the examples provided in the dataset, in this instance, the metrics are P, U, and N. the examples represent both real and negative standards.

Proceeding the substitution phase, an input x (randomly picked vector) corresponds to the value P, the dot product to be determined in w, x should be stated as a value that is either equal to zero (o) or greater than zero. The actual value is not actually, outstanding since the perceptron will only give a yes or no answer.

In another instance, when vector x corresponds to the value N, the calculated dot product gives a zero (o) outcome. The statements above can be represented in one IF situation in a while loop as;

```
while !convergence do
    Pick random x ∈ P ∪ N :
    if x ⊂ P   and   w.x < 0 then
        w = w + x :
    end
    if x ∈ N   and   w.x ≥ 0 then
        w = w − x :
    end
end
```

The deduction from these representations can give two outcomes

The first outcome is when vector x corresponds to the P-value, and the dot product of the two vectors (w, x) is less than zero (w.x < 0).

The second outcome is found when the vector x corresponds to the value of N, and the dot product of the two vectors (w, x) is more significant than zero (w.x>0).

Note that we have to update the w value that has been initialized. In other cases, we are not supposed to mess the value of w, since the two outcomes above are in contradiction with the perceptron rule. For the first outcome, we will summate w and x whereas for the secondary outcome we will deduct the value of x from w.

Assessing the Viability of the Update Rule Above

The basic rule of perceptron has helped us to determine that vector x corresponds to the value P. Therefore,; the remaining part of the task is making the equation to be w.x > 0. The equation can also be interpreted to mean that when vector x corresponds to P, then the angle between the two vectors (w, x) is supposed to be less than ninetydegrees. Why this inference? The cosine of the angle between the two vectors (w,x) is the same as the dot product of the two vectors. Thereby, that angle should be less than ninety degrees.

$$cos\alpha = \frac{\mathbf{w}^T\mathbf{x}}{||\mathbf{w}||||\mathbf{x}||} \qquad cos\alpha \propto \mathbf{w}^T\mathbf{x}$$

$$\text{So if } \mathbf{w}^T\mathbf{x} > 0 \quad \Rightarrow cos\alpha > 0 \quad \Rightarrow \alpha < 90$$

$$\text{Similarly, if } \mathbf{w}^T\mathbf{x} < 0 \quad \Rightarrow cos\alpha < 0 \quad \Rightarrow \alpha > 90$$

From the above interpretation, we get that we don't have to know the vector w given that it makes an angle that is less than ninety degrees with a given feature vector. In this case, the vector must be a positive value. On the other hand, vector w should make an angle that is greater than ninety degrees with a feature vector that has a negative value. This represented, as shown below.

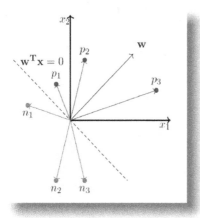

At this point, we can comfortably say that the angle between vectors x and w should be a value less than ninety, for the given case that x corresponds to the value of P.

In the same way, we can conclude that the angle made between vectors w and x should be a value that is more than ninety degrees for a given condition that the vector x corresponds to the value of N.

Moving forward, we take a look at why the update worked. The diagram below presents the explanation as to why the upgrade works. The valuation may be a bit way-out, but the general picture is seen.

(α_{new}) when $\mathbf{w_{new}} = \mathbf{w} + \mathbf{x}$	(α_{new}) when $\mathbf{w_{new}} = \mathbf{w} - \mathbf{x}$
$cos(\alpha_{new}) \propto \mathbf{w_{new}}^T \mathbf{x}$	$cos(\alpha_{new}) \propto \mathbf{w_{new}}^T \mathbf{x}$
$\propto (\mathbf{w} + \mathbf{x})^T \mathbf{x}$	$\propto (\mathbf{w} - \mathbf{x})^T \mathbf{x}$
$\propto \mathbf{w}^T \mathbf{x} + \mathbf{x}^T \mathbf{x}$	$\propto \mathbf{w}^T \mathbf{x} - \mathbf{x}^T \mathbf{x}$
$\propto cos\alpha + \mathbf{x}^T \mathbf{x}$	$\propto cos\alpha - \mathbf{x}^T \mathbf{x}$
$cos(\alpha_{new}) > cos\alpha$	$cos(\alpha_{new}) < cos\alpha$

For the case that vector x corresponds to P, we will have to add the values of vectors x and w. the addition raises the cosine of (alpha) function. This also means that the value of alpha is reduced (which is the angle between two vectors). The diagram below indicates how we can learn the vector w, which meets with a real object to make an angle that is less than ninety degrees and an angle greater than ninety degrees with negative-value objects.

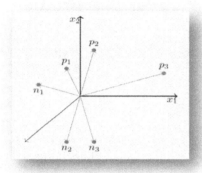

Proof of Convergence

There is no precise explanation to make people believe that the vector studied will converge in the end. This is due to the varying conditions within different sets of data. Even though it looks that there might be cases where the vector fails to converge, the truth is that the algorithm is proven to converge at some point. Many types of research have studied the patterns and deduced these proofs. Videos demonstrating this can be found in YouTube and other platforms.

Summary

In this chapter, I have taken a look at the perceptron algorithm, defined it, and went on to illustrate how it works. In so doing, I have refreshed your minds on the necessary components of linear algebra before proceeding to study the perceptron learning algorithm. This step by step presentation is meant to guide learners in understanding and visualizing the concept of machine learning, taking note of the perceptron. It is my wish that by the end of the chapter, you have gained insight and knowledge to get you started. Additional materials of study are recommended.

Chapter 7: Useful Platforms For Python Programming

Python is ported in several platforms to enable secure access. These platforms have improved over the years to become sophisticated and specialized for users. Useful platforms for Python programming include AIX, ISO, OS, VMS, and PH-UX. Other platforms for Python programming are Cygwin, Java, FreeBSD, Java, OpenBSD, Solaris, and Windows. Python 3 and 2 can be downloaded for AIX for free. Machine learning forms an integral part of artificial intelligence and helps businesses to discover information from run predictions and data. Data scientist writes machine learning algorithms to help users learn data trends. Moreover, it is used to make predictions beyond basic analysis. Other tools used for simple analysis do not make predictions, thereby making work difficult. Therefore, using these platforms for Python programming makes work easy. Python is a programming language used to write machine learning algorithms. It is used by many because of its applicability and simplicity. Moreover, packages written in Python help data scientists perform data visualization, model building, data analysis, and feature extraction. AIX users are free to use machine learning packages to perform data mining, scientific computation, and data analysis. Because the packages are based on Python, users must install the latest version of Python on their AIX systems. They can use YUM to install AIX. It is better to use YUM because it is the easiest way out. Furthermore, it is the fastest way to install an open-source RPM package because you do not need skills to use it. You can download YUM from AIX toolbox repository and install it on AIX. The good thing about this process is that Python2 will be installed by default. Ensure that you update all the packages after installing YUM. To install machine learning packages, users need specific open source packages. These include blas, lapack, gcc, xz, python3, and zeromq. There are additional settings that are required to complete a machine learning package installation. Users need to increase resource limits for successful installation. The data and stack limits should also be increased. There are several web applications that enable users to write code for statistical analysis, and analysis. Jupyter Notebook is one of them and it does an excellent job. To facilitate the installation process, AIX users should use Jupyter Notebook to write data analysis models. To install the Jupyter Notebook, users should run this command: # python3 -m pip install jupyter. In case you do not have it in your folder, run this command, # jupyter notebook - generate-config. Python machine learning tools have gained popularity among data scientists. Moreover, AIX users want these packages on AIX to help them write AI applications. AI applications are demanding and these platforms make it easier to get things into perspective.

Linux is common among geeks and programmers. This operating system is fantastic for everyone, including students. What most people do not know is that Linux is also great for programming. There are numerous reasons why people should consider using Linux for programming. The first great thing about Linux is that it is free. Users do not incur any cost to download and install Linux on their computers. This means that it can be used by anyone, especially those facing financial difficulties, but still want to use a good Python platform. It does not matter whether you are a hobbyist or take programming as a career. The only important bit is that you don't incur any cost to use Linux operating system. The only thing that you need is a Linux compatible machine and chances are that you already have it. Moreover, most of the software that comes with Linux is free, reducing the cost of operation further. This means that you can pick the tools that you want without worrying about extra expenses. Another added advantage of using Linux is the fact that it is easy to install. Many people never get to install an operating system because they do not understand how it works or its significance. The good thing about using Linux is that it is easy to install. Some people think that since it is difficult to install other OS that it is the same case with Linux, but that is far from the truth. A programmer can easily know how to search for a Linux OS and proceed to install it. There is no difficulty pressing the function key and following the prompts. After booting a live USB drive, installing Linux becomes similar to installing a program in windows. Users who want to keep current OS can do so by choosing the dual-boot option. Another reason why you should use Linux for python programming is because it creates time to improve your skills. It is easy to access the source code and in any part of the OS. While it is difficult to use, it allows you to dive in and learn how it works. Furthermore, users are not worried about legal woes when they make mistakes. Linux offers support for programming languages to facilitate learning. It supports CSS, Java, HTML, and C++ and other languages one might be interested in. Operating languages that are not limited to specific operating systems work fine on Linux. In case a language you desire to use is not installed by default, you can get them from the distribution's repository. Linux users have the freedom to choose from a wide range of applications. The common image of a programmer is sitting in from a machine full of green or white texts. Linux offers many tools that programmers can use to have an easy time. It also allows users to pick IDEs or integrated desktop environments. Users also get to experience the power of bash scripting and apply it to python programming. Most of the commands in Linux are extremely powerful which enable users to live in the terminal. Bash script enable users to put commands together to create complex combinations. Many people long to have Linux expertise and the great way to learn it is by using in in Python programming.

Windows is a great platform for Python programming. The first thing you need to do to use Windows for Python is to set up the development environment. For those who are new to Python, it is ideal for getting Python from the Microsoft Store for installation. It utilizes basic Python3 interpreter and comes in handy in an educational environment. In case you are using Python on Windows for web development, create a development environment. Instead it directly on Windows, install Python through the Windows Subsystem for Linux. Installing Python from the Microsoft Store is easy. Press the start bar, and key in Microsoft Store and click the link to open it. Choose search and type 'Python' which will open Python 3.7. When Python has finished the download and installation process, use the start menu to open Windows PowerShell. Pip is part of the Microsoft Store installation process. You can use VS to install visual studio code. Make use of the IntelliSense to facilitate the process. You can also use linting to avoid making errors. Visual studio code comes with a built-in terminal to help you open the Python command line. Download VS Code for windows to install it. To run a Python code, you need to guide VS Code which interpreter to employ. To be on the safe side, use Python 3.7 unless you have a different reason for using something different. Open the Command Palette to select Python 3. Type the command python and choose the command Python. Once you select the interpreter, select the command. The Select Python environment shows a list of interpreters that can be used. Select 'view' to open the terminal in VS Code. Enter the command to open Python in the VS Code. You can decide to install Git or not. For those who plan on collaborating with others on the Python code, VS Code enables this control via Git. You need to download and install Git for windows. An install wizard will ask a series of questions, and it is best that you use default settings. The web installer is an initial download which download components automatically. Two options are given after starting the installer; install now and customize installation. If you choose to install now, it will not be mandatory for you to be an administrator. Moreover, Python will be installed in the user directory, and shortcuts will be limited to current users. On the other hand, if you select 'customize the installation,' you will be able to choose features to install and where to install. Customize installation enables all-users installation, although users are required to prove administrative authority. Furthermore, Python is downloaded in the

438

file directory, and there are optional features to choose from. Available options in the installer UI can be listed from the command line. It is possible to set up these options without interfering with the UI to change some defaults. Users can pass the /quiet option to hide the installer UI. This option also enables them to install Python silently.

Another platform that is useful for python programming is Java. Most Java programmers who make a move to Python find it difficult to handle its object-oriented approach. The truth of the matter is that the approach taken by Python to work with objects and language abilities and that of Java are different. This makes switching between languages hectic and confusing. Java classes are put in files using the same name of the class. Object-oriented languages keep data concerning the object. Data is stored in attributes for Python and Java.

The most notable difference between Java and Python, how classes are defined and managed. It is important to note that some of the issues faced are imposed by the languages. One is supposed to outline attributes in the class when using Java. The number one rule is that you must define class attributes before using it. On the contrary, Python requires users to define and define attributes. You can opt to create instance variables, but it is not a good idea as it leads to confusion. Moreover, you are supposed to declare variables outside a method when dealing with Python. Java is the one that has access to attributes and methods by stipulating the difference between private and public data. Attributes are expected to be private in Java to limit access to them from outside the class. In case you forget to specify the access level, the attribute defaults to package safety to limit access. However, it is not advisable to declare public attributed in Java. One is supposed to declare private attributes but use public access techniques. Whenever Python sees attributes with double underscores, it fixes things by writing the original name using an underscore.

Python and Java have numerous similarities. Both have strong support from cross-platforms and extensive standard libraries. Furthermore, they treat things as objects, compile to bytecode, although Python is compiled at runtime. Both form part of the Algol family, but it is not a must to provide a type whenever someone declares an array in Python. Static type is known for catching type errors during compilation. Therefore, using Java helps to catch a mistake if you did not want to mix integers and strings. Static typing made code run regardless of whether it eliminates errors. Whitespace forms an important part of Python syntax. The declaration creates a block in each case. It not clear whether Python's typing is better than Java, but using them both maximize results. Users who use Python for Java programming benefit greatly. Java has better performance than Python, and incorporating it into programming improves the process. Java has no tuple, an immutable collection of values. Python is used by many because it has a high speed, and is reliable and efficient. It is also dynamic and has an elegant syntax. Users do not need to compile the program before executing it.

The OS module present in Python allows interaction with the OS. OS is a Python standard and offers a portable alternative of employing OS dependent functions. It has many functions that enable interaction with the file system. Functions in OS are many, such as OS name, which gives the name of the operating system module imported. Names registered under this are 'posix' 'java,' and 'nt.' Different interpreters have different outputs. OS also enables the getcwd function, which returns the current working directory to execute the code. OS error is a function of the OS which invalid file names that are not accepted by the OS. OS popen opens a pipe to a command can be read if the mode is 'r' or 'w.' OS module allow users to interface with the OS that is run on by Python. OS is preferred because it returns the actual process ID and information that identify the current operating system. It also allows users to change the root directory when they want to. It returns entries to file directory and names it. It can also rename the file once the command is given. Moreover, OS returns group id and process user id when it receives a command.

Another platform for Python programming is iso, a packaging used to simplify the development cycle linked to building-machine learning models. It also comes in handy during deployment. Iso is commonly used because it is effective and reliable. It promotes mental clarity when designing learning algorithms. Some platforms are hectic to use and can make one give up on the creation process. Instead of helping you come up with something that is unique, it makes you frustrated. The worst thing that can happen during the development of machine learning models is for the creator to become frustrated. It makes the entire process cumbersome and does not yield good results. Instead of using a platform that you unsure of, it is better to use one that guarantees results. There are few platforms that guarantee results, and one should take advantage of them. iso is also effective because it allows developers to understand the problem they are dealing with. It makes everything clear and allows the user to e fulfilled from creating the models. Iso is special because it can define modular data changes that form part of the model, which helps developers to stay organized. It also makes the transition from one model to another easy. Another advantage of iso is that it has tools that can be used for data augmentation. One can also save and deploy models easily. It also enables interactions with the model building process, unlike other platforms. Iso is good because it has tools which enable users to transform responses and predictors in one step. It saves time and allows you to learn a lot from the process. It yields more results when used with other python programming tools/platforms. Moreover, it is flexible and allows users to concentrate on other things while using it. It is not restrictive, and users and free in the platform.

Chapter 8: Decision Trees

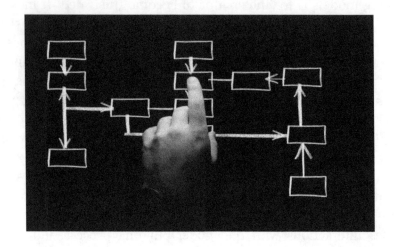

A decision tree is a decision-support tool with a tree that utilizes tree-like graphs to explain concepts. It uses utility, resources costs, and event outcomes. It is suitable for showing algorithms with only conditional control statements. In a decision tree, every internal note symbolizes a test on the attribute while the branch stands for the results of the test. Leaf nodes represent class labels and the distance from the root to the leaf signify the classification rules. Decision trees are helpful in learning algorithms and are widely used. Moreover, tree-based learning algorithms are popular learning methods. Some of the reasons why decision trees are common are because they empower predictive models with straightforward interpretation and efficiency. They are also accurate, stable, and reliable. They are also ideal for linear mapping models, unlike other tools. Decision trees solve all kind of challenges and never disappoint. Many people attest to the fact that this decision-support tool has helped them overcome problems and reach the helm. Decision tree algorithms are known as Classification and Regression Trees (CART). It is useful for tackling data science challenges. In a decision tree, the term Root Node stands for the entire population, which is divided further into homogenous groups. When sub-nodes are split further, they are referred to as decision nodes. Splitting is the act of dividing nodes into sub-nodes.

Pruning refers to the process of removing sub-nodes of decision nodes. Decision trees are made in such a way that they fit easily in programmatic structures. They are laid out to categorize issues when they arise. People can use decision trees to know the species of plants. There are many assumptions people make when creating decision trees. Many people consider the entire training set as a root in the beginning. Records are divided based on attribute values. Most people prefer feature values to be categorical. Below is an example of a decision tree.

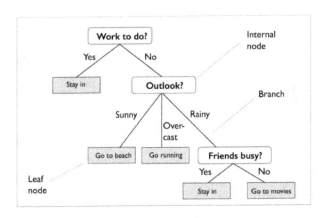

Decision trees are used for several reasons. Data miners use decision trees to analyze data. It is also commonly used in machine learning and similar activities. For example, decision trees can be used to evaluate opportunities for brand expansion using historical sales data. It can also be used to determine possible customers using demographic data. Many companies use decision trees to evaluate their performance in the market and determine their buyers. This allows them to adjust their marketing tactics to suit the target customers. It also informs them of problematic areas and how to approach buyers. Knowing possible buyers enables a firm to limit its advertising budget. Most of the time, companies spend a lot of money creating adverts without knowing where to target. They end up with more losses than profits. They are not able to recover even when a product makes massive sales. Decision trees are also used to predict the possibility of a default borrower using the predictive model. One of the reasons why companies go bankrupt is because of default borrowers. Some people do not keep their word when it comes to returning borrowed money. To evade such individuals, companies can use predictive models obtained from historical data to know such people. Doing this saves both time and operations of the company. Decision trees are also used in operations research to know a strategy that has a high chance of meeting set targets. There is no need in doing a research without knowing its end goal. A decision tree helps in performing decision analysis and makes work easy for researchers. Many industries have used decision trees to interpret data, including engineering, financial, energy, education, and business. People who were using other tools and techniques to analyze data have switched to decision tree because of its benefits.

Decision trees have numerous advantages that make them worthwhile. They are easy to understand. There are several tools that are used to solve problems, but most of them are hectic and need skills. On the contrary, decision trees are simple and do not require a lot of attention to understand. Even people without analytical knowledge can use a decision tree. It is not a must to have statistical knowledge to understand decision tree algorithms. The graphical representations used are simple, and users can relate to the narrative. Moreover, they have a simple hypothesis that users can relate to. Decision trees are effective in data exploration. They are useful in identifying the best variable and links between variables. For the longest time, people used variables that did not yield results. Researchers were frustrated because they could not explore data fully, decision trees changed the narrative. Now researchers can explore data with ease. Moreover, they can create new variables to predict target variables. If we are dealing with an issue where we have data on thousands of variables, decision trees save you from the struggle of finding the most significant one. Another added advantage of the decision tree is that users only put in little effort to prepare data. Less data cleaning for users allows them to focus on other things. It is effective and reliable, compared to other modeling techniques. Furthermore, decision tree is not influenced by missing values or outliers. It is also a non-parametric method which means that they have no assumptions about the classifier structure and space distributions.

444

Despite its benefits, decision tree has disadvantages that users should keep in mind. In some cases, decision-tree learners might create trees that do not generate expected results. In such cases, the user is left wondering whether it was a good idea to use a decision tree. It can be frustrating if misused. The case of creating a complex tree is known as over fitting, and many people fall under this category. Learners solve this problem by setting constraints on model parameters. They can also prune it to deal with the issue. Another challenge with decision tree is the fact that it does not fit continuous variables. If you are working with a continuous numerical variable, you stand a high chance of losing information. Moreover, decision tends to be unstable in case the tree is altered. One is supposed to use the tree as it is because a slight variable can result in a completely different thing. There are greedy algorithms which do not guarantee a return to the decision tree. Learners can eliminate this problem by training several trees. They also have to be careful when creating a decision tree. Decision trees do an excellent job in determining variables, but require careful mitigation to avoid errors. There is no guarantee of a good outcome and the user must constantly monitor it to interpret its performance.

At the bottom of the decision tree lies the terminal nodes. Terminal nodes are bottom because decision trees are drawn upside down. Classification trees and regression trees have similarities and differences. Both work in a similar way only that regression trees in instances where dependent variables are continuous. On the contrary, classification trees are employed whenever dependent variables are categorical. Both trees are known to divide the predictor space into separate regions. They also take a greedy approach and continue until the criteria stipulated by the user are met. Moreover, the splitting process contributes to full developed trees until the set criteria are reached. However, there is a possibility that the grown tree might overfit data, and this is where pruning comes in. Deciding to split a tree affects its performance. It can derail or improve accuracy, based on it is done. The decision criteria vary depending on whether it is for regression trees or classification trees. Several algorithms are used when deciding whether to split a decision tree into sub-nodes. The

445

target variable affects the purity of the node. After splitting the node on present variables, decision trees pick the one with more homogenous sub-nodes.

A tree has several uses in real life, and it turns out that it is also applicable in machine learning. It can be used to represent decisions virtually in decision analysis. The question that running people's minds is how an algorithm can be represented by a tree. Similar to how a real-life tree has many parts, decision trees also have several parts which perform different functions. It is essential to understand all the parts in a decision tree and their role. While the dataset has more features, we cannot overlook the simplicity of a decision tree. For someone to grow a tree, he/she must decide the features to use and conditions that are favorable for splitting. The person also needs to know when to stop. Trimming the tree is important because it grows habitually. You also need to be patient when creating a decision tree. Similar to how a real-life tree takes time to grow and goes through the pruning process, you must be patient when creating a decision tree. Rushing the process may cause overfitting so it is better to take time and do a good job. There are various techniques used for splitting, including recursive binary splitting, where all the features of taken into account a cost function is used to test split points. Many people do not know when to stop splitting a tree. Overdoing it can cause more problems than expected, and it is important to stop at the right time. Huge trees lead to overfitting, and one way of avoiding this is setting a minimum number of training input for every leaf. Some people are skeptical about this strategy, but it works for many. Users need to find methods that work and stick to them. What works for one may not do the same for another user.

Decision trees use algorithms such as Gini Index, and Chi-Square to determine the most homogenous nodes. Gini Index states that if one picks two items from a sample randomly, they must be in the same class and the probability of this happening is 1. The value of homogeneity increases with a high value of Gini. CART utilizes Gini Index technique to create binary splits. Chi-Square is another algorithm used by decision trees to calculate variables. It is used to determine statistical significance between the parent node and sub-nodes. It is measured by the value of squares of standard differences between expected and observed frequencies. You can derive Chi-Square for each node by calculating the deviation for both success and failure. The good news is that impure nodes need less information to describe and vice versa. Some steps can be taken to avoid over-fitting to improve efficiency of decision trees. Over-fitting is one of the problems faced by decision trees. Dealing with it means that users will have wonderful experiences using the decision-making support tool. A model with over-fitting issue when it attempts to reduce training set mistakes, but causes more test set errors. You can deal with the issue of overfitting by pruning and putting limits on the tree size. You can set limits on the tree size by employing numerous parameters that define a tree. The parameters include minimum populations for a node split, minimum sample for the leaf, maximum vertical depth, increased features to weigh for a split, and increased terminal node. Regarding minimum population for the node split, indicate the minimum number of samples needed in a node to qualify for splitting. This sample can be used to control over-fitting. Use higher values to prevent models from learning relations which is significant in the decision tree. Use minimum samples for the terminal leaf. Start by defining the samples needed in a terminal leaf. It is also used to control over-fitting like the minimum samples for node split. Use lower values for class problems that are imbalanced.

Alternatively, use the tree pruning method to deal with the issue of over-fitting. The method of putting limitations is a greedy tactic which looks for the best split available and moves on until the specified point is reached. The difference between putting limitations and pruning is that the former cannot see the danger ahead and adopt a greedy approach to overcome it. The pruning method allows you to see what is ahead and helps you to make the right choice. To implement pruning in a decision tree, we start by creating the tree then start removing leaves at the bottom. Remove the leaves that do not yield good returns when compared with the top. It is important to note that not every problem can be addressed using linear methods. There are amazing non-linear methods that perform wonders and users need to try them. Tree-based models can map non-linearity better than most techniques. Decision trees are ideal because they can also be used to solve classification and regression challenges.

There are two types of decision trees and they are based on target variables available. The first type of a decision tree is Categorical Variable Decision Tree. This is a decision tree with categorical target variables. In the example of which students will play baseball, where the target variable was learners will play baseball or not, that is yes or no. The second type is the Continuous Variable Decision Tree. As the name suggests, this type of decision tree contains continuous target variables. For instance, if there is a problem to predict whether clients will pay their renewal premiums (yes/no), it is apparent that income is a notable variable in them paying premiums, but insurance firms may lack income information about clients. To solve this problem, we can create a decision tree to predict the income of all clients. The insurance company will take into consideration the occupation when creating the decision tree. Values for continuous variable are being predicted in this case. The first thing is to put the best attribute at the root of the tree. Afterward, split the training set and make sure that each subset has data. Start from the root of the tree when predicting a class label for records. Values of the root attribute will be compared with record's attributes. The most important thing during this process is to use the right data to minimize errors. By comparing attribute values with internal nodes, we increase chances of getting the right variable. Decision trees work in a simple way. It falls in the category of supervised learning algorithm with a predefined target variable used to classify challenges. Both continuous input and categorical output variables use decision trees. It divides the population into two homogenous sets, depending on the differentiator. For example, if we have a sample of 20 learners with variables gender (girl/boy), height (4 to 5 ft) and class (IV/V). 10 out of the learners play baseball and we want to create a model to predict who is likely to play baseball. To do so, we have to separate learners who play baseball depending on highly significant input variable and this is where one uses a decision tree. The decision tree separate learners based on the values of the three variables and determine which one makes the best homogenous sets. By identifying the best variable among the three, it helps in

448

solving the problem. It utilizes numerous algorithms to identify the significant variable.

Creating Our Own Decision Tree

Now that we have had a bit of time to talk about the decision trees and how they are supposed to work, it is time to create one of our own. These are actually a lot easier and simpler to work with compared to what it sounds like, but it is going to be so useful to work with. So, let's spend some time taking a look at the steps that we are able to use in order to create one of our own decision trees and make this process work well for us.

Decision trees are going to be one of the most popular algorithms that we can work with, mostly because it is so powerful to use. The algorithm that comes with the decision tree is going to be one of our supervised learning algorithms, and it is going to work with both the categorical and the continuous variables that you use for your output.

In the code that we are going to work with in a bit, there are a number of different packages that we need to import and work with in order to make this work. We will focus on the Pandas, the NumPy, and the sklearn packages to get them to work the best way possible. If you do not have these on your computer already, then now is the time to get them on so that you can use them for your needs.

While we are here, we need to make a few assumptions for the decision tree to work. If these are not true, then the results of our decision tree may not work the way that we want. Some of the assumptions that we have to make with this one will include:

1. When we first start with this, we need to consider all of our set of training data as the root of the tree. We can change that later if needed.
2. Attributes are going to be assumed as categorical for all of the information gain. And when we are working with the gini index, we are going to assume that the attributes are continuous in nature.
3. When we look just on the basis of the attribute values, this means that the records are going to be distributed in a

449

recursive manner.

4. We are also able to work with some of the statistical methods to help order the attributes either as the internal node or as part of the root.

There is also a bit of pseudocode that we need to work with along the way. To do this, we need to work with a number of steps along the way. Some of these steps will include:

1. Find the attribute that looks the best out of all of them and then place it right on the root node of your tree.
2. When this is done, you can split the training set of the dataset into subsets. While you are making one of these subsets you have to make sure that all of the subsets of training the dataset should come in with the same value for that attribute.
3. You are able to find the leaf nodes to all of your branches when you go through and repeat one and two on all of your subsets.

While we are implementing our decision tree, we are going to end up with two phases that we need to focus on. These include the building phase and the operational phase. In our building phase, we are going to do a number of things that include preprocessing our data set, splitting up the set of data that we are working with so that we end up with the training and the testing set to work on the algorithm. Then we are able to train the classifier. And then we can move on to the operational phase. This is the part where we are able to use the algorithm in order to make some predictions, and it is a good way to calculate how accurate things are for us along the way. The next step that we need to work with here is doing a data import. This can be done with the help of our pandas package that we can get with Python. Here, we are going to be able to work with a URL that is going to be directly able to fetch the dataset from the UCI site, and we will not have to take the time to download the set of data. When you try to get this code to execute on the system, it is important to make sure that the internet connection is on and working well. As the set of data is going to be separated out by the ",", so we have to make sure that we pass the sep parameters value as ",". Another thing that we are going to notice when we are working with this one is that the set of data that we are working with is not going to contain the header, so we need to go through and pass the parameter value of our header as none. If we do not pass this parameter for the header, ten it will consider the first line of the set of data for the header.

Then it is time to go through and do some data slicing. Before we train our data and start to use it with the algorithm, we need to make sure that we can split the set of data into both of the options for the training and the testing. In order to go through our set of data and split it up into training and testing, we need to bring out a module from sklearn that is noted as train_test_split. To go through this, we are going to separate out the target variable from the attributes that are found in our set of data. Then we are able to go through and split up the data for the purposes of training and testing. Take your time doing this because it is going to make a big difference in how well the algorithm is going to be prepared to do some of the work that we want it too.

There are a few other things that we need to go through and understand a bit more as we work with this process. First, we have the idea of entropy here. This is going to be an important thing to measure because it will tell us the uncertainty of our random variable, and it is going to be able to help us to characterize the impurity of our arbitrary collection of examples. In our decision tree, the higher we see the entropy, the more the information content that is there. The entropy typically changes when we work with a node in the decision tree to help us create a new partition for the training instances, making them into smaller subsets. We have to do a few different iterations of the training and then testing, going back and forth, so we need to divide these up so we can accomplish that a few more times. Then there is the information gain, which is going to help us o know a bit more about measuring the change in entropy. Sklearn is going to be useful here because it is able to support the criteria of entropy for our information gain. We do need to make sure that we go through and use the method of information gain, and we have to actually mention that we want this explicitly. Along with this, we are going to be able to work with the accuracy score, which is going to be there to help us figure out how accurate the trained classifier is. And finally, we can use the confusion matrix in our code to help us to understand the behavior of the trained classifier over the test set of data or to validate the set of data that we are working with.

Now that we have had some time to go through the different parts that are necessary when we work with our decision trees, it is time for us to take this to the next part and look at some of the coding that we are able to work with. Some of the coding that a programmer is able to use to create our own decision trees, and use all of the steps that we had above, will include:

```python
# Importing the required packages

import numpy as np

import pandas as pd

from sklearn.metrics import confusion_matrix

from sklearn.cross_validation import train_test_split

from sklearn.tree import DecisionTreeClassifier

from sklearn.metrics import accuracy_score

from sklearn.metrics import classification_report


# Function importing Dataset

def importdata():

    balance_data = pd.read_csv(

'https://archive.ics.uci.edu/ml/machine-learning-'+
```

```
'databases/balance-scale/balance-scale.data',

    sep= ',', header = None)


    # Printing the dataswet shape

    print ("Dataset Length: ", len(balance_data))

    print ("Dataset Shape: ", balance_data.shape)


    # Printing the dataset obseravtions

    print ("Dataset: ",balance_data.head())

    return balance_data


# Function to split the dataset

def splitdataset(balance_data):

    # Separating the target variable

    X = balance_data.values[:, 1:5]

    Y = balance_data.values[:, 0]


    # Splitting the dataset into train and test

    X_train, X_test, y_train, y_test = train_test_split(
```

```
    X, Y, test_size = 0.3, random_state = 100)


    return X, Y, X_train, X_test, y_train, y_test


# Function to perform training with giniIndex.

def train_using_gini(X_train, X_test, y_train):


    # Creating the classifier object

    clf_gini = DecisionTreeClassifier(criterion = "gini",

        random_state = 100,max_depth=3, min_samples_leaf=5)


    # Performing training

    clf_gini.fit(X_train, y_train)

    return clf_gini

# Function to perform training with entropy.

def tarin_using_entropy(X_train, X_test, y_train):


    # Decision tree with entropy

    clf_entropy = DecisionTreeClassifier(
```

```python
                criterion = "entropy", random_state = 100,

                max_depth = 3, min_samples_leaf = 5)


    # Performing training
    clf_entropy.fit(X_train, y_train)
    return clf_entropy


# Function to make predictions
def prediction(X_test, clf_object):


    # Predicton on test with giniIndex
    y_pred = clf_object.predict(X_test)
    print("Predicted values:")
    print(y_pred)
    return y_pred
# Function to calculate accuracy
def cal_accuracy(y_test, y_pred):


    print("Confusion Matrix: ",
```

```python
    confusion_matrix(y_test, y_pred))

    print ("Accuracy : ",

    accuracy_score(y_test,y_pred)*100)

    print("Report : ",

    classification_report(y_test, y_pred))

# Driver code

def main():

    # Building Phase

    data = importdata()

    X, Y, X_train, X_test, y_train, y_test = splitdataset(data)

    clf_gini = train_using_gini(X_train, X_test, y_train)

    clf_entropy = tarin_using_entropy(X_train, X_test, y_train)

    # Operational Phase

    print("Results Using Gini Index:")
```

```
# Prediction using gini

y_pred_gini = prediction(X_test, clf_gini)

cal_accuracy(y_test, y_pred_gini)


print("Results Using Entropy:")

# Prediction using entropy

y_pred_entropy = prediction(X_test, clf_entropy)

cal_accuracy(y_test, y_pred_entropy)


# Calling main function

if __name__=="__main__":

    main()
```

Chapter 9 : K-Nearest Neighbors (KNN)

The K-Nearest Neighbors is the simplest and the most used learning algorithms in classification and regression problems. This type is straightforward and easy to master. The value of a result for the solved puzzle is based on the selection made by the neighboring values. The purpose of this is to classify the most common class, following its K-nearest neighbors. KNN is sometimes used in a regression where the value of output is predicted as per the most continuous value. The output value can be a mean or median of the entire class (k-nearest neighbors). In both regression and classification problems, the value input that corresponds to k and is used for training is usually found in the feature space. The desired result depends on the type of machine learning for which KNN has been used, that is to say, either classification r regression.

In simple terms, the KNN algorithm can be defined as one that classifies objects by putting them to the group they are close to. The method takes into account the features and data points in a set. Fr the algorithmic function, the process will try to find out a group in which object X belongs to by looking at the ends near object X in the same state. A result is founded by determining where the majority features lie. For example, if most of the points of an object fall in group Y, then object X is classified in group Y. This method of identifying a group in which item X belongs is used in classification. It works in the same way as a plural vote for the neighbors, and then the item is allocated a group in which the majority of its k nearest neighbors fall in. When the evaluation is done, and the value of k comes out as 1, then the object is classified in that same class.

KNN is sometimes referred to the lazy learner because it takes time to compute values. KNN is based on estimations, and the mathematical analysis is usually left pending up to the last step of classification.

In both regression and classification problems, a single unit should be set as the average of a class. This is to ensure that the closest neighbor in that unit contributes to the metric more than the neighbors that lie far from the class. For instance, a good model will set a value at $1/x$, where the x is the distance between the nearest neighbors.

For classification problems, the neighbors are chosen from units with a known value in terms of features and other parameters. The group can be considered as training datasets even though less training is done in the K nearest neighbor theory. A distinctive characteristic of the k nearest algorithm is its sensitivity to the components and the composition of a dataset. An example of training data that can be used for k nearest neighbor algorithm is a labeled vector, usually applied in feature space that has many dimensions. The algorithms learn by isolating feature vectors and the labeled classes in the training dataset. In the process of classifying objects, the value of k is usually constant and set by the user of the system. In the process, a vector without a label (used a testing data) is assigned a group by looking at the labels that frequently appear throughout the training set and is the closest to the vector. The training data set is also called the k sample.

For a continuous variable, the Euclidean distance is the commonly used parameter for solving range related problems. For variables that are not continuous, also referred to as separate, a different setting is used to solve the problem. The performance of the nearest algorithm can be enhanced by the incorporation of other unique algorithms to study the elements that define the distance space.

Finding the Value of K in the K Nearest Algorithm

In the opening segment of this chapter, I mentioned that the k value is a constant that is set by the user of the system. That statement remains the case. However, it takes a lot to choose the value that best represents k. I this sector I want to raw a theory that can help in settling for the real value of k. the first thing to note is that the selection of k factor is dependent on the type and weight of data. Another metric that influences the choice of k is the type of function, that is, whether the task is classification or regression. The features of the object also play a more significant role in choosing the k value. Lastly, the choice of k is primarily put on the shoulders of the user (that is why the algorithms are mostly prone to bias). From all this we can conclude that the k factor has a close relationship with the system in which it is used. The most applicable implication is the weight of data.

When the set value of k is significant, there are chances that noise will be reduced within the datasets. However, an important k factor results in undifferentiated boundaries within classes. Therefore, the best value of k can only be arrived by a trial and error method that is based mostly on experiments. The experiments are. In other words, called optimization processes. These processes are aimed at correcting deviations of metric values form the low point, leading to a point where a unit can be predicted to be the closest to the k sample. At this point, the value of k should be 1. This is the process referred to as the nearest neighbor algorithm.

Noise, bias, or any other undesirable parameter can significantly alter the accuracy of the K- nearest neighbor algorithm. Efficacy is also complicated by the inconsistency of features to the roles of the system. For example, a system that is supposed to predict whether part of the population is men or women may not be accurate in predicting other metrics. Such parameters may be whether the same section of the community is rich or poor. This problem, however, can be solved by isolating features to reflect the functions of the algorithm and the desired result. The isolation can be done by the use of an evolutionary algorithm or by mutually incorporating the k sample (training dataset) with the data to be classified.

In a joint classification problem, also called binary, the k value is recommended to be an odd number. In that way, we avoid the problem of seeing a tie between elements. If the k value proves challenging to estimate, it is recommended that you use a bootstrap method to evaluate it.

Comparing the K Nearest Neighbor with the K Means Clustering

I cannot summarize this chapter without comparing the most commonly used algorithms in machine learning. The two algorithms (k- means clustering and k nearest neigh our), are usually mistaken for each other because of the k letter in their names. The clearest distinction between the two algorithms is that k-means is an unsupervised algorithm while the k-nearest neighbor is a supervised algorithm. The functions also can be used to differentiate the two complex algorithms. The c means is used for clustering while the k nearest algorithm is used for classification and sometimes in regression problems.

The K-Nearest Neighbors Algorithm

The first thing to note is that this is a supervised algorithm it is used for both classification and regression problems. Being a supervised algorithm, the k nearest uses learning data that are labeled. The KNN learns from the data and is thus able to classify unlabeled data by looking at the value of k in the nearest data points within the class. The k value in the algorithm is set by the developer of the system, as mentioned above.

The K-Means Algorithm

Compared to the KNN algorithm, the K-means algorithm is an unsupervised type that is used for clustering problems. Being an unsupervised algorithm, the k-means do not rely on labeled data to make predictions.

The k means algorithm can cluster objects by studying the distance between the data points in a class over time. Here, the value of k is said to reflect the number of classes that are supposed to be analyzed — the k-means works by minimizing error.

Differences Between the KNN and the KM

K-means algorithm is used in situations where the attributes of the data are not known, such as estimating the fall and rise of stock value over time. On the other hand, the K-nearest neighbor algorithm is used for classification and regression purposes, where the metrics are clearly stated. The function of the k-means can broaden to cover the results of the k-nearest neighbor algorithm. This is to say that, when the k-nearest algorithm predicts an event, the k-means can be used to analyze the result further. Analyzation may be in ways that give a more in-depth understanding of the features and the outcome.

For this reason, both algorithms are vital in components of machine learning. Nonetheless, the two algorithms are used in different circumstances to solve various problems, while deriving the function k and what it represents in the system. Using the k factor, this statement can be shortened as;

i.   K-means, being an unsupervised algorithm, works by collecting data in groups to form a k number of clusters.

ii. K nearest neighbor, being a supervised algorithm, works by producing new data using the metrics in the learning data. KNN does this to assign points according to the k value, which represents the nearest point of data.

Despite the difference in scope and functions, both the k nearest neighbor algorithm and the k means algorithm work by considering distance within the dataset.

Limitation of the K Nearest Neighbor Algorithm

A significant limitation of the classification method of k nearest neighbor is the existence of bias among the classes. If the distribution of elements in the class is twisted, the majority of items within the unit will tilt the metrics to their side. For instance, the dominant feature within the feature space will attract the estimating to their points because they are found almost everywhere within the unit. However, such bias can be alleviated in many ways. The most common method of overcoming prejudice is by setting an average metric point in the class. The balance is found when the distance between the k nearest neighbor is considerably weighted.

Solving the problem of bias in regression requires a different approach. A unit of the k nearest neighbors is crossed by an average weight value that is inversely proportional to the distance between the two points in the group. This is the distance from the nearest neighbor to the test point. An additional method to be used can be the generalization of the data representing each class. A case in point is representative nodes in the self-organizing map, which represent the core point of the dataset. The central location is, Therefore, regardless of the distribution of elements in the class.

Advantages of K Nearest Neighbors

Being the easiest and the simplest of all machine learning algorithms, the k nearest neighbor's algorithm boasts of many positives.

The k nearest neighbor is also referred to as the lazy learner. This name comes from the fact that the algorithm does not learn anything during the training period. However, it gains on occasions where it is required to perform a task. The lack of training period can be seen as a win on its side. The algorithm stores sets of learning data and uses it when it is required to make predictions. The process ensures that the KNN algorithm is the fastest among the machine learning algorithms, which need training.

Additional sets of data can be induced in the k-nearest neighbor flawlessly without altering the prediction accuracy. This is supported by the fact that it does not require training.

The k nearest neighbor algorithm only requires two metrics to function. The two parameters are the k factor and the distance function. This makes the algorithm simple and easy to device.

Disadvantages of K nearest neighbor

The algorithm cannot be effective when handling large amounts of data. Large sets of data present a wide range between points, which make the algorithm ineffective.

As seen in the paragraph above, the algorithm cannot work with large dimensions. When the distribution of data is broad, the estimation of the distance between the nearest points becomes a challenge.

K nearest neighbor algorithm is susceptible to noise and other irregularities in data. For effectiveness, manual methods are incorporated to remove outliers and induce values that are not in the system.

The algorithm usually requires regular feature scaling.

Creating Our Own KNN Algorithm

Now it is time for us to go through and create one of our own KNN algorithms and use this for our own needs in our data analysis. The KNN algorithm that we have been talking about so far is going to use the feature similarity, which is going to help predict the values of the new points of data, which further means that all of the new points of data are going to be assigned a value based on how well they are able to match the points that are found in our training set. We are able to better understand this with some of the following steps along the way.

1. First, we need to make sure that we start with implementing our algorithm. And this is going to require us to have a set of data to work with. So, while we are working with the first step of this algorithm, we need to load the training and the testing data that we want to use.
2. Next, we have to go through and choose what the value of K should be. This can be any integer that we want, but will help us to separate out the data we are working with.
3. For all of the points that are going to be in our test data, there are a few things that we need to accomplish, and these steps will include:
    a. We have to start with this one to calculate the distance between the data for the testing, and then each row of the training data with the help of any methods that you want to use. These include options like Hamming or Manhattan distance, and the Euclidean distance. The most common of these is going to be the Euclidean distance.
    b. Now, based on the value that you place with the distance, we want to go through and sort this out in ascending order.
    c. When that order is all done, it is time for us to go through and choose out the top K rows based on the

sorted arrays that we are working with.

    d. And then, we can end this part by assigning a class to our point for testing. The class that we are going to assign here is going to be based on the class that is the most frequent for these rows.

4. When we are done with all of this, then the algorithm is going to end, and we should be able to take a look at the clustering and how it is going to work for us.

This is going to take a bit of work to accomplish, but you will find that it is going to help us get a lot of things done in the process. And when it shows up, the graph or the chart will show us where our data points are supposed to go, and that will help us to take a look at where these points go, and learn some of the new options that we could explore to make this work for us.

Chapter 10: Random Forest Algorithms with Python

This type of algorithm is the most available and common in recent years. There are several factors that you need to comprehend this type of algorithm. The main objective of this algorithm is to help with the regression and classification computations using the raw natural data. When you talk of a random forest, you refer to a collection of learning methods with multiple decision trees. Random forest improves in outcome prediction by calculating the average of the decision trees impacts. With this, you can make several predictions using the various models provided in this algorithm. Examples of models you can correctly use include the logistic regression, which mainly deals with binomial data. The other examples might include k-nearest neighbours, naïve Bayes and even support vector machines. In most cases, it works best where different features of a model comprise of predictive power which is very weak but shows stronger power in a combination. The following illustrations will help you understand this topic very well.

The Decision Trees
They refer to predictive models for calculating some target values using binary rules. It comprises of two forms or types, for example,

466

regression trees and classification. Regression trees are applicable in creating any continuous data like those data sets used in tree cover percentage and also in biomass. On the other hand, classification trees deal with sets of data which are very definite and specific. Examples are data found within the land cover. It is good to note that any typical tree composed of leaves, nodes and even branches. As a result of all these features, it will lead to a simple model. In this case, the nodes comprise of some unique attributes that are entirely applicable in the functioning of your algorithm. You also need to take a look at the random forest so that you increase your level of understanding about this topic.

The Random Forest

From the layman's language, you can deduce that random forests consist of a collection of tree predictors in that every individual tree will strictly depend on random vector values which have been independently sampled and distributed equally to all different trees within the forest. You can also say that random forest can be a form of a classifier comprising of a group of trees which have been arranged structurally as classifiers. Therefore, in brief, you can conclude that random forest has the abilities to build up various multiple trees decisions and later on fuse them to come up with the stable prediction and which is highly accurate. It is also good to note that this kind of machine learning algorithm entirely relies on ensemble learning. Therefore, ensemble learning is a form of learning where you can categorically join all algorithms of different types or same types so as to come up with a model which is very powerful in terms of predictions. Funny enough, random forests come as a result of the combination of multiple different trees used in decision making. Therefore, you can also refer to it as 'forest of trees.'

Merits of Random Forest

- It is certainly applicable to both regression problems and classification.

- It helps in reducing overfitting, especially within the trees. All these are possible through performing averaging.

- It is the most accurate algorithm since it will only give a wrong prediction if, at all, more than half of the data used are wrong.

- It is easy to use since you can easily detect the level of importance or instead of the significance of every feature, especially within the prediction. In this case, Sklearn boasts of its powerful library in performing that task.

- The algorithm reduces the traces of biasedness within the analysis since it mainly depends on the entire crowd of the forest for its maximum prediction.

- It is a highly stable algorithm which you can trust with all your computations. A slight mistake will only affect a small portion of the prediction. Therefore, the whole prediction will still be correct.

- This type of algorithm can perform its duties using numerical and categorical features.

Demerits of Random Forests
- It has an annoying and overlapping trend of overfitting on some sets of data, especially the ones with regression tasks and also the noisy classification.

- It's a costly and highly complex algorithm as compared to other algorithms such as decision tree algorithm.

- Its training takes long since it comprises a large combination of decision trees.

Decision tree and random forests algorithms have different roles in data computations and outcome predictions. Again, the two have a specific time of implementation. That's, the exact time you can eventually apply them in real life. Below illustrations give us enough explanations on when to use these two aspects of data prediction algorithms.

When do we apply the decision tree:
- You can use the decision tree when you prefer the simplicity of your model with many explainable attributes.
- You can also use this method, especially when you want your model to be non-parametric.
- You can also apply this when you are not worrying any form of multicollinearity or something to do with regularization or feature selection.

When do we apply random forest:
- When you require good data prediction accuracy even though you don't worry about model interpretations.
- When you are looking for accuracy while using a validation data set.

How to Perform the Random Forest Algorithm
The illustrations below show a clear step by step guideline on how to accomplish this kind of algorithm.

1. You can start by picking a random number like say X from the random records within the sets of data.
2. Try as much as possible to come up with a decision tree, basing your computations on X records.
3. You can now choose the number you require especially the number of trees. Then, you can repeat these steps that's step 1 and 2.
4. For example, if you are solving a regression problem, dealing with a new record, every individual tree in those particular forests will have an output value of Y. In this case, you can quickly get the final value by computing the average of all the predictions.
5. Also, if it is a classification problem, the predictions narrow to an individual tree that's, every tree takes part in categorical predictions which comprise of new recordings. Eventually, the category with the majority votes will have the power to handle the new records.

Feature Selection Methods in Random Forest

Random forests boast of being popular within the technological world. The main attributes towards this are their robustness, accuracy and also you can use them more easily. It provides two strict methods that you can employ in your feature selection, as shown in the illustrations below.

The Mean Decrease Impurity

Random forests comprise of various decision trees. Each node in that decision trees represents a situation of only one single feature. The primary function of this node here is to split those datasets into two equal parts in that same set will have similar values at the end. All these happen at the optimal level condition which you can refer to as impurity. However, in classification, you can call it Gini impunity or instead information gain, which is also entropy.

In most cases, you can call it variance in regression. Therefore, when having some sorts of tree training, you can eventually compute the amount reduced by each feature on the impurity, which is weighted. In the case of a forest, you can calculate the decreased impurity by getting their average and later on ranking them using the same measure.

However, in this method, there are things of great importance to keep in your mind. The first one is that when you compute more categories, the chances of getting biased is high. The next thing to keep in mind is that it treats all the correlated features equally, but when you take one as a predictor, then the importance of the rest reduces. This is because one feature reduces the impurities of the other features.

The Mean Decrease Accuracy

This category involves getting the accuracy of impacts features by measuring them directly. The main objective here is to detect the level of reduction inaccuracy caused by the permutation, especially within the accuracy model.

Creating Our Own Random Forests

Now that we have had a chance to go through and learn about the random forest, it is time for us to go through and actually perform one of these algorithms for our own. There are a few options and steps that we want to be able to work with in order to get the Random Forest to behave in the manner that we would like. Some of the steps that we are able to use n order to work with the random forest algorithm include:

1. Pick out the N random records that are a part of our set of data.
2. Then we are able to take those records and then build up the decision tree to start with. Remember that we need to have several of these decision trees in order to end up with a random forest, so starting with one is important.
3. We can then go through and choose how many trees we would like to have with our algorithm before going through and repeating the first two steps again with each one.
4. If we are doing this to work with one of the regression problems for a new record that we want to use, each tree in the forest is going to be able to predict the value of Y, which is going to be our output. The final value is then going to be calculated by taking the average of the values predicted by all of the trees that you have in your forest.
   a. Or, if you are going to use this to work with a classification problem, each tree that is in the forest needs to be able to predict the category that our new records are able to belong to. Finally, the new record is going to be assigned to the category that is able to win the vote of the majority.

#' reg_rf

#' Fits a random forest with a continuous scaled features and target

#' variable (regression)

```
#'

#' @param formula an object of class formula

#' @param n_trees an integer specifying the number of trees to
sprout

#' @param feature_frac an numeric value defined between [0,1]

#'              specifies the percentage of total features to be used in

#'              each regression tree

#' @param data a data.frame or matrix

#'

#' @importFrom plyr raply

#' @return

#' @export

#'

#' @examples # Complete runthrough see:
www.github.com/andrebleier/cheapml

reg_rf <- function(formula, n_trees, feature_frac, data) {


  # source the regression tree function

  source("algorithms/reg_tree_imp.R")
```

```r
# load plyr

require(plyr)


# define function to sprout a single tree

sprout_tree <- function(formula, feature_frac, data) {

  # extract features

  features <- all.vars(formula)[-1]


  # extract target

  target <- all.vars(formula)[1]


  # bag the data

  # - randomly sample the data with replacement (duplicate are possible)

  train <-

    data[sample(1:nrow(data), size = nrow(data), replace = TRUE)]


  # randomly sample features

  # - only fit the regression tree with feature_frac * 100 % of the features
```

```
features_sample <- sample(features,

                size = ceiling(length(features) * feature_frac),

                replace = FALSE)


  # create new formula

  formula_new <-

    as.formula(paste0(target, " ~ ", paste0(features_sample,

                        collapse = " + ")))


  # fit the regression tree

  tree <- reg_tree_imp(formula = formula_new,

                data = train,

                minsize = ceiling(nrow(train) * 0.1))


  # save the fit and the importance

  return(list(tree$fit, tree$importance))

}


# apply the rf_tree function n_trees times with plyr::raply
```

```
# - track the progress with a progress bar

trees <- plyr::raply(

  n_trees,

  sprout_tree(

    formula = formula,

    feature_frac = feature_frac,

    data = data

  ),

  .progress = "text"

)


# extract fit

fits <- do.call("cbind", trees[, 1])


# calculate the final fit as a mean of all regression trees

rf_fit <- apply(fits, MARGIN = 1, mean)


# extract the feature importance

imp_full <- do.call("rbind", trees[, 2])
```

```
# build the mean feature importance between all trees

imp <- aggregate(IMPORTANCE ~ FEATURES, FUN = mean,
imp_full)



# build the ratio for interpretation purposes

imp$IMPORTANCE <- imp$IMPORTANCE /
sum(imp$IMPORTANCE)



# export

return(list(fit = rf_fit,

      importance = imp[order(imp$IMPORTANCE, decreasing =
TRUE), ]))

}
```

In Summary

Random forests form a large part in the methods used to solve day to day problems and tasks using a computer. They are high in terms of feature ranking since you can easily apply them. It is also good to note that Random Forest minimal engineering techniques towards its feature. Also, it doesn't need much care of its parameter tuning. As a result, you will realize that there is an exposure of mean decrease impurity, especially on these libraries. However, all these have serious problems, especially when you are dealing with data interpretation. In that, in correlated features, chances of getting low scores with stronger features are high. Due to this, you end up having affected by issues of biasedness towards variables comprising of several categories. Nevertheless, you can keep all these critical issues in your mind and use this method on your data.

It is also good to note that sometimes, the predicted outcome might have some errors and less accurate. However, there are several ways we can always use to improve our outcome. The first one involves fine-tuning of the used parameters within the algorithm. In this case, the vital parameters include the split features, the tree depth and also the total number of the trees.

Chapter 11: Perceptron Algorithm

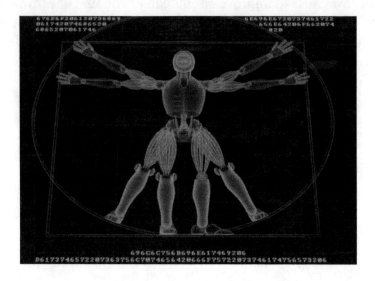

In this chapter, I have taken a look at the perceptron algorithm, defined it, and went on to illustrate how it works. In so doing, I have refreshed your minds on the necessary components of linear algebra before proceeding to study the perceptron learning algorithm. This step by step presentation is meant to guide learners in understanding and visualizing the concept of machine learning, taking note of the perceptron. It is my wish that by the end of the chapter, you have gained insight and knowledge to get you started. Additional materials of study are recommended.

Limitations and Precautionary Measures
In the training phase of the system, the perceptron algorithm should be helped to learn from acclimating data. This is to ensure that the prediction is accurate and errors barred. The presentation of input vector should reflect a due-diligent process. This ensures that the perceptron is set at par with the metrics and that the system can self-correct in case of errors as it just goes back to the provided input vector. The recommendation here is to ensure that any problem that needs solving through a linear separation has solved a set go based on the learning process. Another method to induce learning to the

algorithm is by the use of a functioning train. This method set up networks within the algorithm and then produces input vectors to the perceptron. Afterward, the setup can correct the system depending on the number of errors to be fixed. Unfortunately, this method is faced by the uncertainty of convergence. There are no precise ways that can lead to convergence in the perceptron. For this reason, it is not advisable to use the function train method in training perceptron.

Despite the hype surrounding the use of perceptron learning algorithms, they do not fall short of limitations. The first limitation is that the output result in a perceptron network can only assume either a zero (0) or one (1) value. There are no in-between values. This can be seen as a biased outcome or an inaccurate one because sometimes we expect other values. The second drawback of the perceptron is that it can only be used to solve problems that require linear distinction. This implies that perceptron is only capable of working out issues that involve vectors that can be separated by a vertical plane. If a straight line cannot separate the vectors, then learning them becomes a hutch for the perceptron network. It is, however, worth noting that experts have proof to show that for linear separable quantities, perceptron learning algorithms can solve them in no time.

Perceptron may portray limitations. However, it is fair to note that a combination of networks (having numerous perceptron can be applied in complex problem-solving. For instance, say we have a unit of four problems to solve (four-vectors) by separating them with a straight line. In the process that we have two perceptrons in the network, it will create a two-dimension boundary that splits the vectors into four different groups.

Conclusion

An algorithm is a system that gives solutions and answers to question on a step by step basis. In computer science, algorithms provide results to search questions, offers recommendations on contents in accordance with the history of the user. Additionally, algorithms pool a large set of data to detect sequences and make forecasts about the habits of the user.

Algorithms can also be used to underpin prevailing partialities, particularly on digital media. For instance, double-tapping an online editorial that an acquaintance displayed on Instagram, which portrays political opinion, would show the Instagram algorithm that you have an interest in the political opinion posted. In the forthcoming, Instagram may set up your feeds to include the impression liked and filter out conventional feeds and views.

As a vital component of Python Machine Learning, the knowledge of algorithm involves; identifying the personal partialities in computer software design; analytically assessing the information available in the internet, and taking in to account the fact that the best news is always ranked first in the search results. All these are drawn from the digital media perspective. However, the knowledge of algorithms stretches far than just the digital media arena.

Almost every sector of the economy is applying the techniques of machine learning in day-to-day activities. The knowledge of python machine learning algorithms thereby becomes an essential tool for tackling dynamic problems in the real world.

Though not entirely looked at in this book, the question that draws debate is whether machine learning algorithms have a political character. As suggested by Tarleton Gillespie, it is vital to cross-examine the rationalities of premeditated populaces, by understanding the scope of influence of the digital tools and how the use of python machine learning algorithms have impacted our knowledge and if it may have political consequences.

The usefulness of agonistic nature in terms of machine learning may widen our understanding in areas where neural networks are structured. This broad understanding draws the conclusion that people make intelligent machines, and they are in fluidity and rooted infused places. Therefore, it essential to view the areas where the models are built as productive spots of research.

As discussed above, machine learning algorithms have become a significant part of our interactions and activities both in the social media and socio-economic platforms. And to answer the question of "can algorithms be agonistic?" It is crucial to take a look at past instances where algorithms have been considered to be combative. A good example was when the ML algorithms of Reddit provided a platform for most upvoted articles to be on top of search results thus promoting the spread of fake news at the time of the Boston Bombing in 2013.

As a result, a missing student, Sunil Tripathi, was mistakenly accused of carrying out the attacks.

Nowadays, almost all technical skills are influenced by the transformational model brought forth by the introduction of machine learning. This fact does not change the truth that the essential natural and human resources are limited. Therefore, the incorporation on intelligent machines in social activities should be done with precautionary measures taken to alleviate any potential risk.

Progressive procedures of machine learning may be useful in guiding the industrial processes towards an ideal way out. The methods, however, should not be programmed to find solutions to the same optimization problems in the same ways. A torrent of new sets of data and information is necessary to help this course. In the same spirit, developers and users of the software with algorithms of neural network should continue the innovative processes and research to find the ideal fit for every problem. This book is structured to guide my readers, among them with the necessary knowledge of python machine learning and relevant algorithms. It is hence essential to find additional sources to enhance the skills already acquired from this book.

Notes

www.ingramcontent.com/pod-product-compliance
Lightning Source LLC
LaVergne TN
LVHW051219050326
832903LV00028B/2165